The Regulatory Agency and the Public Corporation

The Regulatory Agency and the Public Corporation

The Canadian Air Transport Industry

John R. Baldwin

Ballinger Publishing Company • Cambridge, Mass.
A Subsidiary of J.B. Lippincott Company

This book is printed on recycled paper.

International Standard Book Number: 0–88410–262–9

Library of Congress Catalog Card Number: 75–8916

Printed in the United States of America

Library of Congress Cataloging in Publication Data

Baldwin, John Russel.
The Regulatory Agency and the Public Corporation.
A revision of the author's thesis, Harvard, 1973.
Bibliography: p. 239;
1. Aeronautics and state–Canada–Case studies.
2. Government business enterprises–Canada–Case studies.
3. Independent regulatory commissions–Canada–Case studies. I. Title.
HE9815.A4B34 1975 387.7'0971 75–8916
ISBN 0–88410–262–9

Table of Contents

List of Figures

List of Tables

Preface

Until recently economists have tended to treat the institutions that shape the performance of our economic system as being exogenously determined. This has changed. A literature now exists that examines the reasons for the development of alternative property rights structures. Economists have begun to devote themselves to the question of the efficacy of different legal rules. The determinants of group behavior and the formation of collective institutions have also garnered attention. Finally, positive theories of non-market institutions—from public bureaucracies to state-owned firms—have been developed using the assumption that they are utility-maximizing entities subject to certain constraints.

This book attempts to contribute to the literature explaining the development and behavior of non-market institutions. It is based on my Ph.D. dissertation, which was completed for Harvard in 1973. Initially I had begun a standard analysis of the distortions occasioned by the combination of regulation and a state-owned corporation in the Canadian airline industry. As the work progressed, the question I was asking gradually shifted from what to why. The result was the adoption of a positive approach to the behavior of both institutions. This book, therefore, contains a mélange of both theory and a description of the actual behavior of each entity. The latter is meant to test the relevance of the model that is developed to explain the behavior of the Canadian regulatory agency and the Canadian state-owned airline.

For this approach, I owe a debt of gratitude to A. Breton of the University of Toronto. The formative stages of this work coincided with a year he spent at Harvard. His emphasis on the need to explain the behavior of political institutions is responsible for the methodology I adopted. However, I am most indebted to R.E. Caves and M. Roberts for their perspicacious comments on rough drafts of the thesis. They have continually pointed out that the world is not as simple as my model makes it out to be. Articles by R. Posner, G. Stigler, and S. Peltzman that also dealt with positive theories of regulation and state-owned corporations appeared as the thesis reached completion. A year spent at the University of Chicago on a post-doctoral fellowship provided the opportunity to make improvements in my manuscript. I am grateful to all members of the Industrial Organization Workshop at Chicago who pointed out numerous shortcomings in my approach—most of which probably still remain in this book.

Credit must also go to members of the Micro-Economic Workshop at Harvard, to participants of the NBER Conference on Regulation held in the Autumn of 1973 at Chicago, and to my colleague R. Fraser whose comments were invaluable. The Institute for Economic Research at Queen's University funded the typing and preparation of this manuscript. I wish to thank the librarians in several government agencies who proved most cooperative in unearthing material. Finally, my wife Adrianne Marie deserves credit for editing numerous drafts. I hope I shall receive similar credit at her first gallery showing.

Introduction

Government agencies, important as their influence is on the market system, are seldom studied with the rigor or within the framework usually adopted in economic analysis. These institutions most frequently receive the attention of economists only insofar as they distort the operation of the market system. Policy recommendations are therefore either couched in terms of admonishments that such agencies should pay more attention to the public interest [1] or consist of pleas for their abolition on the grounds that the affected markets require no interference.[2]

Resolution of conflicting recommendations as to the desired form of government involvement requires not only a study of whether a particular institution leads to satisfactory results, but also the development of a theory to explain the behavior of existing institutions. Otherwise, it is impossible to explain the manner in which objectives, posited as desirable, might be achieved.

This study adopts the premise that merely exhorting government agencies to maximize social welfare is inadequate. Different institutions, acting consistently in response to basic behavioral motivations, may produce dissimilar policies. Elsewhere in economics, normative and positive theories of the market process have been intertwined to great advantage. As justification for their support of a particular type of market structure, economists have long relied on evidence that that market structure, combined with profit-maximizing behavior on the part of firms, will produce a "desirable" outcome. If the decisions of non-market institutions can be explained on the basis of a behavioral model constructed on the assumption of generally accepted motivational postulates, then cogent arguments for or against specific types of agencies may be developed.[3]

This study develops a positive theory of two institutions—a Crown airline and a regulatory agency—both of which have influenced the performance of the Canadian air transport industry. The government-owned airline has been the dominant domestic firm since its inception in 1937. Policy affecting the Crown airline generally has been made at the Cabinet level, not by the regulatory agency. At first primarily responsible for frontier aviation, the regulatory agency has come to play an increasing role in fostering the development of a group of regional carriers. A study of these two organizations provides an opportunity both to model the behavior and to compare the results of two institutions often used to influence the performance of an industry.

Not only is this study interested in the larger issue of whether a positive theory can be developed for such institutions, but it is also designed to demonstrate the use to which such models can be put in analyzing the effect of changes in existing institutions. For instance, it has been suggested that the Canadian regulatory agency be granted wider powers; in particular, that it be given absolute control over the government-owned airline. Yet, without an appreciation of the objectives and behavior of both bodies, little can be said about the likely effects of such action. In particular, if their objectives should coincide, there may be little point in the exercise. While the behavioral models can be used to predict the results of proposed changes, they can also serve to evaluate certain policies that have already been implemented. For example, the Canadian government-owned airline has seen its dominance substantially reduced via new entrants—an action justified in terms of the benefits to be derived from a reduction in its "monopoly" power. Yet, such emotive terminology is implicitly based on the premise that the model of a privately owned firm applies to public corporations. If it does not, this justification of the government's competitiion policy is ill-founded. The development of a behavioral model of a "public" firm offers an opportunity to resolve this issue.

The following chapters develop for both the Canadian regulatory agency and the government-owned airline the type of model to which an economist is accustomed—a model whose major purpose is to extract only those motivations and structural attributes necessary to predict the general characteristics of each process. In so doing, it utilizes both the economist's motivational assumptions of self-interest and his analytic technique of maximization subject to constraint. The theory of regulation is contained in Chapters one through four. The theory of the Crown airline is pursued in Chapters five through eleven. In each case, the model first extracts the reason for a government's adoption of each institution and then develops the model of the institution's behavior. Following each theoretical section, evidence from actual behavior is adduced to corroborate the hypothesized model. Finally, the conclusion briefly compares the performance of the American industry to that of the Canadian. In addition, it utilizes the positive theories developed herein to evaluate certain changes that have occurred in, or that have been proposed for, the structure of regulation in Canada.

Part I

The Regulatory Agency

Chapter One

Towards a Positive Theory of the Regulatory Process in Transportation Industries

THE CREATION OF REGULATORY AGENCIES

Specialization of function yields advantages not only in the production process but also in the political system. Utilizing this premise, this section explains the creation of the transportation regulatory agency as a rational act on the part of the participants in the political process. This, in turn, provides the background necessary for an understanding of the objectives the agency is forced to adopt.

Adoption of a motivational hypothesis is central to a model of non-market decision making. The self-interest motive serves as the frame of reference around which this study is organized. For operational effectiveness, it is transformed into a variant of the survival motive. The regulatory agency is hypothesized to act so as to perpetuate its own existence. This implies that a regulatory agency will try to satisfy the government by divising policies which benefit government supporters and thereby improve the chances of the government's re-election.[1]

Two major problems face any government pursuing re-election: accurate determination of (1) the desires of the electorate and (2) the strategy of the opposition.[2] Numerous devices have been employed to minimize the first problem. The use of such intermediaries as lobbyists, the development of ideologies,[3] and the selective dissemination of information [4] have all been utilized to this end. But even if individual preferences can be ascertained or influenced by a government, their variation across individuals may make the formulation of a winning election platform difficult.

Some models of the political process, which have concentrated on the extreme case, show that, even with perfect information about voters' preferences, the existence of the Condorcet voting paradox or the cyclical majority guarantee certain defeat.[5] However, a government's uncertainty as to the probability of its re-election arises not so much from the static theoretical constructs of cyclical majorities as from a dynamic process that imposes net negative benefits on certain groups. The continuous growth of the government's budget,[6] in combination with the unequal incidence of benefits from many of the "non-appropriable" programs, means that perceived benefits and tax costs tend to increasingly diverge for some individuals.[7] Coalitions, for this reason, may be unstable and new ones formed to redistribute the net benefits of government programs.

Recognition of both the dynamic nature of the legislative process and the nature of the disequilibrium has led to a study of the ways by which governments forestall defeat. The work of Buchanan and Tullock [8] emphasized the importance of vote-trading or "logrolling" as the method by which externalities imposed on minority groups are internalized via the barter system. Logrolling is most commonly treated as an explicit trade-off between one policy and another by a rational voter.[9] It is the explicit nature of the bargaining process that has garnered the most attention.[10] But this approach, in treating the political process as bargains struck between individual voters, neglects the high costs to the voter of both information as to the implications of particular policies and the costs of participating in the political process. As a result, bargaining occurs under the aegis of agents rather than by the participatory bargaining of the principals themselves.[11]

A regulatory institution should be regarded as one type of agent adopted by the government to effect particular bargains. The circumstances that have led to the creation of the agency suggest not only the objectives it is expected to fulfill, but also certain aspects of behavior likely to be adopted in order to meet them. While no attempt will be made to develop a comprehensive list of the circumstances that have led to the creation of all regulatory boards, the following two encompass the reason many such agencies have been established.

First, governments are often called upon to arbitrate rancorous disputes between parties whose interests are diametrically opposed. The recriminatory nature of these conflicts stems from the nature of the confrontation—that is, any gains accruing to one party are made at the expense of another. These types of conflict are in essence constant or negative sum games. The most common example of this type of confrontation is that of consumer–business conflicts. The monopolist, if unable to freely set prices, faces the loss of excess profits; the consumer, if forced to pay monopoly prices, faces the loss of income that could have been used for other purposes.

The literature on externalities has focused attention on whether in similar conflicts a voluntary agreement between the contending parties may be reached—an agreement that produces a social optimum.[12] Recourse to the existence of high transaction costs in the case of multi-person conflicts or to the uncertainty of an agreement in bilateral confrontations [13] suggests such agreements may not be made. It might then be argued that regulatory agencies are created in order to assist or to impose the optimal solution.

This interpretation of the rationale behind the creation of a regulatory agency, I would suggest, neglects the essence of the conflict and thus the problem the legislature is called upon to solve. Once again, reference to the externality literature serves to clarify the issue. Because of what are essentially income effects, neither the optimum solution to the amount of externalities that should exist nor the resulting distribution of welfare is independent of the legal rights of the opposing parties.[14] It is therefore in the interests of each party to seek from the state those rights that most favor him. It is this type of confrontation that gives rise to regulatory boards. Therefore, the essential nature of the conflict that gives rise to a regulatory agency is the refusal of one of the parties concerned to accept the optimum that might be established via bargaining, given the existing structure of legal rights. Even if bargaining were costless, a conflict would still exist. It is this problem that the political process is called upon to arbitrate.

Regulation is adopted because the government does not want to risk alienating either group, and logrolling in its usual form cannot be used. Usually the costs of a specific logrolling program are spread across a sufficiently large number of voters that their share either goes unperceived, or else it is insufficient to counteract the surplus benefits they already receive from all other government programs.[15] But in the case of the confrontation at issue, any gain experienced by one party is at the expense of the other. Regulatory agencies must, therefore, not only arbitrate a compromise but also arrange for side-payments to those who suffer negative effects. As such it is an agency-specific variant of the logrolling process.

That regulation has recognized the right of parties to compensation for damages is discernible both from a history of its establishment as well as from the subsequent policies of regulatory agencies.[16] The request for regulation has come from "groups that have been hailed as vital to the preservation of freedom and capitalism."[17] Much of the agitation for early railroad legislation originated from mercantile interests who felt themselves to have suffered from the railroads' pricing policy.[18] They were unlikely to demand that "due process" be abrogated or confiscation be implemented. In fact, the implicit application of the welfare condition that neither party should suffer after compensation was much in evidence. Railroad regulation may have reduced the discrimination imposed on one party to the dispute, but it increased the profits of the other. For example, as railroads discovered, the "anti-discrimination law rigidly imposed on a cartelized market provides the means for effective cartel control."[19]

The second type of confrontation giving rise to regulation results from inter-firm conflicts. Since coalitions of firms may be unstable, and since each firm acting separately may reduce total profits below the industry's joint profit-maximizing level, an arbitrator, such as a regulatory agency backed by the coercive power of the state, may increase the pay-off to all existing firms. It is not uncommon to hear the complaint that regulation merely aids the "regulated" [20] or to have it suggested that the regulated industry actively supported the enactment of regulatory legislation.[21] However, care must be exercised not to confuse this result with the reason for the creation of the agency. The reason the regulatory agency is chosen in this instance is the same as that suggested above. Once again the government is faced with an opposing group—consumers—whose interests are diametrically opposed to those of the industry. Again an indirect form of logrolling is required. In order to succeed, the agency must work out a satisfactory solution for the parties concerned. Should its very creation serve to obscure the costs to consumers of the successful implementation of a cartel, then its chief duty will be to arbitrate inter-firm conflicts as to who receives special privileges in the form of franchise or monopoly rights. Otherwise, the agency will also be forced to find some method of compensating at least some of the opposing group of consumers.

These examples illustrate one of the primary means by which the regulatory agency achieves success. Regulation enables the government to turn what was a constant or negative sum game into one with a higher pay-off. Since this is accomplished either directly by payments to the industry via taxation of the general public [22] or indirectly through resource misallocation, regulation really just amounts to a variant of the logrolling process. However, equally important is the notion that the increase in pay-off need not all accrue to industry. There are two sides to the conflict that necessitated the appointment of the regulatory agency, and to ignore the way in which the agency garners support from some consumer groups is to ignore an important aspect of the policies implemented by regulatory institutions.

Just as the government has cause to adopt the regulatory framework, so too do the participants. Apart from expecting higher net benefits from this process, they have another reason for submitting to regulation. When collective decisions are likely to result in confiscation of property or abrogation of human rights, Buchanan and Tullock have stressed the rational tendency of society to adopt decision rules that would require greater unanimity of the decision-making group.[23] If such matters do arise, there is the likelihood that both sides will attempt to substitute for the usual majority rule a form of decision making that requires more unanimity. It has often been remarked that regulatory agencies only continue to function effectively when both sides essentially concur in their decisions.[24] The regulatory agency, it is claimed, depends for its existence upon agreement from both sides. In effect, these observations recognize that the regulatory process has introduced a form of the unanimity rule into the decision process.

The regulatory framework, then, is agreed upon by the contending parties, because its existence implicitly promises to make each party better off. It is adopted by the government, because, if successful, the agency will have alienated neither side to the dispute and will have reduced the probability that either group can be welded by the opposition into a "coalition of minorities."

Descriptions of the enabling legislation readily demonstrate the nature of the process. Rather than outlining specific objectives, the regulatory statute generally is "a vaguely worded compromise of conflicting attitudes" that fails to establish "a workable set of goals."[25] Regulation is described as no more than a "pragmatic process of searching for the appropriate answer."[26]

The literature on the regulatory process often emphasizes the necessity of the "independence" of the regulatory authority.[27] Independence is justified because of the complexity of the decisions required,[28] because of the need to simplify administrative procedure,[29] because of the necessity to provide continuity in decisions, and because of the desire for impartiality.[30] But if the framework developed here is correct, this stress on independence is more readily explained. It is in the self-interest of any government to stress the independence of its regulatory agencies. The nature of the compromise, which is likely to require side-payments, means that some segment of the population, perhaps originally external to the issue, will bear the costs of this policy. The government will want to reduce the possibility that this group can discover the effect upon them of regulation. If unsuccessful in disguising these costs, the government will want to disclaim responsibility for the result. If citizens can be persuaded that technical decisions in the public interest are being made by an agency one step removed from the government, they are, first, likely to find it harder to evaluate the results and, secondly, less likely to link the costs imposed upon them by the regulatory process to the party in power.

"Independence" of the agency is sought for a second reason. If regulatory agencies were created to achieve a compromise, appeals of their decisions to the government would negate the advantages of this institution. To be drawn back into the dispute as mediator is to risk alienation of a significant minority of the electorate. The success of the regulatory agency must basically be measured by its ability to prevent just such an occurrence. But even when the agency manages to bring the two parties together at a point on their contract curve, the temptation on the part of competing applicants to invest in further strategic bargaining may still exist. By developing the tradition that regulation should be non-political, the government attempts to prevent itself from being drawn back into the process.

Not only will this tradition reduce the chance that appeal to the government will be considered, but it also diminishes the probability that any dissatisfied party will be estranged from the present government. This tradition increases the information costs to a dissatisfied party as to the effectiveness of alternate action. It can no longer be certain that actual defeat of the government will change regulatory policy. As a result, as long as the regulatory agency is receptive to argument, investment in strategic bargaining costs is more likely to be resorted to at that level.

In both the United States and Canada, association of the judiciary with the regulatory system has helped to develop its independent character.[31] The development of railway regulation in Canada supports the theory outlined above. Pressures for rate regulation led, in 1886, to the creation of the Railway Committee of the Privy Council–a subcommittee of the Cabinet.[32] The Cabinet found itself embrawled in one battle after another until, in 1903, an independent agency, the Board of Railway Commissioners, was established–as "an independent body not subject to the policy fluctuations of the party in power."[33] While the procedures for appealing its decisions are not the same as those in the United States,[a] a similar guarantee for threatened property rights was established by stipulating that the Board was "a court of record with all the rights and privileges of a superior court,"[34] and that the Chief Commissioner had to be a Justice of the Exchequer Court.[35]

THE BEHAVIOR OF REGULATORY AGENCIES

Treating the creation of regulatory bodies as a purposive act on the part of government and recognizing that regulatory agencies are an integral part of the political process provides the framework for a positive theory of regulatory decisions. If the government is regarded as choosing institutions to further its own self-interest, an agency will be considered useful only insofar as it achieves that goal. Survival of the agency depends on the degree to which it successfully solves the problems that led to its creation.

The theme of survival is not uncommon to studies of bureaucracy. Downs recognizes that a bureau, if it is to survive, must continually "demonstrate that its services are worthwhile to some group with influence over sufficient resources to keep it alive."[36] Similarly, studies of regulatory agencies implicitly recognize the importance of the survival motive by describing both the sensitivity of regulatory agencies to their environment and their awareness of the precarious nature of their existence.[37] For instance, Redford implicitly acknowledges the existence of the survival motive by proposing to evaluate the success of regulatory agencies in terms of their ability to avoid criticism and demand for change [38]–which is a curious substitution of a normative criterion for a positive description of behavior.

However, what most of these studies ignore is the manner in which the agency's decision set is constrained by the social function it is meant to play. For instance, Tullock claims that "an administrative structure will not perform the task for which it is designed."[39] What this ignores is that survival is accomplished, not by frustrating the political process, but by adjusting to its demands. Thus, a study of regulatory policy should focus on the determinants of the way in which its social function is carried out.

[a]Appeal in Canada could only be made on questions of law or jurisdiction, not of fact. See Arthur R. Wright, "An Examination of the Role of the Board of Transport Commissioners for Canada as a Regulatory Tribunal," *Canadian Public Administration* VI, no. 4 (1963):365.

Since it has been argued that a regulatory authority is created to satisfy the conflicting demands of two opposing parties, the agency should be treated as the vehicle by which "acceptable" compromises are reached. Failure to achieve such compromises leaves the commission's decisions susceptible to appeal and increases the probability that it will be bypassed in the decision process and eventually replaced. If appeal is to be avoided, one would rarely expect either party to achieve all they desire. If the agency could safely "penalize" one party by awarding it nothing, there would be no need for regulation in the first place. A government department could safely have been assigned the task of ensuring compliance with precise legislation.

Students of the regulatory process have noted the failure of agencies to prosecute or penalize one party in order to accomplish some objective.[40] This failure has been rationalized in terms of the relative costs of such a policy.[41] However, it is more easily understood if the importance of compromise is appreciated. The imposition of penalties and sanctions do not imply compromise, and the general use of these instruments would quickly lead to demands for a new regulatory framework. They might occasionally be used in an attempt to stabilize an existing agreement; but persistent application would indicate that one party no longer accepts the situation and that a new agreement has to be reached.

If the energies of the regulatory process are devoted to the formulation of an acceptable compromise, the determinants of this process should be analyzed. One way to do this is to deduce from the final outcome the apparent weights given to the opposing interests.[42] There is, however, the danger that this will lead to the regulatory agency's being treated as perpetually succumbing to pressures from industry groups.[43] The commission, as we have argued, should not be expected to aid only one party. As others have stressed, it may build on "shared" purposes to achieve success.[44] Focusing on whether one party to the dispute has been unduly aided,[45] serves only to ignore the way in which support from both sides is solicited.

One way a regulatory agency might gain such support is by offering to substitute a certain benefit for the uncertain outcome of the legislative process. Participants, whose preferences satisfy the Von Neumann–Morgenstern axioms and who exhibit risk-averse utility functions, would accept the regulatory agency's proferred result if it approximates their expectations as to the outcome of the legislative process. However, if the expectations of the participants differ, both cannot be simultaneously fulfilled. Nevertheless, the regulatory agency may still succeed in satisfying both, if their expectations do not differ by more than the sum of their insurance premiums. Any point between the expected outcome and the outcome plus the amount of the insurance premium, if it were achieved by the agency, would result in a higher level of satisfaction to each party.

In Figure 1–1, M and N represent the two outcomes being sought in the legislative arena. That the legislative process is treated as having only two

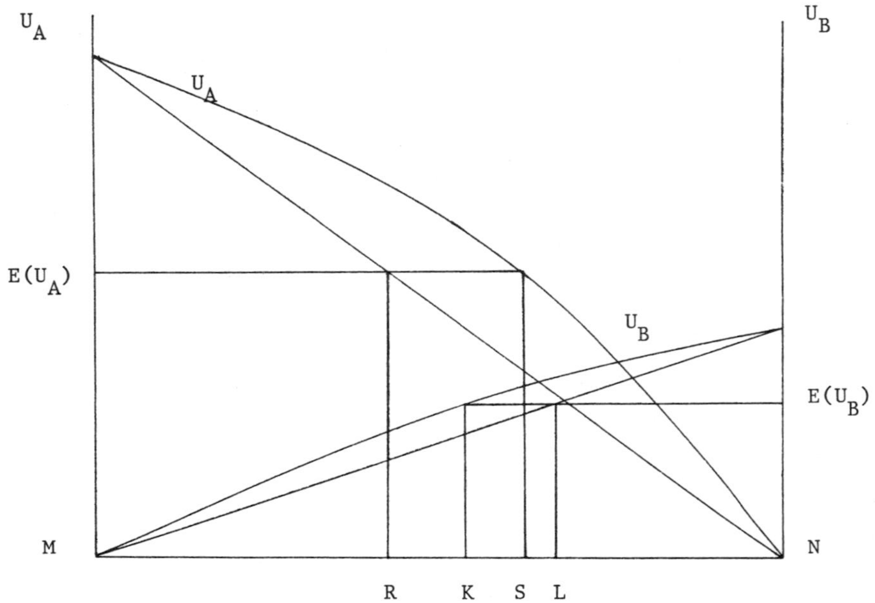

Figure 1-1. Regulation as the Substitution of a Certain Outcome for the Uncertain Outcome of the Political Process.

outcomes may not be unrealistic in light of the type of conflict that it was argued gave rise to regulation—that is, conflict revolving around the assignment of property rights to one or another of two opposing parties can result in a two-outcome situation.[b] The axis *MN* measured in monetary terms represents the trade-off of benefits between the two parties.[c] *R* is the value of the expected outcome for individual *A*; *RS* is the amount he would be willing to pay for the certainty of *R* and still be equally well off. *L* is the value of the expected outcome for *B*; *KL* his insurance premium. As long as *RL* is less than *RS* plus *KL*, a point can be found between *K* and *S* where both parties are better off than under the uncertain situation characterized by the legislative process.[d] If

[b]Of course, the issue is rarely this simple. A company is unlikely to be forced to accept a monopoly price or a competitive price, but some point in between.

[c]This diagram is based on the assumption that the conflict is constant sum. The conflict may be negative sum as in the case of a deadweight loss arising from a misallocation of resources due to monopoly pricing.

[d]That the two parties in this instance could gain from mutual agreement on a point between *K* and *S* does not obviate the role of a regulatory agency. For there is no presumption that they will reach an agreement. See Kenneth Joseph Arrow, "Political and Economic Evaluation of Social Effects and Externalities," in *The Analysis of Public Output*, ed. by Julius Margolis, Universities–National Bureau Conference Series, no. 23 (New York: National Bureau of Economic Research, distributed by Columbia U. Pr., 1970), p. 10.

this should not be the case, mere interjection of a regulatory agency into this conflict will not be successful.

This treatment of the agency's role in garnering support assumes that regulation provides both parties to the dispute with an outcome that is certain. Regulation might instead by hypothesized to substitute one uncertain outcome for another—but with the limits of the possible outcomes of the conflict being altered by the regulatory process. Suppose that, while the issue was before the legislature, a group seeking specific legislation would receive a pay-off of zero if they failed, or some positive value—K—if they won. But, it has been argued that the purpose of regulation is to reach a satisfactory compromise. It is possible to regard the compromise as being accomplished by setting new limits for the game at $(1\text{-}m)K$ and mK where $\frac{1}{2} < m < 1$. In this way both parties are guaranteed a positive return, even if they lose. In this formulation, there is still a measure of uncertainty as to the outcome for each party.

Let $P(E)$ represent the probability that mK, the higher return, is achieved. It is written as a function of effort (E). Pressure groups, lobbying, voting, and side payments are all ways in which the probability of success can be increased. Let $C(E)$ be the function that relates the costs of political participation to the effort expended. Then the expected benefits to each participant can be written:

$$B = P(E)mK + [1 - P(E)]\ (1 - m)K - C(E). \qquad (1\text{–}1)$$

If the regulatory agency can be regarded as changing m—restricting the limits within which the game can be played—the sign of $\delta B/\delta m$ will determine whether the regulatory process will be acceptable to the participants in the dispute.[e] From (1–1)

$$\frac{\delta B}{\delta m} = [2P(E^*) - 1]\,K.$$

Now $2P(E^*) - 1 \lesseqgtr 0$ as $P(E^*) \lesseqgtr \frac{1}{2}$ where E^* is the optimum degree of political effort originally chosen.[f] If $P(E^*) < \frac{1}{2}$, then $\delta B/\delta m < 0$ and the actions of the regulatory board in reducing the limits of the game increase the utility of the participant.

If $P(E^*) > \frac{1}{2}$, then the regulatory agency cannot be certain that its actions will achieve a level of acceptance from the participant necessary for the survival of the agency. If both the probability of success and the costs of political effort are functions not only of effort but also of the procedures followed by the regulatory board—that is, $P(E, R)$ and $C(E, R)$ where R is an institutional factor—then the introduction of these procedures may be sufficient to yield

[e] Assume for the moment that the functions $P(E)$ and $C(E)$ are not affected by the regulatory process.

[f] If we assume that $P(E)$ and $C(E)$ are independent of the procedures of the regulatory board, $\delta E/\delta m > 0$ or reducing the limits of the game leads to a reduction in lobbying effort.

positive benefits to this participant. However, such an adjustment is likely to affect the expected utility of the other party. In effect, the probability of success and the costs of political participation depend on the perceived actions of rivals. The indeterminacy of these reactions may be sufficient to leave the regulatory agency uncertain as to the exact adjustment necessary and the likelihood of its success.

Both these examples serve to indicate that interjection of the agency into the bargaining process by itself cannot guarantee a solution acceptable to both sides. However, the regulatory process will increase the probability of its success if it can transform the initial confrontation of the participants from a constant or negative sum to a positive sum game. Where "insurance" premiums are insufficient to bridge the gap between each party's expected value of the outcome of the legislative process, the introduction of a positive sum paid to one or the other of the parties may be sufficient to yield positive net benefits to both. Or, in the second characterization of the regulatory process, where $\delta B/\delta m > 0$, a sufficiently large positive sum paid to this participant would accomplish the same objective.

There is a second reason for expecting side-payments to be a characteristic of the regulatory process—a more compelling one in the light of the discussions of the origins of a regulatory agency. The previous example assumed a compromise might be acceptable to both sides and that side-payments increased the probability of reaching an agreement. In fact, we have previously suggested that the conflict may in fact stem from the unacceptability of the compromise to one party. In this case, the introduction of side-payments will not just increase the probability of an agreement; it is likely to be the only way to reach an agreement.

Two sources of funds for these side-payments are available to a regulatory agency. The first consists of direct grants, often in the form of subsidies. Even when such funds are limited, the agency may still be able indirectly to bestow privileges upon the regulated firm. It has been remarked that the issuance of a certificate of "public convenience and necessity" apparently makes it difficult for an agency to see a firm succumb to competitive pressures.[46] In effect, this is a recognition of the primary way in which indirect benefits can be conferred upon a regulated firm—via restriction of entry of new firms to the industry.

While side-payments may be the means employed to obtain the support of the industry, consumers are wooed by other means. The determinants of regulatory policy in this area have been variously catalogued as consisting of the system of social values, the technology, the institutional framework, and the power of different interest groups. For instance, the nature of the constraints placed upon the regulatory agency is recognized by Fainsod who claims that "regulatory agencies may, within limits, generate consumer support for their activities, but such activity is hedged about by the resources of the agency and the pressures of other interests."[47] What should be stressed here is that the prime determinants of the policy chosen by the agency are the costs to different groups of information concerning specific policies, and the costs to the regulatory agency of alternate sources of funds.

The existence of information costs leads to the hypothesis that only those groups, whose stake in the matter is greatest, will rationally inform themselves as to the effect of various policies and exert time, energy, and funds attempting to influence the regulatory process. One would, therefore, expect the industry groups to be the most vociferous, well-organized, and successful. Although the influence of these pressure groups has been recognized, their importance as the sole determinants of the process has been distorted. For instance, Bernstein claims that "regulations . . . are usually keyed to acceptability by regulated groups." [48]

Concentration on the relationships between the regulator and the regulated ignores the fact that regulatory agencies, in their quest for survival, do evince public support.[g] If the government can be persuaded that the regulatory agency is supported by a body of the electorate external to the industry, then the agency will have reduced its vulnerability to any strategic bargaining behavior that the industry might attempt. Admittedly, the subset of the "public" to which the agency turns may not be unique; but the policy they choose to follow is influenced by the relative costs of information. Certain policies are easily appreciated by certain consumers and, therefore, render themselves likely candidates for adoption. "High visibility" issues will be pursued to the benefit of particular consumer groups. "Low visibility" items can be sacrificed for the benefit of the regulated companies. In the case of transportation regulation, two issues appear to be highly visible and to engender intense emotion: (1) the prevention of "discriminatory" pricing and (2) the provision of service. The benefits of both are easily discernible to specific groups in the electorate. Whether prices are higher than costs or the quality of service is suboptimal is far more difficult to judge. Thus it is in the area of these low visibility items that the regulatory agency can favor the industry.

Just as the relative level of information costs affects the policies chosen, so also does the relative cost of different sources of funds determine the extent to which the regulatory agency will rely on each. Direct subsidies are not costless to the survival-minded agency. They lead to continuing appraisal and occasional interference in its programs by other participants in the political process.

[g]This process should not be regarded as deterministic. Additional support may be sought from outside those groups originally concerned directly with regulation. The creation of the agency often reduces the costs of pressure groups seeking specific favors by providing a convenient focal point for their actions. It is this phenomenon that leads to policies not originally envisioned by the government. Provision of air service to outlying areas is a case in point. Prior to the establishment of a regulatory agency, these communities could do nothing but lobby generally for air service. Following the creation of the Air Transport Board, they were able to argue that the agency was "required" to do something about their demands.

Interference can come from investigating subcommittees of the legislature or central budget-review agencies. Autonomy from such interference is an acute necessity if "consistent" programs aimed at garnering public support are to be developed.[49] On the other hand, cross-subsidization, or permitting the regulated companies to earn "monopoly" profits on certain routes, does not suffer from this drawback. Therefore, its use reduces the threat of arbitrary cancellation of programs that results from a reliance on direct subsidies. In addition, travellers have difficulty in discerning its effect upon them, whereas subsidies are highly visible to the tax payer. These considerations suggest the regulatory agency will prefer to rely on cross-subsidization rather than upon direct subsidies.

CONCLUSION

This chapter has stressed that the objectives of the regulatory agency can best be comprehended if the rationale for its creation is understood. Only with these objectives established can the efficacy of alternate policies be examined. Using this approach, it was argued that the determinants of the policies likely to be chosen by the agency were the ability of the public to discern the effects of different policies as well as the relative costs of alternate sources of funds to the agency. However, the discussion has so far failed to produce an operational model applicable to the Canadian air transport regulatory agency. It is to this task that the next chapter addresses itself.

Chapter Two

The Transportation Regulatory Agency: A Model

The behavioral model predicts not only that a regulatory agency will cultivate a group of supporters in order to survive, but also the manner in which this is likely to be accomplished. On the one hand, it suggests that industry support will be sought by the imposition of entry controls that increase earnings or protect existing firms from the uncertainties associated with the entry of new firms. On the other hand, it is hypothesized that the agency will attempt to develop consumer support by increasing the level of some services and by establishing a rate structure that does not fully reflect the distance-related taper in transportation cost functions. Both practices will produce cross-subsidization[a]—that is, the use of profits derived from one part of the system to support another part.

The regulatory agency will not only seek supporters from outside the industry itself, but it will also tend to favor particular groups. In the first place, provision of service is neither equally perceived nor equally appreciated by all consumers. In the second, groups will differ in their political power and thus in their importance to the regulatory board. These considerations suggest that much of the support the transportation regulatory agency seeks to develop will be generated on "local" or "regional" routes. The agency has been hypothesized to rely upon such high visibility instruments as the provision of service or the manipulation of rate structure in order to generate consumer support. Both of these items are most likely to be distinctly recognizable to those groups with an interest in service to outlying areas. Isolated communities, by their very nature,

[a]The appearance of cross-subsidization may result in the absence of regulation—when a natural monopoly engages in price discrimination. What should be emphasized here is that the pattern under regulation need not correspond to that existing in its absence. Indeed, a possible test of this model against one that argues that regulatory agencies do no more than aid the regulated industry would be to examine the pattern of price discrimination before and after regulation in an industry characterized by a natural monopoly. Since the airline industry is not so characterized, this test cannot be utilized here.

tend to have fewer transportation alternatives. Therefore, they have greater ability both to recognize and to appreciate any improvement in transportation services. There has also been a long-standing tradition—at least in railroad pricing in Canada—that such communities should not have to suffer from higher rates per mile than exist on "mainline" routes, even though the cost of service to them might be greater. There is an additional reason to postulate that the Canadian regulatory agency, in particular, will tend to seek support from "regional" routes. As we shall see, this agency was restricted to deal almost exclusively with the industry outside of the mainline route structure—that part external to the government-owned airline. Thus, it is natural that its interest in the provision of service should have been concentrated in this area.

Both the targets of the regulatory agency—the rate structure and service level—and the instruments available to it—industry profits and direct subsidies—are hypothesized to enter its objective function. The reasons have already been set forth as to why the two targets are a promising means of attracting a group of ardent supporters. However, inclusion of direct and indirect subsidies in the objective function requires an explanation. Direct subsidies should be entered in the agency's utility function because their use diminishes the independence of the regulatory agency and concomitantly increases the risk that its programs may be arbitrarily altered or cancelled. In addition, acquisition of subsidies will entail effort on the part of the regulatory agency—via appearances before legislative committees and via competition with other government bureaus for a limited budget. Similarly, cross-subsidization does not provide the agency with a costless source of funds. Some travellers may react adversely to cross-subsidization, although their ability to detect the practice suggests this is likely to be of little importance. More costly to the agency will be the pressures brought to bear by firms seeking a breakdown of entry barriers on routes where profits are being generated. The agency that sanctions monopoly earnings on mainline routes faces the problem of arbitrating between competing firms equally desirous of sharing in these profits. The successful regulatory agency must settle upon an acceptable division of market shares in the profitable sectors.

The theory of bargaining is not so well advanced that a definitive outcome can be predicted. Harsanyi suggests that an equal distribution of the privileges between two parties may result.[1] Schelling points out the importance of focal points in any bargaining process.[2] He argues that, in the case of two competitors, the focal point toward which the outcome of negotiations will tend to gravitate is the fifty-fifty split. This is in fact what has happened in Australia. There, the regulation of a state-owned and a private airline has resulted in an equal division of traffic between them.[3] Whatever the outcome, it is likely that the larger the profits the agency permits to be earned on mainline routes, the greater will be the pressures exerted on the regulatory agency to permit entry and the less successful the agency will be in satisfying all competing applicants. Therefore, while higher industry profits garner support from this group, they also lead to increasing difficulties for the agency.

Acceptance of these assumptions permits the behavior of the regulatory agency to be represented by the following model. The transportation network will be treated as consisting of two sectors: those on which profits are generated (sector 1) and those on which losses are incurred (sector 2). It has been argued that the primary way in which the regulatory authority develops a core of ardent supporters outside of the industry itself is via the provision of greater services and lower rates to sector 2 than would otherwise have existed—which policy will lead to losses in this area. Some of the funds utilized to offset these losses will be generated in sector 1 by permitting the airlines to establish higher than normal load factors via a restriction in the frequency of service or by permitting excessive fares to be charged. The agency's interest in frequency of service to the profitable sector will be minimal. Since this sector consists of dense, high-frequency routes, it is virtually impossible for consumers of such services to appreciate the effect regulatory policy may have upon them. The price level on these routes ordinarily can be ignored by the regulatory agency for a similar reason. In most instances, whether the prices on these routes are above what they would have been in the absence of regulation is too costly for consumers to investigate relative to any gains that might accrue to them from a change in regulatory policy.[b]

The provision of service to sector 2 will be represented by the frequency of flights thereon (F_2), the rate structure by the difference in fares per mile between the two sectors ($P_2 - P_1$). Both variables are chosen because of their degree of visibility to the public.[c] The higher the frequency (F_2) and the lower the price spread ($P_2 - P_1$), the greater will be the support accruing to the regulatory agency from consumer groups in outlying regions. The level of profits generated on profitable routes (R) will determine the degree of industry support as well as the effort required by the agency to adjudicate between competing applicants desirous of entry. The level of subsidies (S) also enters the agency's utility function because of the effort required to obtain them. Then the transportation regulatory agency's utility function can be written:

$$U \left\{F_2, P_2 - P_1, R, S\right\} .$$

[b]The exception occurs when there is a ready standard for comparison of prices. For Canada, the obvious comparison is to fares in the United States. As such, it is possible that the price on the profitable routes was constrained by the price on similar routes in the United States. To treat it as such would not change the essence of the model.

[c]Apart from frequency, quality as measured by plane type is also extremely visible and might therefore be encouraged by the regulatory agency. For simplicity, we will continue to refer to F as standing for frequency, though it should be understood to refer to service quality in general.

The regulatory agency might be characterized as setting frequency and prices in both sectors as well as the level of subsidies in such a way as to maximize its utility function, subject only to the constraint that subsidies plus profits earned on the mainline routes equal losses incurred in outlying areas. But such a representation of the regulatory process ignores the constraints imposed by the political system on most regulatory agencies. This procedure is far too costly and would be a more appropriate representation of the behavior of a public enterprise in complete control of the industry. Instead, the agency shall be regarded as setting prices in both sectors (P_2 and P_1) and the amount of subsidies (S) it will offer to support loss services in sector 2.[d] Given the price on the profitable sector, the airlines are assumed to adjust frequency thereon (F_1) in order to maximize profits. Thus, we shall regard the regulatory agency's power to set prices on sector 1 and its ability to restrict entry as enabling it to control the profits earned thereon (R). The airlines, it is suggested, strike an implicit bargain with the regulatory agency. In return for protection and perhaps a level of profitability they would not otherwise have earned, they provide services that the regulatory agency finds desirable. In this case, the price on the loss sector (P_2), the profits earned in sector 1 (R), and the amount of subsidies (S) determine the frequency of service the airline will offer on the loss sector. Then, the frequency on the loss sector can be written:

$$F_2 = F_2(R[P_1], P_2, S),$$[e]

and the utility function of the regulatory agency becomes:

$$U\left\{F_2(R\ [P_1], P_2, S); P_2 - P_1; S; R[P_1]\right\}$$

The rational authority is assumed to maximize this function with respect to the parameters under its control (P_1, P_2, and S). In what follows, it will be assumed that $R_{P_1} > 0$–regulation maintains prices below the profit-maximizing point on the profitable sector–and that $F_{P_2} > 0$–a similar condition holds on the loss sector.[f]

[d] Even this amount of control did not always exist for the Canadian regulatory agency, since often the level of P_1, the price on the profitable mainline sector, was controlled not by the agency but by the Crown airline.

[e] While not necessary to write the function in this form, the simplest way to regard the process by which F_2 is determined would be if F_2 were maximized subject to the constraint that the net losses on sector 2 are offset exactly by profits earned on sector 1 plus subsidies. The actual bargain struck between the industry and regulatory agency is likely to be more complex. Both F and R will be assumed to possess the necessary properties for a maximum with respect to each of their arguments.

[f] Ordinarily one would expect F_{P_2} to be less than zero. But what is being assumed here is that as long as the price in this sector is below the profit-maximizing level the increased profits due to a price increase will be used to increase service because of the implicit bargain struck between the regulatory agency and the airlines.

Differentiating the agency's objective function with respect to P_1, P_2, and S gives the first order conditions:

$$U_{F_2} F_R R_{P_1} - U_{(P_2 - P_1)} + U_R R_{P_1} = 0 \qquad (2\text{–}1)$$

$$U_{F_2} F_{P_2} + U_{(P_2 - P_1)} = 0 \qquad (2\text{–}2)$$

$$U_{F_2} F_S + U_S = 0 \qquad (2\text{–}3)$$

These three equations yield:

$$U_{F_2} = -\frac{U_{(P_2 - P_1)}}{F_{P_2}} = -\frac{U_S}{F_S} = -\frac{U_R}{F_R + \frac{F_{P_2}}{R_{P_1}}}. \qquad (2\text{–}4)$$

In the previous chapter, it was argued that funds derived from subsidies were more visible to the public than those derived from cross-subsidization and might well yield the agency more public disapproval. Therefore, there was a presumption that the latter source would provide most of the funds that the regulatory agency would devote to the provision of service and control of the rate structure. But there is a second dimension to the disutility the regulatory agency suffers when raising funds—which dimension makes the relative attractiveness of cross-subsidization less certain. Both sources of funds will lead to pressures—on the one hand from communities, on the other hand from firms—for the benefits to be derived from the appropriation of these funds. The competition for the limited resources of the agency requires onerous and time-consuming arbitrations.[g] The behavior of the Canadian regulatory agency confirms the existence of this problem, for it has been reluctant to release information to the general public either as to which routes have received support or the reasons a particular route benefited from a subsidy.

The pressures emanating from communities for the benefits to be derived from each source of funds should be greater for subsidies because of their greater visibility. This would lead the agency once more to prefer cross-subsidies over direct payments. On the other hand, while the industry's information about the existence and size of each source of funds should not differ as it does for consumer groups, the value of a dollar derived from supra-normal profits earned on mainline routes is probably worth more to a firm than a dollar derived from direct subsidies. Generally, a firm may count on retaining more from funds that

[g]Ross Eckert, "Regulatory Commission Behavior: Taxi Franchising in Los Angeles and other Cities" (unpublished Ph.D. dissertation, University of California, 1968) suggests that the gradual reduction in the number of taxi firms as a result of local regulatory action might well be explained by the desire of these boards to minimize time spent arbitrating amongst competing applicants for what have become monopoly rights.

were generated internally than from subsidies paid for specific services. The public accountability of the regulatory agency reduces the extent to which subsidies can be used to generate supra-normal rates of return for a firm. Therefore, the relative importance of the pressures that will develop from the agency's use of the two sources of funds is no longer as certain. However, if the neutral assumption is made that there exists no difference between the disutility functions of each source of funds, then the first order conditions suggest that the regulatory agency will rely more upon profits generated on the mainline routes than upon subsidies. Rearranging two of the first order equations yields:

$$\frac{U_S}{U_R} = \frac{F_S}{F_R + F_{P_2}/R_{P_1}} \, . \tag{2–5}$$

If F_S is assumed equal to F_R (a dollar from either source is equally effective in providing service), then since F_{P_2}, $R_{P_1} > 0, U_S/U_R < 1$. In equilibrium, the marginal disutility from subsidies will be less than that from the profits devoted to cross-subsidization. This occurs because raising funds by permitting prices in sector 1 to rise above the competitive equilibrium reduces the price spread between the two sectors, thereby offsetting to some extent the disutility occasioned the agency by the funds themselves. Providing funds via direct subsidies has no comparable offsetting effect. If similar disutility functions are postulated, then greater marginal disutility from cross-subsidies implies greater reliance on this source of funds.

But F_S will not equal F_R if the fraction of an increase in mainline profits that is appropriated for internal use by the industry is greater than the fraction of subsidies that suffers a similar fate. However, it can still be proven that the regulatory agency will rely more upon such internally generated funds than upon direct subsidies. In the above formulation, internally generated funds directly enter the agency's utility function only once—as the net effect of industry support less the problems brought on by the supra-normal profit level. This may be modified by entering total profits (in order to represent the disutility suffered by the agency from having to arbitrate amongst competing applicants) and that portion of those profits that goes to the industry as separate terms. In addition, the constraint that total profits equal those retained by the industry plus those used to support services in the loss sector must be imposed. Then, by using the same procedure as was adopted above, it can be proven that in equilibrium the marginal disutility of subsidies to the agency will be less than the marginal disutility of total funds internally generated from the allowance of non-competitive prices on mainline routes.

This model may also be used to explore the effects of different exogenous events upon the level of prices, the extent of subsidy payments, and the degree of cross-subsidization sanctioned by the regulatory agency. In order to do this, certain additional properties of the objective function $U[F_2\ (P_2, P_1, S); P_2 - P_1;\ S;\ R(P_1)]$ previously ascribed to the regulatory agency will be assumed.

Consider this function to measure the units of support that an agency will receive from different combinations of the variables under its control. Units can take on a positive or negative sign. It will be assumed that all second order derivatives (U_{ii}) are negative. This requires that the number of units of support increases with frequency but at a decreasing rate and that as the price spread, and subsidies and cross-subsidization rise, units of support lost increase at an increasing rate. Secondly, it will be assumed that the marginal value to the agency of a unit of support derived from increasing frequency or decreasing the price spread (U_1 or U_2) is independent of the marginal utility (disutility) from subsidies or cross-subsidization (i.e., $U_{ij} = 0; i = [1,3]; j = [3,4]; i \neq j$).[h] This is reasonable if the agency is regarded as maximizing units of support and it is recognized that the difficulties which arise in the course of generating funds and the support arising from the industry in return for a portion of these funds does not affect the number of units of support arising from provision of service or control of the rate structure.[i]

However, since both frequency (F_2) and price spread ($P_2 - P_1$) serve the same constituency, U_{12} cannot be treated as zero. Treating the two policies as substitutes gives $U_{12} > 0$ (since $U_2 < 0$). Finally, the partial derivatives F_{P_2}, F_{P_1}, F_S will be treated as functions of P_2, P_1, and S, respectively. This is reasonable if the amount of funds available from one source does not affect the additional service that one dollar of funds from another source provides.

Four major events have stimulated the Canadian regulatory agency's interest in and modified its policy toward those scheduled carriers that primarily serve regional points. The history of the resulting "regional aviation policy" is recounted in Chapter Four. In this section, the model is used to predict how the regulatory agency might have been expected to alter the variables under its control in response to these events.

The first set of events that stimulated the development of a regional aviation policy involved a decrease in either the frequency or the quality of service in the loss sector. As Chapter Four will indicate, the immediate cause of these events varied. In one case, the cause was a decline in government contract work in the North, in two others, the immediate cause was the reduction in cost of a substitute mode of travel through the creation of a highway network. Thus, the agency was faced with a decline in frequency, not because of the decreased effectiveness of either source of funds used to support these services, but because of a shift to the left in the demand for service on these routes.

[h]The numbering 1 through 4 represents frequency on route 2, the price spread, subsidies and profits generated on mainline routes, respectively.

[i]Ordinarily, the survival decision rule determines the existence of interdependence effects amongst policies. With a 51 percent voting rule, it is possible that the marginal value of a policy falls to zero once the majority number of votes has already been assured. However, with the lack of such a clear cut decision rule, it is not unreasonable to assume that the agency maximizes the support it can get from each group.

The second event that stimulated the development of regional aviation policy caused the marginal utility the agency received from the provision of service to increase. During the 1950s, the introduction of turbo-equipment on the mainline routes of the Crown airline increased the disparity in the quality of service between these routes and those the agency treated as its prime constituent. Since it was argued that the support accruing to the agency from consumer groups depended upon their perception of benefits, the sudden increase in disparity that was beyond the control of the agency should have increased the support it would gain from an additional unit of service provided to these regional centers.

While the first two events led the agency to attempt to formulate a regional aviation policy, the third was instrumental in the implementation of the policy. The third event caused the marginal disutility suffered by the agency in obtaining funds to decrease. A major change in government policy in the mid 1960s—unrelated to the efforts of the aviation regulatory authorities—made subsidies easier for the regulatory agency to obtain. At the same time, greater opportunities for cross-subsidization were also opened up to the regulatory agency.

The final event of interest occurred during the implementation of the regional aviation policy. As we shall see, several of the regulated firms, which had begun receiving subsidies, decreased the effectiveness of these funds. This strategic maneuver was designed to pressure the agency to permit them greater entry to the mainline sector.

CASE 1: A SHIFT IN THE FREQUENCY FUNCTION (F_2)

Suppose that the frequency of service function in sector 2 shifts, but that F_{P_2}, F_{P_1}, and F_S are not affected. Such a result is possible if the demand curve in sector 2 shifts leftwards. F_2 should now be regarded as a function not only of P_2, P_1, and S, but also of a shift parameter α. Then differentiating the first order conditions gives:

$$\begin{bmatrix} \\ A \\ \\ \end{bmatrix} \begin{bmatrix} dP_2 \\ dS \\ dP_1 \end{bmatrix} = \begin{bmatrix} (-F_{P_2}U_{11} - U_{21})F_\alpha d\alpha \\ (-F_S U_{11})F_\alpha d\alpha \\ (-F_{P_1}U_{11} + U_{21})F_\alpha d\alpha \end{bmatrix}$$

where A =

$$\begin{bmatrix} F_{P_2P_2}U_1+U_{22}+F_{P_2}{}^2U_{11}+2F_{P_2}U_{12}\ ; & F_{P_2}F_SU_{11}+F_SU_{21}\ ; \\ \quad F_{P_2}F_{P_1}U_{11}-F_{P_2}U_{12}+F_{P_1}U_{12}-U_{22} & \\ F_SF_{P_2}U_{11}+F_SU_{12}\ ; & F_S{}^2U_{11}+F_{SS}U_1+U_{33}\ ; \\ \quad F_SF_{P_1}U_{11}-F_SU_{12} & \\ F_{P_1}F_{P_2}U_{11}+F_{P_1}U_{12}-F_{P_2}U_{12}-U_{22}\ ; & F_{P_1}F_SU_{11}-F_SU_{21}\ ; \\ \quad F_{P_1P_1}U_1+F_{P_1}{}^2U_{11}-2F_{P_1}U_{12}+U_{22}+U_4R_{P_1P_1}+R_{P_1}{}^2U_{44} & \end{bmatrix}.$$

Solving these equations by assuming the second order conditions are fulfilled yields:

$$sgn\ \frac{\delta P_2{}^{j}}{\delta\alpha} = sgn\ \frac{\delta P_1}{\delta\alpha} = sgn\ \frac{\delta S}{\delta\alpha} = -sgn\ F_\alpha > 0\ .$$

Therefore, the model predicts that the regulatory agency will seek to increase P_2, P_1, and S in response to a decrease in the frequency of service in sector two.

CASE 2: AN INCREASE IN THE MARGINAL UTILITY DERIVED FROM SERVICE TO THE LOSS SECTOR

Suppose the marginal support from a given service level to the loss sector increases. It has already been suggested that this could result from an increase in the perceived difference in quality between this sector and the mainline sector. If the objective function is now written so as to include a term $F_2 - F_1$ rather than just F_2 alone, then including a shift parameter α in F_1 yields results equivalent to those reported above. As in case 1, the regulatory agency is hypothesized to seek to increase P_2, P_1, and S.

[j]This and all subsequent results for P_2 require as a sufficient condition that $F_{P_2}U_{11} + U_{12} \leqslant 0$. It can be shown that this holds if the objective function is rewritten $U^2\{T[P_2 + G(F[P_2,P_1,S])];S;R[P_1]\}$ T, the support derived from regional routes, is a function of total cost–out of pocket cost P_2 and time cost G. Time cost G is a function of the frequency of service F. Providing $U_TT_{P_2} \neq 0$ and $G_{FF} \geqslant 0$, it can be shown that the above condition holds. $U_TT_{P_2} \neq 0$ requires nonsatiety on the part of the agency and the public. $G_{FF} > 0$ requires that as F increases G_F decreases–a condition that is fulfilled by functional relationship between time required per trip and frequency that is reported by Douglas and Miller in "Quality Competition, Industry Equilibrium, and Efficiency in the Price-Constrained Airline Market," *American Economic Review* LXIV, no. 4 (1974):663.

CASE 3: EASING THE DISUTILITY FROM SUBSIDIES

Suppose the difficulty in obtaining subsidies encountered by the regulatory agency is eased. Returning to the initial model, U_S or U_3 may be treated as functions of S and of a shift parameter α –that is, $d(U_3) = U_{33}dS + U_{3\alpha}d\alpha$ where $U_{3\alpha} > 0$. Differentiating the first order conditions gives:

$$\begin{bmatrix} \\ A \\ \\ \end{bmatrix} \begin{bmatrix} dP_2 \\ dS \\ dP_1 \end{bmatrix} = \begin{bmatrix} 0 \\ -U_{3\alpha}d\alpha \\ 0 \end{bmatrix}$$

Therefore, $sgn \dfrac{\delta P_2}{\delta \alpha} = sgn \dfrac{\delta P_1}{\delta \alpha} = -sgn\ U_{3\alpha} < 0$

$$sgn \frac{\delta S}{\delta \alpha} = sgn\ U_{3\alpha} > 0\ .$$

Thus, the regulatory agency should be expected to let the price in both sectors fall while permitting subsidies to increase. Since we are assuming $R_{P_1} > 0$, this implies subsidies are substituted for cross-subsidization. Using the same framework, any increased difficulty in obtaining subsidies would lead to a rise in prices in both sectors and a decrease in the amount of subsidies paid.

CASE 4: A DECREASE IN THE EFFECTIVENESS OF SUBSIDIES

Suppose the airline industry suddenly raised the costs of providing service via subsidies – that is, F_S is affected by a shift parameter α. Assume this is done in such a fashion that neither F_{P_2} nor F_{P_1} is affected. Then the equations become:

$$\begin{bmatrix} \\ A \\ \\ \end{bmatrix} \begin{bmatrix} dP_2 \\ dS \\ dP_1 \end{bmatrix} = \begin{bmatrix} 0 \\ -F_{S\alpha}U_1 d\alpha \\ 0 \end{bmatrix}$$

and $sgn \dfrac{\delta P_2}{\delta \alpha} = sgn \dfrac{\delta P_1}{\delta \alpha} = -sgn\ F_{S\alpha} > 0; sgn \dfrac{\delta S}{\delta \alpha} = sgn\ F_{S\alpha} < 0$

Combining this result with that reported in case 1 yields the prediction that the agency will attempt to increase the price in both sectors. Whether subsidies increase or decrease depends upon the magnitude of the offsetting effects of the decrease in frequency (case 1) and the increase in the costliness of this instrument (case 4).

In summary, a decrease in the frequency provided by the airlines should cause both sectors' prices to rise and subsidies to increase. In addition, anything that gives a sudden urgency to increasing support from the loss sector by improving the quality of service thereon should lead to a similar result. On the other hand, a decrease in the disutility experienced by the regulatory agency from subsidies should result in their substitution for cross-subsidization, while both sectors' prices should fall. Finally, if the effectiveness of subsidies decreases, the agency should be expected to increase prices in both sectors thereby increasing the amount of cross-subsidization.

Throughout this discussion it was assumed that profits available for cross-subsidization (R) were a function of price only. But the profits available to regional carriers are also a function of their participation in mainline markets. The previous analysis might equally well have been performed assuming R instead of P_1 was the control variable. In Canada, the regulatory agency does not have absolute jurisdiction over the Crown airline, which has the predominant share of these markets.[k] Nevertheless, the agency can still be hypothesized to respond to events in much the same manner as described above—but by changing the share of the mainline market taken by the regionals rather than by changing fares on this sector.

CONCLUSION

By its very nature, the formalized model introduced in this section cannot depict the entirety of the regulatory process. The regulatory agency may be able not only to choose the level of certain variables such as prices and subsidies but also to affect its environment in such a way as to influence the value of the parameters implicit in the utility function derived above. On the other hand, there may be other parameters in the utility function over which the regulatory agency has only loose control. For instance, implicit in the last case of the previous section was the assumption that the industry might unilaterally decrease the effectiveness of subsidies. The bargain struck between the industry and the regulatory agency in reality is renegotiable in response to numerous exogenous factors.

This model, along with the discussion of the first chapter, is meant to provide the framework within which the effect of these events can be understood. But it

[k]Chapter Three discusses the reasons for the evolution of this situation.

is more than a descriptive shell—empty of predictive content. The first two chapters have emphasized the nature of the compromise the agency is called upon to settle and the instruments available to it. The discussion in these chapters developed the prediction that the agency would rely primarily upon funds generated internally by the industry. It forecast the policies likely to be chosen in order to develop a group of consumer supporters. It predicted the reaction of the agency to certain exogenous events. With this background, the following two chapters explore the salient aspects of the history of aviation regulation in Canada. For along with an understanding of why the agency reacted to past events in a particular way comes predictions as to the likely result of alternative courses of government policies that might be adopted in the future.

Chapter Three

Interaction between the Regulatory Agency and the Political Process

The relationship between regulation and the larger political process of which it is a part was used to outline the problems the regulatory agency was called upon to solve and the instruments it was most likely to utilize. But this description of the decision set of an agency and its control variables should not be misconstrued to imply that the agency is a passive participant in the political process. The model suggests that the creation of regulatory agencies is a rational act only in terms of general tendencies. Governments may call upon a regulatory institution to perform a task for which it is inherently not suited, or they may deny the agency the instruments that have been suggested as being of critical importance. In either case, the survival-minded agency will find itself at variance with government policies and should be expected to seek the change them.

This chapter outlines, first, the failure of the initial framework chosen for the regulation of the Canadian air transport industry and, secondly, an attempt in the late 1950s by the government to deregulate a segment of the industry. The first episode illustrates the reaction of an agency when it is assigned a function for which it is inherently unsuited. Due to a change in market structure, its task changed from one of arbitrating issues in such a way as to satisfy all parties concerned, to one of imposing a course of action completely unsatisfactory to one participant. Placed in an untenable situation by a government that was slow to react to these events, the regulatory agency forced the issue with a route decision that contravened government policy. The second episode emphasizes the importance of entry controls to a regulatory agency. Faced with a new governing party that implemented deregulation of a segment of the industry, it was able to reverse this policy and regain control over entry.

INAUGURATION OF CANADIAN AIR TRANSPORT REGULATION

The demise of the initial regulatory framework is illustrative of the fate of an unsuccessful regulatory agency. The initial agency lasted only six years–from 1938 to 1944. Its failure has a twofold significance. First, it illustrates the importance of the survival motive–even in failure–for its dissolution was the result not of an irrational agency unmindful of survival, but of a changing industrial structure that led the agency to make decisions unpalatable to its chief constituent–the government. These decisions permitted survival but not in the field of airline regulation. In the second place, the failure must certainly have emphasized to the succeeding regulatory agency the consequences of failure and reinforced the immediacy of the self-perpetuation objective. As such, the early history of regulation reinforces the relevance of the positive model.

Both the regulatory framework and the government-owned airline were created almost simultaneously in the late 1930s. In 1936, the newly created "Department of Transport" inherited responsibility for civil aviation from the Ministry of Defence. At the time, the industry was composed of a large number of operators, the largest of which was Canadian Airways[a] (see Table 3–1). Initially, the federal government proposed that a new company be created around Canadian Airways to provide trunkline transcontinental services. The new company was to have three directors from the government railway (Canadian National Railways–CNR), three from its privately owned competitor (The Canadian Pacific Railway Company–CPR),[b] and three from the government.[c] When Canadian Pacific refused to participate on this basis, the Trans-Canada Air Lines Act [1] was passed, thereby creating a national carrier separate from Canadian Airways and funded entirely by the government. A year later, the Transport Act of 1938 gave the Board of Transport Commissioners, the traditional rail regulatory agency, jurisdiction over aviation as well.

Under the 1938 legislation, the Board was given the power to grant a license for new air services only after a finding that the service was necessary for "public convenience and necessity." Without fully defining the meaning of the term, the act did specify general guidelines to be followed. The Board was directed to "coordinate and harmonize the operations of all carriers" and to look favorably on those licenses that would develop "complementary rather than competitive functions of transport."[2] In granting a license, the Board was specifically directed to consider the harmful effect of competition upon existing operators.

In 1938, the regulatory board was faced with a large number of privately

[a]Canadian Airways had been formed in 1930 from a merger of lines serving the St. Lawrence Basin, the Prairies, and the Pacific Coast.

[b]Canadian National and Canadian Pacific had equal investments in Canadian Airways. However, together their joint holdings amounted to only a minority position.

[c]The government argued this would preserve the relative status of each railway, but permit it to have overriding say in the matter of the expenditure on facilities it would be called upon to make.

Table 3–1. Number of Operators and Distribution of Aircraft Ownership in the Private Sector of the Air Transport Industry, 1936–1944

Year	*Number of Operators*	*Number of Aircraft*	*Canadian Airways Aircraft*	*Canadian Pacific Aircraft*
1936	49	163	42	. . .
1937	59	206	36	. . .
1938	61	215	35	. . .
1939	43	178	37	. . .
1940	24	137	36	. . .
1941	24	142	34	. . .
1942	13	144	. . .	86
1943	14	137	. . .	76
1944	14	152	. . .	84

Source: Canada, Department of Reconstruction and Supply, Directorate of Air Development, "Development of Commercial Air Services in Canada, 1919–1944" (unpublished paper prepared by H. Cunningham, Ottawa, 1946, mimeographed), pp. 124–49.

owned airlines. Its role was to promote frontier aviation and to ensure feeder services into Trans-Canada Air Lines' transcontinental system. However, within six years the structure of the industry was drastically transformed. Between 1938 and 1944 the number of major operators fell from 61 to 14 (Table 3–1), as a result of the war and an acquisition program initiated by Canadian Pacific. By 1942, the railroad's airline subsidiary, Canadian Pacific Airlines, had acquired 10 companies including the previously dominant firm Canadian Airways.[3] Table 3-1 indicates that in 1938 the largest privately owned airline controlled only 16 percent of the aircraft used. By 1944, Canadian Pacific Airlines (CP Air) controlled over 55 percent of the aircraft operated. Table 3–2 shows the same trend in revenue plane-miles. Whereas in 1938 Canadian Airways flew only 19 percent of total revenue plane-miles, in 1944 CP Air flew over 33 percent of the total. If Trans-Canada Air Lines (Air Canada)[d] is excluded from the total, CP Air performed 78 percent of all private plane-miles flown in 1944. Of the 59 commercial licences issued as of December 31, 1944, exclusive of those held by Air Canada, CP Air possessed 54.[4] As the map in Figure 3-1 illustrates, by 1945, CP Air had acquired a series of regional networks across Canada that, if joined, would have created a transcontinental system closely paralleling that of Air Canada.

With the emergence of CP Air as virtually the only carrier besides Air Canada, the task of the regulatory agency was fundamentally altered. In essence, it had become the arbitrator between the government airline—Air Canada—and the private airline—CP Air.[e] The Board was experienced in this role since it had

[d] Trans-Canada Air Lines was renamed Air Canada in 1964.

[e] By 1944, it had submitted a number of applications for new routes that, if granted, would have connected its regional networks. See Canada, Parliament, House of Commons, *House of Commons Debates,* 5th Sess., 19th Parl., 8 George 6, Vol. V (1944), p. 4609.

Table 3–2. Relative Size of Trans-Canada Air Lines and Its Principal Competitor, as Measured by Revenue Plane-Miles Performed, 1936–1944 (000)

Year	*Total*	*Canadian Airways*	*Canadian Pacific*	*Trans-Canada Air Lines*
1936	7,200	1,900	.....	.....
1937	7,000	1,900	.....	.....
1938	9,000	1,700	.....	1,900
1939	8,100	1,700	.....	2,800
1940	10,000	2,000	.....	4,800
1941	11,500	1,800	.....	6,300
1942	12,800	.....	4,600	7,200
1943	15,000	.....	5,200	8,300
1944	15,900	.....	5,300	9,100

Source: Canada, Department of Reconstruction and Supply, Directorate of Air Development, "Development of Commercial Air Services in Canada, 1919–1944" (unpublished paper prepared by H. Cunningham, Ottawa, 1946, mimeographed), pp. 124–49.

played a similar one in the area of railroad regulation where it had long been occupied with problems involving the government-owned CNR and the privately owned CPR.[f]

Its success in the area of railroad regulation presented the Board with a dilemma once the structure of the industry had changed. With the entrance of Canadian Pacific into the airline industry, the Board's constituents in the rail and airline industries were no longer mutually exclusive. Decisions in both areas affected Canadian Pacific and therefore this firm's acceptance of the Board. Having spent decades developing industry and public acceptance in the field of railroad regulation, the Board was not likely to jeopardize its jurisdiction in this area merely because it had been given the fledgling airline industry to regulate. If the airline industry were removed from its purview, it would as least continue to function in the field of railroad regulation.

CP Air's parent company, the CPR, had already begun to exert considerable pressure on the government. Evidence suggests its power was not insignificant. For instance, following a request by the President of the CPR to the Prime Minister during this period that CP Air be permitted a greater role in domestic and international routes, the Cabinet was immediately convened to consider governmental aviation policy.[5] Even when existing policy was reconfirmed, the CPR returned once again to present its position, this time directly to the War Committee of the Cabinet.[6] While only these direct overtures have been fully documented, the CPR undoubtedly presented their case to the Board of

[f]The Board of Railway Commissioners became by the Transport Act of 1938 the Board of Transport Commissioners.

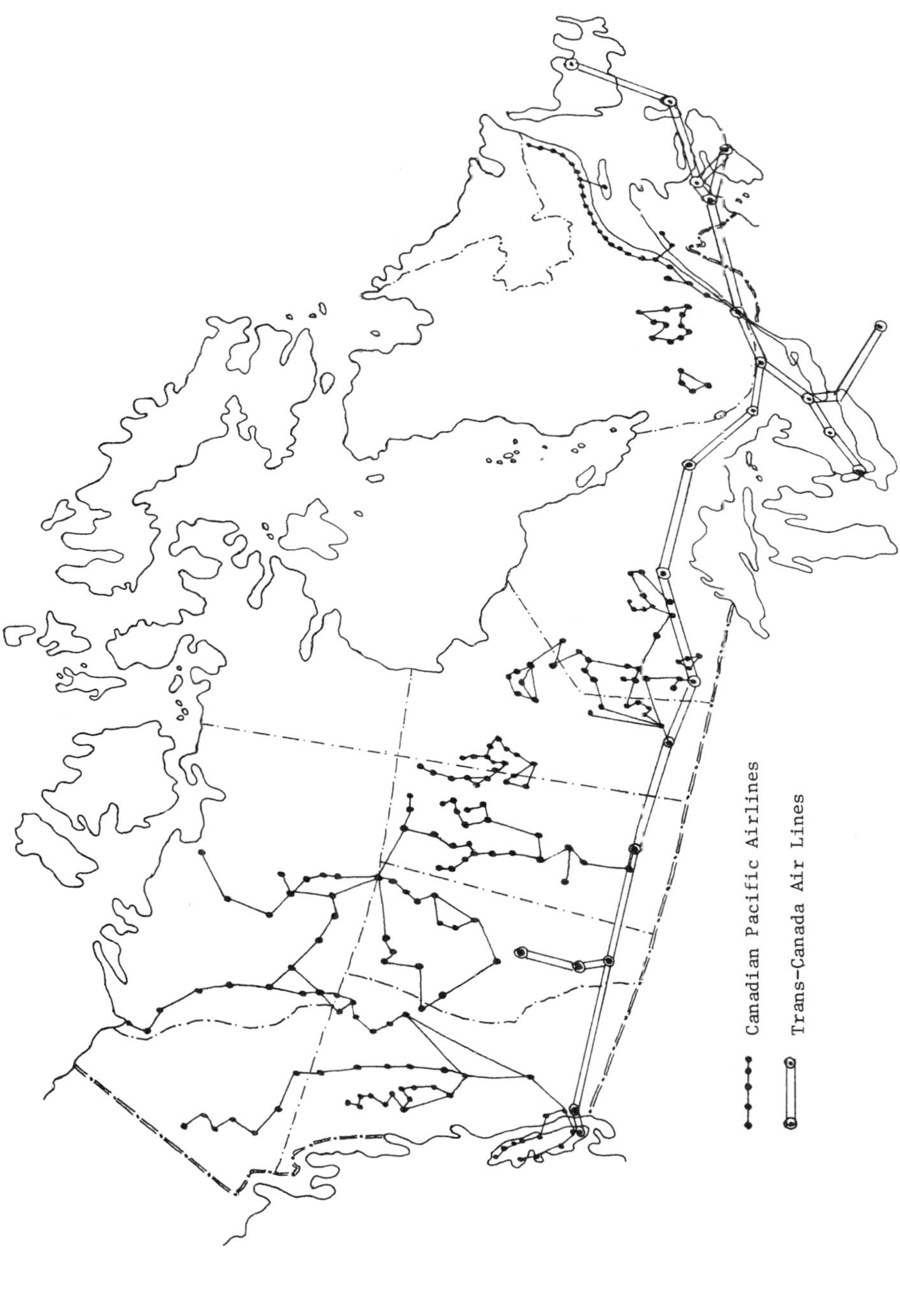

Figure 3-1. Map of Trans-Canada Air Lines (Air Canada) and Canadian Pacific Airlines (CP Air) Route Systems, 1945.

Transport Commissioners, with whom they had long ago established contacts because of the latter's regulatory function in the field of railway transportation. In fact, the Prime Minister, at the time the Rt. Hon. W. L. Mackenzie King, had indicated that he was aware of intense lobbying efforts being made in Ottawa by the CPR to change the government's aviation policy.[7]

The Board had been accepted by the industry only after it had succeeded in having itself regarded as an independent, impartial agency rather than as an arm of the government.[8] The pattern of its decisions in airline regulation were thus to parallel those which had proven to be successful in railroad regulation. Impartiality is most obvious in the case of route awards, it has been argued, if they are reasonably equally divided. However, with Air Canada having initially been granted transcontinental routes, impartiality in route awards was bound to conflict with the government's originally stated policy of having Air Canada remain the sole transcontinental carrier.

In 1943, the Board of Transport Commissioners made the decision that immediately brought it into conflict with avowed government policy—a decision whose ramifications must have been obvious to the agency. From Air Canada's inception, it had been the government's stated intention that the Crown airline was to operate a transcontinental run from Halifax, Nova Scotia to Victoria, British Columbia. Initially, Air Canada had subcontracted its mail contract between Vancouver and Victoria to the existing carrier—Canadian Airways—because the airport facilities in Victoria were temporarily inadequate. However, in 1943, when the Crown airline was ready to inaugurate its service, the Board of Transport Commissioners ruled that it could fly this route to carry mail, but that it could not transport passengers on this segment. As justification for this decision the Board argued that a carrier—by then owned by Canadian Pacific Air Lines—already existed thereon and there was insufficient traffic for two carriers.

Under the 1938 Transport Act, flights on new routes could be inaugurated only after the routes had been "designated" by the Governor-in-Council as requiring service and the Board had awarded them to an airline. But by the 1937 Trans-Canada Air Lines Act, the Governor-in-Council also had the power to enter directly into a contract with the Crown airline to fly specific routes. The Victoria decision meant the Board had still to approve the final designation of Air Canada if it was to do anything other than fly the mail over such routes. By 1944, CP Air not only had five operating divisions spread across the country, but also had made applications for services which would link these together.[9] In light of the Board's decision in the Victoria case, the possibility was very real that any new routes in the transcontinental system designated by the government would be awarded to CP Air.

This ruling also complicated government policy with respect to the designation of international routes. The north-west staging route (from Canada to Alaska) was slated to be operated by Air Canada in preparation for eventual expansion to the Orient.[10] However, by 1942, CP Air controlled the airline—the Yukon Southern—that already flew the Vancouver and Edmonton to Whitehorse routes. With the Board's decision on the Victoria route, there seemed to be no way to expand the Air Canada transcontinental system to Asia.

The government was as yet unwilling to countenance a division of transcontinental air traffic between Air Canada and CP Air.[11] A Gallup Poll indicated that public opinion was very much against expanding the role of CP Air and downgrading that of the government airline.[12] More important, the Prime Minister worried that a lessening of government support for the Crown airline would provide the CCF—an opposition party—with an issue that would enable them to make considerable gains at the expense of the government in the forthcoming postwar elections.[13] On the other hand, it could not force the Board of Transport Commissioners to follow government aviation policy more closely, both because of the safeguards that had evolved to protect the Board's independence and because acceptable behavior on the part of the Board would require it to favor the government airline and cause the Board considerable difficulties in the regulation of the railways.

Therefore, in 1944, the government recognized that the structure of the industry had changed sufficiently that the Board of Transport Commissioners was no longer the institution to regulate the air transport industry. It gave sole responsibility for aviation regulation to a new agency, the Air Transport Board.[g] Separation of responsibilities for rail and aviation regulation should have reduced the pressure on the Air Transport Board to treat both private and public airlines alike. But, as has been argued, this would not suffice in the long run. Therefore, the government moved to constrain the agency's decision set—at least vis-à-vis the Crown airline. Not only was the new Board made directly responsible to the Minister of Transport,[h] but it was made clear that any Order-in-Council, which was used to assign routes to the Crown airline, was to be final and not subject to review by the Air Transport Board.[14] Thus, the new Board was left only with the task of regulating the aviation industry outside of the Crown airline.

The regulatory crisis in this particular instance evolved essentially because of a recognition lag on the part of the government. A changing market structure meant the original institution required change, and that very institution took the action that forced the government to evolve a more satisfactory framework for regulation. But crises in regulatory institutions may also be caused by errors made by governments whose information as to the likely benefits of regulation is incorrect. The next episode illustrates this phenomenon.

[g]The Board of Transport Commissioners continued in its previous role of regulating the railway industry.

[h]The Minister, in answer to a question as to whether this was contrary to the tradition of transportation regulation in Canada, responded that the decisions required (in the case of conflict between Air Canada and CP Air) were not "judicial" and should not be so treated. See Canada, *House of Commons Debates,* Vol. V (1944), p. 4946.

ENTRY RESTRICTIONS AND THE AIR TRANSPORT BOARD

The model proposed herein does not purport to explain every event, nor to claim that certain excluded variables might not at times be relevant. Strong personalities will occasionally succeed in diverting policies from the direction the model would otherwise predict. The power of the model lies in its ability to predict that these deviations will be temporary and to catalogue the forces that should counteract these aberrations. The attempt by the Minister of Transport to deregulate the industry in the late 1950s is just such an aberration.

The behavioral model has suggested the importance of entry controls to the transportation regulatory agency. Without such controls evidence on the lack of scale economies and other barriers to entry [15] suggests that the amount of profits that can be created for cross-subsidization purposes will be insignificant. Restriction of entry is the primary instrument by which the regulatory agency creates support for itself—both inside and outside the industry. Therefore, the agency will resist any attempt to weaken its control and is likely to seek controls when it either loses them or does not initially possess them. The brief Canadian experiment with deregulation illustrates not only the extent to which entry controls have been relied upon by the Canadian regulatory authority, but also its predictable reaction to the threatened loss of this instrument.

The legislation that created the Air Transport Board in 1944 gave it substantial controls over the industry. All commercial air services were to require a licence issued by the Air Transport Board. Only in the case of Trans-Canada Air Lines (Air Canada) was the licence to be automatic.[i] All other services were to require a finding of "present and future public convenience and necessity."[16] In issuing a licence, the Board was given not only the negative rights of disallowance, but also the positive right of prescription on such issues as rates, schedules, type of traffic carried, and actual route followed.

Although the 1944 Act did not define "public convenience and necessity," the Transport Act of 1938 suggested some considerations the then Board of Transport Commissioners might take into account in awarding new licences. Apart from those provisions requiring financial and technical competence of the applicant, these conditions placed upon an applicant the onus to demonstrate the required need for the new service.[j] Foremost amongst the considerations that were suggested for possible examination by the Board of Transport

[i] Canada, *An Act to Amend the Aeronautics Act, 1944,* 8 George 6, ch. 28, *Statutes of Canada,* 1944. "The Board shall upon application grant to T.C.A. Lines [Air Canada] a licence to operate a commercial air service in such terms and subject to such conditions as will enable Trans-Canada Air Lines to perform any agreement made between the Minister of Transport and Trans-Canada Air Lines under section 15 of the Trans-Canada Air Lines Act, 1937."

[j] Contrary to the history of airline regulation in the United States, no "presumption in favor of competition" ever existed in Canada.

Commissioners were whether new services would result in overcapacity, whether tolls were "reasonable," whether other transportation modes would be affected, and whether the new service would be "complementary" rather than "competitive."[17] Thus, legislation accorded the agency the means by which it could erect barriers that would protect the existing firms in the industry. The procedures adopted by the Air Transport Board reinforced this emphasis. Except for a few categories of specialty licences, only "interested" parties were informed of new applications and allowed to make written submissions. Public hearings were held only at the discretion of the Board.

For purposes of licencing, the Air Transport Board classified aircraft by maximum authorized take-off weight and carriers by type of service offered. Aircraft of less than 2,500 pounds were classified in Group C; those from 2,500 to 18,000 pounds were placed in Group B; and those in excess of 18,000 pounds made up Group A. Class 1 carriers were defined as those offering unit toll service in accordance with a regular schedule. Class 2 carriers differed only from Class 1 insofar as their service was offered less frequently. Class 3 was also a unit toll service, offered infrequently—virtually service on demand. Class 4 included all carriers offering charter services from a designated base. Contract air carriers were placed in Class 5. Class 6 consisted of non-profit flying clubs, while Class 7 included all firms engaged in specialty and photographic work.

In 1957, the Conservative party regained control of the government for the first time since 1935. While in opposition, they had called for greater competition in the air transport industry. In July of 1958, the Conservative Minister of Transport, the Hon. G. Hees, announced that, as part of his policy of encouraging greater competition, he was decontrolling all operations involving the smallest classification of aircraft—Group C.[18] The announcement referred only to class of aircraft, not type of service. However, the Air Transport Board regulations when published made clear that the policy applied only to Class 4 (charter operations) and to Class 7 (specialty licences). A year later, in December 1959, the Minister proceeded one step further by deregulating Group B aircraft for the same two classes of service.

How effective the entry controls had been is evidenced by a marked rise in the number of carriers in the charter and specialty classes. Table 3–3 indicates that 1958 marked the beginning of a large expansion in both these categories—the major users of Group C aircraft. This expansion cannot be explained by a general upsurge in traffic. As Table 3–4 indicates, capacity ton-miles for bulk or charter operations did not increase markedly during this period. Before deregulation, entry controls appear to have been sustaining firms at levels larger than the market alone would have permitted.

The reaction was almost immediate. The Air Transport Industries Association on October 26, 1959, urged the old restrictions on entry be re-implemented.[19] Following the extension of deregulation to Class B aircraft in 1959, they went so far as to bypass the Minister of Transport and approach the

Table 3–3. Number of Air Carriers with Class 4 and Class 7 Licenses, 1945–1964

Year	Class 4	Class 7
1945	18	. . .
1946	85	21
1947	159	243
1948	166	282
1949	161	248
1950	150	233
1951	133	225
1952	124	201
1953	144	216
1954	152	221
1955	156	235
1956	171	254
1957	180	274
1958	205	323
1959	233	459
1960	254	524
1961	272	642
1962	284	687
1963	315	736
1964	304	725

Prime Minister directly.[20] Little is known about the Air Transport Board's position at this time. Since the Minister was adamant in his stand,[k] the Air Transport Board did not, at first, openly oppose him. However, by 1963 the Board was actively campaigning to reimplement the controls it once enjoyed. Its president openly criticized government policy with the statement that "it is impossible to contemplate further prolonging an air transport policy which does not make sense."[21] Deregulation was approved of by neither the industry nor the Air Transport Board.

It was suggested that entry controls would be used by the Board not only to obtain support from the industry, but also because they were necessary if the cross-subsidization of services was to be developed in order to garner the support of a politically important subset of users. The arguments used by the industry in its effort to have controls reimposed do indeed suggest cross-subsidization was being used to benefit a specific group of users.

Class 4, the charter carriers that were affected by the new regulations had previously received "base protection" from the Air Transport Board. Under this policy each carrier was designated a home base. Carriers could originate flights out of the home base of another carrier only if the home operator had refused

[k]The Minister stated publicly that "the Air Transport Industry is interested in maintaining a monopoly." See Canada, *House of Commons Debates,* 3rd Sess., 24th Parl., 8–9 Elizabeth 2, Vol. II (1960), p. 1856.

Table 3–4. Capacity Ton-Miles, Bulk Operations, 1952–1963, by Aircraft Category (Capacity ton-miles in 000)

Year	*Group A*	*Group B*	*Group C*
1952	16,958	5,112	593
1953	23,445	6,486	780
1954	10,281	5,041	1,075
1955	93,624	6,521	1,770
1956	114,661	8,676	2,899
1957	78,005	8,377	2,540
1958	39,085	6,618	1,915
1959	43,552	6,958	2,046
1960	48,448	7,490	2,657
1961	44,022	7,029	2,341
1962	53,647	6,972	2,614
1963	85,747	10,087	384

Source: Estimate prepared from reports of air carriers to the Air Transport Board.

the charter. With free entry this protection disappeared. The industry argued that this meant many of the smaller communities would lose their local company. The summer business would be skimmed by the larger carriers, and these communities would be left without year-round service. In effect, the small carriers were arguing that without the lucrative summer traffic which others were prepared to carry at a lower price, they would be unable to offer year round services—at least at existing fares.

The combined weight of the industry and these communities was sufficient to overcome any increased political support that the Conservative government might have received from those consumers who benefited from deregulation. In February 1963, following Hees' resignation from the Cabinet over an unrelated matter, the Conservative government quickly reversed its position by reregulating all Group B aircraft.[22] Although Group C aircraft were for the moment left untouched, the dividing line for classifying aircraft in Group B or Group C was lowered from 2,500 to 1,100 pounds, thereby reclassifying the Cessna 180 to Group B and reregulating most of the industry.[1] By November 1963, the remaining aircraft in Group C were included in regulation, while the only category—specialty licences—still unregulated, had all applications frozen.[23] In April 1967, specialty services re-entered the regulatory umbrella.

This episode provides corroborative evidence for our behavioral model of the regulatory agency. The successful regulatory agency will develop a group of supporters—from both industry and consumers—that makes its continued existence important to the government. The Conservative government's inability to deregulate the industry provides evidence of the Air Transport Board's

[1] This accounts for the sudden jump during 1963 in Group B's capacity ton-miles as reported in Table 3–4.

successful use of entry controls. Moreover, it tends to substantiate the earlier contention that the support of a subset of users—a group which is politically important because of either its intensity of emotion or geographic distribution—combined with the support of the industry can be worth more to a government than the displeasure of those consumers who suffer under regulation. The government actively sought support from the public for its policy, only to find that the political costs of doing so outweighed the benefits.

CONCLUSION

These two incidents serve to emphasize that the role for which a regulatory agency is ideally suited is a limited one. Its function is to resolve a conflict between two parties in such a way that neither party is inordinately alienated from the government. This automatically restricts both the decision set and the control variables available to it. It can utilize threats, unpopular solutions, and fines or penalties only rarely. As such it is most likely to succeed where it can divide the benefits "equitably" among the participants, and if it cannot do so, where it can compensate one party with side-payments. The first episode, the demise of the initial institution, indicates how important equity is in the bargaining process. The agency essentially could not function when government policy called for one policy, and one participant, whose support was required in another facet in the agency's operations (railway regulation), refused to accept this policy. The second episode illustrates how important entry controls are to the agency. It is essentially via offers of rewards that the agency can create support. But the best evidence of the Canadian Air Transport Board's behavior lies in the relationship it has had with its chief constituent—the "regional" airlines. It is to this topic that we now turn.

Chapter Four

Regional Aviation Policy

The growth of the regional air carriers in the late 1960s occurred under the aegis of the government's "regional aviation policy." First announced in 1966, the policy was meant to facilitate the development of airline service to regional points both in terms of number of points served as well as quality of service.[a] Five carriers were singled out to be the "chosen instruments" for the implementation of these objectives. Pacific Western Airlines (PWA), Transair, Nordair,[b] Quebecair, and Eastern Provincial Airways (EPA) were chosen as the carriers to "provide regular route operations into the north" and to "operate local or regional routes to supplement the domestic mainline operations of Air Canada and Canadian Pacific Airlines."[1] The map in Figure 4–1 outlines their route systems as of 1970.

Stimuli both external and internal to the industry have affected the formulation of "regional aviation policy." The development of the model of the transportation regulatory agency recognized the importance of the environment in which this institution operated. The environment of the political system determines both the agency's objectives and the instruments under its control. A changing environment may place more or less pressure on an agency to fulfill certain objectives if it is going to survive. It may also change both the cost to the regulatory board of the different policies as well as the efficiency with which

[a] Although not specifically outlined in the announcement of policy, these objectives may be culled from the two public documents, both issued by the Air Transport Board. They are Canada, Air Transport Board, *Report to the Minister of Transport on Transcontinental Air Services* (Ottawa, December 1958) and K.W. Studnicki-Gizbert, *The Regional Air Carriers' Problem,* a study prepared for the Air Transport Board (Ottawa: Queen's Printer, 1966).

[b] In the discussion that follows, Nordair will be ignored because, although officially designated as a "regional," government policy in this area had very little impact upon it. In fact, although it was designated as a "regional" in 1966, the government's own statistical publications do not include it in this category until 1970.

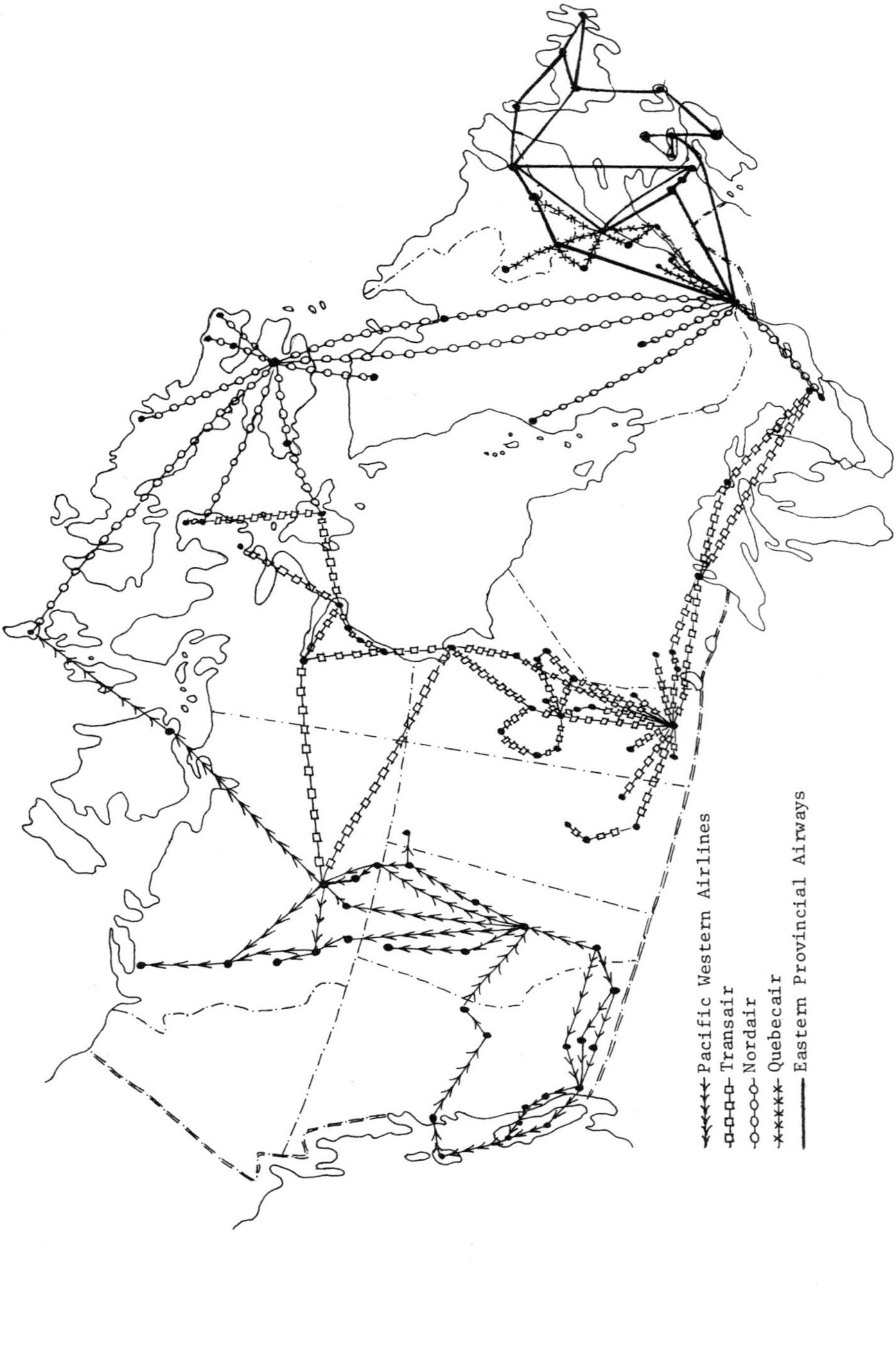

Figure 4–1. Map of Regional Carriers Route System, 1970.

they can be used to achieve the agency's objectives. Thus, a model of a regulatory agency risks being sterile without a discussion of the environment in which a particular agency operates. The previous chapter stressed that the agency could and did interact with the rest of the political process to influence both the task it was called upon to perform as well as the instruments available to it. This chapter describes the manner in which the regulatory agency has reacted to changes in the economic health of the industry, to changes in government policy, and to "strategic" behavior on the part of regional carriers. In doing so, it uses the model of a transportation regulatory agency developed in Chapters One and Two as a framework for the discussion.

THE EMERGENCE OF A "REGIONAL AVIATION POLICY"

The early demise of the Board of Transport Commissioners' authority over aviation regulation served to emphasize to its successor, the Air Transport Board, the susceptibility of a regulatory agency that failed to develop a cadre of supporters. This, combined with the fact that the new agency had its purview restricted to that part of the industry lying outside of the main transcontinental routes, should have guaranteed that the agency would actively develop support in this segment of the industry—from both the public and the industry. The controversy over deregulation of what was essentially the charter segment of this market confirms this hypothesis. But, the Air Transport Board should have taken an equal interest in promoting regularly scheduled services to off-line points. This section substantiates the existence of this concern and traces the stimuli that led to the emergence of a "special" policy for a small group of airlines that were to be earmarked as the regional carriers.

The initial impetus giving rise to the agency's perception of a need for a "regional aviation policy" was the economic crisis that struck this segment of the industry in the late 1950s. A brief description of the historical development of regional carriers is required to understand the situation confronting the regulatory board at that time.

By 1945, Canadian Pacific Airlines (CP Air) had come to dominate the private sector of the industry—primarily through their acquisition of competitors during the war years.[c] The Air Transport Board was, however, faced with the problem of returning wartime flyers who desired entry to the industry. The Board used its control over entry to strike an implicit bargain with CP Air. It announced that CP Air's future role lay in scheduled operations using multi-engined aircraft.[2] The airline stood to benefit in two ways. First, the uncertainties it had faced in expanding into scheduled services were reduced. Secondly, since it was the only carrier designated for expansion of scheduled

[c]See Chapter Three.

services, it was implicitly being promised a protected position.[d] The Board stood to benefit by being assured of regular services to frontier points backed by the resources of Canadian Pacific. In turn, the Board made it clear that it expected this policy would cause CP Air to turn over some of its local services, expecially the charter licences, to new entrants.[e] Providing CP Air turned over more than just its unprofitable routes, the agency would succeed in creating a new group of local carriers.[f] Thus, in the initial postwar era, the development of local carriers was to be governed by the rate at which Canadian Pacific divested itself of its local services as well as the growth of the natural resources frontier upon which most of these services depended.

As a result of the announcement of its new role, Canadian Pacific began to withdraw from its non-scheduled "bush" operations in 1947.[3] Table 4–1 indicates that this marked the beginning of entry by new carriers. Between 1946 and 1947, the number of small charter carriers (Class 4) almost doubled. In addition, the number of scheduled carriers in Class 1 made a discontinuous jump as CP Air abandoned some of its more insignificant routes in this classification and as new carriers were created to serve the new routes which CP Air no longer aggressively sought to control.

The Air Transport Board made no attempt to impose rigid restrictions upon the new airlines as to the type of traffic (passenger versus freight) or the type of service (regularly scheduled as compared to charter operations) permitted. As a result, carriers were readily able to adapt to varying demands placed upon them by changing market conditions. Table 4–2 outlines the relative growth of the privately owned scheduled and non-scheduled (charter) sectors of the industry. While those airlines that concentrated their services in scheduled operations flew four times as many passenger-ton-miles as goods-ton-miles,[g] the division of traffic between passengers and freight was more equal for the non-scheduled

[d]Maritime Central Airways—operating in the Atlantic Provinces—was promised similar status and eventually developed into the regional carrier Eastern Provincial Airways. However, operating in a completely different region of the country, it offered no threat to CP Air whose operations were based in the west at this time.

[e]This wording, in place of a direct order, emphasizes how important voluntary agreement is to the functioning of the regulatory agency. See Canada, Air Transport Board, *Report on Review of Licences Respecting Commercial Air Services Pursuant to Section 13 of the Aeronautics Act* (Ottawa, April 1947), p. 13.

[f]This situation left some uncertainties for the Board. In particular, the Board could not be certain the services that CP Air vacated would be maintained at the same level. But such uncertainty is characteristic of the regulatory process. Because the effectiveness of these policies depends upon the response of the industry, the Board must learn the efficacy of route awards and subsidy programs only after the fact. The Board could reduce its uncertainty by directly setting the level of service expected of the new entrants. But this would imply that we are dealing not with a regulatory agency but with the beginnings of a Crown airline.

[g]To make this comparison, the arbitrary but commonly used figure of 200 pounds per passenger is used to convert the passenger-miles figures found in Table 4–2 to passenger-ton-miles.

Table 4–1. Number of Operators in Classes 1 to 4, 1945–1964

Year	*Class 1*	*Class 2*	*Class 3*	*Class 4*
1945	...	1	...	18
1946	1	7	...	85
1947	8	5	...	159
1948	9	8	...	166
1949	10	18	...	161
1950	11	21	...	150
1951	10	12[a]	8[a]	133
1952	8	13	9	124
1953	8	15	11	144
1954	8	16	14	152
1955	8	19	15	156
1956	8	14	19	171
1957	10	17	20	180
1958	9	17	30	205
1959	8	17	32	233
1960	7	16	31	254
1961	7	14	30	272
1962	7	13	36	284
1963	7	15	34	315
1964	6	14	36	304

[a]In 1951, Class 2 was divided into (a) regular specific point or new Class 2 and (b) irregular specific point or Class 3.

Table 4–2. Comparison of the Size of Domestic Scheduled Carriers (Exclusive of Air Canada) to Domestic Non-Scheduled Carriers, 1946–1951, by Passenger-Miles and Goods Ton-Miles Performed

Year	*Scheduled*		*Non-Scheduled*	
	Passenger-Miles (000)	*Goods Ton-Miles (000)*	*Passenger-Miles (000)*	*Goods Ton-Miles (000)*
1946	33,700	1,200	4,000	100
1947	35,000	1,300	8,600	800
1948	46,100	1,200	12,300	1,000
1949	57,100	1,300	9,700	800
1950	67,600	1,400	10,200	800
1951	84,500	2,100	13,400	1,100

Source: K. W. Studnicki-Gizbert, "The Structure and Growth of the Canadian Air Transport Industry," *Papers of the Canadian Political Science Association Conference on Statistics* (Toronto: U. of Toronto Pr., 1960), pp. 248–49, and 246, 253.

sector. But these percentages varied considerably across carriers in each group. For the scheduled carriers, bulk or charter revenues as a percentage of total operating revenues varied from a high of almost 40 percent, for carriers like Maritime Central and Central Northern, to a low of 9 percent for CP Air.[4]

The growth both in the non-scheduled and the scheduled private carriers not owned by CP Air reduced the latter's predominant position in this segment of the industry. In 1946, as Table 4–3 indicates, CP Air accounted for 84 percent of all domestic flying revenues earned in the private sector. By 1951, its share had fallen to only 43 percent.

Although CP Air had withdrawn from chartered bush operations, and no longer completely dominated the private sector, the extension of its scheduled services was to influence the pattern of expansion of the remaining scheduled carriers. In 1947 and 1948, it expanded its operations from Vancouver northward to Prince Rupert and Prince George and onwards to Whitehorse in the Yukon. In 1947, it connected Winnipeg with the northern Manitoba communities of The Pas and Flin Flon. Subsequently, it expanded this route to Churchill on Hudson's Bay. Similarly, in 1948, it expanded northward from Edmonton to Dawson Creek. In the east, Montreal was linked to the Northern Quebec communities of Val-Dor (1948) and Noranda (1949). Starting in the early 1950s, it attempted to link these north-south feeders. In 1950, it expanded from Edmonton east through Lloydminster and North Battleford to link with its Prairie route down through Saskatoon and Regina. In 1952, it joined Vancouver to Calgary, with intermediate stops in the Okanagan Valley of British Columbia. In the east, it extended its Montreal-Quebec services (Quebec Airways) west to Toronto via northern Ontario (1952), and east to Sept Isles (1953).

In the meantime, the other scheduled carriers underwent rapid expansion particularly in the area of northern freight operations, which culminated in the

Table 4–3. CP Air's Declining Importance in the Private Sector, 1946–1951, as Measured by Its Share of Domestic Flying Revenues

Year	*Flying Revenues All Domestic Carriers Exclusive of Air Canada ($000)*	*Domestic Flying Revenues CP Air ($000)*	*CP Air Revenues As % of Total*
1946	8,700	7,300	84
1947	10,200	6,200	52
1948	12,700	6,100	48
1949	12,200	6,000	49
1950	13,700	6,600	48
1951	17,600	7,700	43

Source: K. W. Studnicki-Gizbert, "The Structure and Growth of the Canadian Air Transport Industry," *Papers of the Canadian Political Science Association Conference on Statistics* (Toronto: U. of Toronto Pr., 1960), pp. 248–49, and 246, 253.

Table 4–4. The Growth of Regional Carriers: Operating Revenues; Passengers, Goods, and Mail Carried, 1952–1963

Year	*Operating Revenues*	*Passengers Carried*		*Goods Carried*	*Mail Carried*
	($)	*(No.)*	*(Tons)*	*(Tons)*	*(Tons)*
1952	18,740,379	497,658	49,800	18,873	2,033
1953	21,596,048	528,824	52,900	29,780	2,292
1954	18,080,165	550,875	55,100	19,247	2,654
1955	47,321,751	644,685	64,500	68,290	2,813
1956	53,111,256	738,562	73,900	87,165	2,668
1957	42,111,916	737,895	73,800	47,569	3,187
1958	34,728,734	643,001	64,300	30,976	3,422
1959	41,063,984	804,017	80,400	44,446	3,383
1960	43,691,249	773,418	77,300	46,832	3,531
1961	43,411,619	789,765	78,900	34,511	4,084
1962	48,351,816	887,820	88,800	28,559	4,336
1963	50,139,422	954,469	95,400	39,840	4,625

Note: This group includes more than the five carriers designated as "regionals" in 1966.
Source: Compiled from the Reports of the Commercial Air Carriers to the Air Transport Board.

defence contracts for the DEW line construction in the mid-1950s. Table 4–4 indicates the rapid growth in freight traffic that resulted. But these resource booms also resulted in great volatility in the amount of total traffic carried. Most of this was the result of the fluctuations in freight traffic. For instance, on the basis of weight, goods traffic was one-third as large as passenger traffic in 1952; by 1956 it had surpassed passenger traffic, only to fall to one-half that of passenger traffic by 1958 and 1959.

Although the high percentage of variable costs in airline operations permits ready adjustments to changing levels of demand,[5] the post-1956 depression initially led to substantial reductions in the operating profits of Quebecair, Transair, and Pacific Western. As Table 4–5 indicates, Pacific Western had little difficulty in adjusting its costs, while both Quebecair and Transair required two years to overcome the operating deficits that resulted.

Not unnaturally, the regional carriers reacted to this adverse turn of events by seeking to expand their scheduled services—in particular their passenger operations. However, two carriers—Air Canada and CP Air—already operated a network of scheduled services. Our discussion of the regulatory agency's objectives suggested that the Air Transport Board would make every effort to assure the health of the carriers under its jurisdiction in order to maintain operations to the points these carriers already served. The impetus behind a review of policy vis-à-vis entry to the scheduled market was afforded by the newly elected Conservative government's order in 1957 to review the competitive relationship between Air Canada and CP Air.

Table 4–5. Operating Results—Revenue and Profits—of Pacific Western, Transair, Quebecair, and Eastern Provincial Airways, 1956–1969 ($000)

	1956	1957	1958	1959	1960	1961	1962	1963	1964	1965	1966	1967	1968	1969
Pacific Western:														
Operating Revenues	10,430	6,781	7,073	7,864	8,628	6,782	5,942	6,291	8,870	11,537	12,256	14,934	17,618	31,574
Operating Income (Loss)	498	73	640	241	(195)	50	(148)	249	373	982	927	1,078	1,066	1,361
Net Income (Loss) after Taxes	159	68	650	415	(412)	10	(317)	115	331	601	1,425	642	285	562
Transair:														
Operating Revenues	3,115	2,769	3,048	2,868	2,861	4,202	5,238	5,645	5,039	5,054	6,011	5,736	6,254	8,501
Operating Income (Loss)	(1)	(407)	(49)	156	154	223	330	390	199	74	(243)	(254)	(633)	(1,780)
Net Income (Loss) after Taxes	274	(235)	(160)	51	45	110	193	197	180	233	(256)	(185)	(652)	(2,057)
Quebecair:														
Operating Revenues	2,696	2,124	2,046	3,187	3,603	3,254	3,697	3,654	3,679	4,119	5,399	5,499	6,277	8,534
Operating Income (Loss)	69	(110)	(46)	242	(16)	(615)	249	16	60	(16)	(595)	(344)	(999)	(788)
Net Income (Loss) after Taxes	7	(150)	(46)	137	(146)	(923)	130	(46)	151	(153)	(770)	(585)	(630)	(970)
Eastern Provincial[a]:														
Operating Revenues	10,041	7,739	2,766	2,898	3,245	2,987	2,660	5,647	5,755	5,307	6,311	7,514	9,147	11,405
Operating Income (Loss)	2,086	1,113	(813)	231	285	95	(307)	319	(182)	(953)	(84)	(178)	438	141
Net Income (Loss) after Taxes	835	519	(894)	134	466	249	(193)	(1,094)	(309)	(690)	(383)	(611)	76	(350)

[a]Maritime Central: 1956–1962
Eastern Provincial: 1963–

Source: Canada, Dominion Bureau of Statistics, *Civil Aviation–Annual,* Cat. No. 51–202, 1956–1969.

A commissioned study of the industry, although directed primarily at transcontinental competition, responded to the "problem" of the regionals by proposing that certain routes be transferred to them and that a policy of direct subsidies be implemented.[6] This study reflected the Board's anxiety about the financial position of these carriers and rationalized an extension of their services on the grounds that they would be able to operate "regional" routes at lower cost than the dominant carrier—Air Canada.[7]

In the subsequent hearings held by the Board to determine the extent to which CP Air would be permitted to expand into the transcontinental route system in direct competition with Air Canada, the regionals (with the exception of PWA[h]) requested the rejection of Canadian Pacific's transcontinental ambitions and the strengthening of their own systems. The Board was obviously sympathetic to their position for, although ostensibly investigating the issue of competition between CP Air and Air Canada, it dealt at length in its final report with the need for expansion of the regional carriers. Its stated objective was the maintenance and improvement of the quality of services provided by the regionals, and it argued that expansion was urgently need to finance re-equipment of the carriers.[8]

The Board did, however, recognize that subsidies could not be used, because of their political unacceptability. Therefore, it conditioned the possibility of route transfers on the regionals' ability to operate such routes without resorting to subsidies.[9] Nevertheless, it was able to argue in favor of a transfer of some routes by suggesting that even though Air Canada claimed it was losing money on many of these routes, the regional carriers would not require subsidies because of the probability that their operating costs would be lower.

Meanwhile, the very success of the regionals in adjusting to lower traffic levels and the existence of a substantial regional domestic network served by CP Air and Air Canada obviated any immediate action on the part of the government. While the regulatory agency's interest in service to regional points did not diminish, it was unsuccessful in evincing any fundamental change in policy. However, events combined to increase the importance to the agency of strengthening the regional carriers.

As CP Air expanded both domestically and overseas, it divested itself of several regional routes. In 1955, CP Air transferred its Northern Ontario and Quebec system to Air Canada in exchange for Air Canada's rights from Toronto to Mexico City.[i] In 1957, PWA took over the CP Air North Prairie route from Edmonton through North Battleford, Prince Albert, Saskatoon, and Regina, while Transair received Winnipeg-Dauphin-The Pas-Flin Flon in northern Manitoba. CP Air had long argued that strong international routes were needed to cross-subsidize its domestic route system. Although CP Air itself has

[h] PWA's support was obtained by CP Air's promise to transfer to PWA some of its "regional" routes.

[i] Chapter Eight explains why the Crown airline willingly accepted this route transfer.

Table 4–6. The Ratio of CP Air's Operating Expenses to Operating Revenues, by Sector, 1942–1944

Sector	*1942*	*1943*	*1944*
St. Lawrence	118	111	162
Northern Quebec	64	105	101
Northwest	96	90	98
Prairie	134	156	144
Mid-West (Central)	123	137	132
Yukon Southern	89	105	123
Vancouver	142	155	108

Source: Canada, Department of Reconstruction and Supply, Directorate of Air Development, "Development of Commercial Air Services in Canada, 1919–1944" (unpublished paper prepared by H. Cunningham, Ottawa, 1946, mimeographed), pp. 101–22.

published little in the way of route results, we may glean from several sources the nature of its losses. Table 4–6 outlines the results for CP Air's operating divisions during the Second World War. It is noteworthy that the sectors that were first relinquished—the St. Lawrence, Prairie, and Mid-West—incurred the largest deficits (as a percentage of revenues). More informative are PWA's operating results on the North Prairie route that it inherited from CP Air. On August 20, 1957, PWA succeeded CP Air with a once-a-day DC-3 flight from Edmonton to Regina. Losses up to late December 1960 were some $865,000 or about $250,000 per year.[10] This loss was probably slightly larger than was experienced by CP Air, since on May 31, 1958, the mail contract on this route ($75,000) was cancelled.[11]

The Board had no reason to oppose CP Air's route transfers for they did not obviously threaten the continuation of service to these points. Pacific Western had, in fact, received lucrative routes northward out of Edmonton down the Mackenzie River, as well as the North Prairie route from CP Air. However, in 1960, one of PWA's more lucrative northern DEW line contracts was terminated and the carrier promptly threatened to suspend services on the southern route. As an ad hoc measure, temporary subsidies of $25,000 per month or $300,000 per year were implemented in early 1961.[12] After two years and some $600,000,[j] the service lapsed when the government refused to renew the subsidy program.[13] This episode provides an excellent example of the hazards faced by a regulatory agency in relying on subsidies that can be arbitrarily terminated. The government would not countenance a permanent subsidy program, and the Board had failed to find another carrier to continue service. But it had learned that communities expected it to maintain air services they enjoyed and that an ad hoc subsidy program was inadequate because of the probability of its being terminated by forces beyond their control.

[j] This was calculated by multiplying the subsidy $25,000 per month by the time period of 24 months. Since $25,000 was the maximum that could be paid, $600,000 would be an upper limit.

While CP Air's withdrawal from a regional route gave rise to the Board's first problem, Air Canada provided the second. In 1961, as a result of a change in government policy on transcontinental competition, Air Canada proposed to discontinue its local run from Winnipeg to Brandon, Yorkton, Regina, Swift Current, Medicine Hat, and Lethbridge because its equipment and the decline in traffic on this route no longer warranted the losses that it was incurring.[k] Hearings on the "South Prairie Route Case" established that discontinuance of service to Swift Current and Medicine Hat and transfer of the local run from Winnipeg through to Saskatoon and Prince Albert to a regional carrier (Transair) would require a subsidy at least as large as the $300,000 loss being incurred by the government airline.[14]

The Prairie route cases involving Pacific Western and Transair presented the Air Transport Board with a perplexing dilemma. Route strengthening for the regionals had been encouraged so as to guarantee continuance and improvement of the frontier services. But by now it appeared that the transfer of the remaining routes, which CP Air and Air Canada were ready to hand over, would have no such effect. PWA, after five years, had been unable to operate the North Prairie services at a profit because of the extension of highway networks in the area and because their predicted advantage in operating costs failed to materialize. On the other hand, the Board was now faced with the problem of route abandonments—a problem that the affected communities expected it to solve. The continued provision of service had to be important to the survival-minded agency, and the regionals were the only carriers prepared to take on these services. The South Prairie Route Case emphasized to the Board the necessity of subsidies when every applicant conditioned its offer on the provision of subsidy payments. Either subsidies would have to be implemented or new profitable routes would have to be found if the Board was to provide service to the threatened points.

Route transfers from CP Air and Air Canada would have required Cabinet approval, since such transfers inevitably meant entry of new carriers to the transcontinental market. The Cabinet, however, was still recovering from the repercussions of its decision to permit CP Air entry to this market[l] and was unlikely to sanction a further expansion at that time. Thus, recognizing the limited possibilities of route transfers, the Board appeared to favor the only alternative open to it—that is, implementation of direct subsidies.[m]

Direct subsidies were still unacceptable to the government. Proof of this is provided by a statement made by the Minister of Transport. In 1964, he defined

[k]Chapter Nine deals at length with the reason for the discontinuance of this service.

[l]Both Air Canada and CP Air experienced large deficits in 1960, 1961, and 1962, and controversy centered around whether this was the result of the government's having allowed CP Air to enter the transcontinental market.

[m]Studnicki-Gizbert, *The Regional Air Carriers' Problem,* p. 68, recommended relying more upon direct subsidies than on route transfers.

the role envisaged for regional carriers as one "which will give regional air carriers a reasonable chance to operate without government subsidies."[15] However, in order to handle the dilemma brought about by Air Canada's decision to abandon its south Prairie run, ad hoc indirect subsidies were implemented. The Board was able to avoid service discontinuance when Air Canada and Transair reached an agreement that provided this regional with free equipment (a Viscount, two DC-3's, spare parts) and provision of maintenance for the Viscount based on Air Canada's marginal costs. In return, Transair promised to provide service on the route for three years.[n]

No other major route transfers took place in the early 1960s and no general subsidy program was implemented. The initial impetus behind the Board's attempt to find a "solution" for the regional "problem" had been occasioned by the 1957 recession. Route transfers of the type arranged were not strengthening the regionals. In addition, less pressure was placed on the Board since the regionals, as Table 4–5 indicated, were able to weather the 1957–58 recession because of the ease with which costs can be adapted in the intermediate run to changing revenues and because traffic growth generally resumed across the country. More importantly, government policy in the early 1960s was more concerned with the relationships—both domestic and international—between Air Canada and CP Air.[16]

Thus the Air Transport Board responded to the events of the late 1950s and early 1960s as predicted. Two sets of events caused it to seek greater funds—both in the form of direct subsidies and indirectly via cross-subsidization—to support local carriers. First, several events threatened a decrease in the frequency of service on those routes the Board regarded as its natural constituency. In 1957, a downturn in Northern development activity threatened reductions in service. Then, in the early 1960s, first PWA and then Air Canada abandoned several Prairie routes. But what gradually increased pressure upon the Board was the growing disparity in the quality of service provided on the regional and the mainline routes. Air Canada, by 1961, was flying virtually an all turbine fleet while the regional airlines generally operated DC-3's. The Air Transport Board's study of the regional carriers was particularly emphatic in its desire to improve the "quality" of the equipment used by the regional carriers.[17] However, the regulatory agency was not successful in expanding the instruments under its control until the mid 1960s.

In 1966, the government's policy regarding the relative acceptability of direct subsidies for the transportation industries was radically altered. The Royal Commission on Transportation (1960) had recommended that direct compensation be paid any mode of transportation for duties imposed upon it by public

[n]Presumably, Air Canada entered such an arrangement because it reduced the onus it would have borne for discontinuation of service, and as a government agency it was not insensitive to such matters.

policy.[18] This recommendation—essentially requiring that cross-subsidization be replaced by direct subsidy—was included in the National Transportation Act [19] of 1967.[o]

The Board had already indirectly placed itself on record as favoring direct subsidies.[20] With the government having accepted the general principle of subsidies for transportation systems because of developments in the railway industry,[p] the Board faced an easier task of persuading the government to implement a subsidy program specifically for air transport. The result was that as part of a new "regional aviation policy," a subsidy program for regional air carriers was announced in late 1966.

Under the terms of the subsidy program,[q] direct payments could be made on the recommendation of the Air Transport Board and after approval by the Treasury Board to provide support for services on scheduled[r] routes where (1) service was needed to a remote area not adequately served by other means of transport, (2) a developmental activity was involved, (3) a regular route operation required only temporary support in the early stages of its implementation, (4) an established route needed to be slowly phased out, (5) by payment of subsidized route was required to generate a minimum of five passengers per an alternate transportation system.[21] In addition, each point served on a subsized route was required to generate a minimum of five passengers per flight.[22] Although other conditions were stipulated so as to prevent the use of uneconomic aircraft or the subsidization of unnecessary costs, the next section dealing with the interaction of the regulatory agency and the regional carriers suggests these were relatively ineffective.

The new regional aviation policy, which announced the subsidy program, contained two additional means of strengthening the regional carriers: (1) limited competition with Air Canada and CP Air and (2) route transfers from these carriers to the regionals. That the agency was at last able to persuade the government to consider route expansion at the expense of the trunk carriers must be attributed to the healthy state of these carriers by the mid-sixties. As we shall see, the Crown airline develops support for itself in a manner similar to that adopted by a regulatory agency—that is, by providing service to specific regions via funds generated on profitable sectors. Thus, if the Crown airline were using all such profits to subsidize these support-generating services, any entry to or transfer of its profitable routes would either cause it to abandon certain of these

[o]Although this bill was not finally passed until 1967, its initial introduction preceded the announcement of a regional aviation subsidy program.

[p]Growing competition between railroads and trucking forced abandonment by the government of its reliance on cross-subsidization in the railroad industry.

[q]Although termed "temporary," this adjective has been omitted from the description of the program since it is still continuing as of 1974.

[r]This was defined as including only Class 1 and 2 services.

services or require the government to finance the resulting deficit. In the former case, the government risked the certainty of creating ill-will against only uncertain returns from expanding the regionals. If it financed the deficit, it was indirectly subsidizing the regionals from the public purse—a policy that we have already seen was unacceptable. However, by the mid-sixties, the Crown airline was for the first time retaining substantial earnings (see Table 6–2). There now was virtually no cost to the government from expanding competing carriers, whereas such an action might yield increased support. Thus, the Air Transport Board was given the possibility of a substantial increase in the source of funds available to it—both via an extension of any cross-subsidization that already existed and via the implementation of a subsidy program.

In terms of the model developed in Chapter Two, the marginal disutility to the agency from both sources of funds decreased. This should have led to an expansion in both. However, as we shall see, it was the introduction of subsidies that was to serve as a catalyst to changes in the regional carriers' position.

Although the Board had succeeded in acquiring the incremental resources required to stimulate scheduled services to secondary centers, the two instruments at hand—new routes and subsidies—differed with respect to the immediacy with which each could be implemented. Although the government had sanctioned transfers, it did not order them. Thus, the regulatory authority still had to rely upon an agreement being worked out with the trunk carriers before transfers or entry could be arranged. On the other hand, subsidies could be unilaterally implemented by the Board.[s]

The regional carriers were, however, not passive participants during the implementation of the new policy. Like CP Air before them, they were desirous of entry to the longer more lucrative transcontinental routes. Since government-imposed entry restrictions created a major barrier to these desires, several of the regionals reacted to the new policy in a strategic fashion designed to overcome these restrictions. As we shall see, the implementation of the subsidy program improved the pay-offs to a particular strategy that the regional airlines then utilized to force the granting of route extensions.

The following section presents the course of the resulting regional aviation policy. The survival function of the regulatory agency, developed in Chapter Two, serves as a framework for the exposition. To serve this purpose, it must be interpreted not as having fully defined immutable parameters connecting instruments available to, and the objectives of, the regulatory agency, but as possessing a specification that changes as the Board learns the efficacy of certain policies and as the regional airlines react to these policies.

[s]This does not contradict the earlier argument that the Board might prefer cross-subsidization to subsidies. As a static formulation, this conclusion applies to long run equilibrium. Implementation of the regional aviation policy involved short-run dynamic adjustments.

INTERACTION OF THE REGULATORY AGENCY AND THE REGIONAL CARRIERS

Transair

Transair's post-1966 growth illustrates the way in which the regional carriers responded to the new policy in order to break down the entry restrictions to the scheduled market which had previously faced them. It also affords an opportunity to trace through the dynamics of the interaction between the regional carriers and the regulatory agency that resulted from the implementation of the "regional" policy. Originally operating bush services in Manitoba and northern Ontario, Transair received the Northern Manitoba routes of CP Air in 1957. However, northern development in this region did not permit continued expansion. Edmonton, not Winnipeg, tended to be the natural supply point for northern development. Table 4–7 shows Transair's bulk or charter operations gradually decreasing not only relative to its scheduled service, but also in terms of absolute revenues earned. Transcontinental or east-west routes appeared to offer both greater growth and greater profit opportunities.

As previously described, Transair took over Air Canada's local run from Winnipeg to Regina and Prince Albert in 1963 with the aid of indirect subsidies from the Crown airline. In 1966, Transair's contract with Air Canada expired and the Board was faced with the difficulty of maintaining service. This time, subsidies were sufficiently acceptable (the regional subsidy program was about to be announced) that the government felt able to introduce them to prevent discontinuance of service—albeit on an ad hoc basis.[t] Under this arrangement, subsidies were incurred at the rate of $300,000 per year for the next two years.[u]

In 1968, Transair made a formal application under the announced regional program to have the subsidy placed on a permanent basis.[23] Its proposal involved a doubling of both services and the subsidy required. Subsidy requested was $1.1 million, $989,000, and $818,000 respectively in the first three years of service.[24] The Board was faced with a carrier drastically increasing the costs of subsidized service. It rejected the application on the grounds that the fares were inappropriately low, the traffic forecasts were unreasonably high, and the aircraft type was unsuitable.[25]

Transair continued to operate the route but incurred substantial losses in 1968 and in 1969.[v] In the summer of 1969, as losses mounted both on the

[t] The ad hoc subsidies awarded to Transair in 1966–67 should be considered as part of the new regional policy since the National Transportation Act had already been published in preliminary form and the subsidy program was already finalized but not yet announced.

[u] Subsidies amounted to $283,999 for the last 9 months of 1966 and over $151,000 for the first 6 months of 1967. See Canada, *House of Commons Debates,* 2nd Sess., 27 Parl., 16 Elizabeth 2, Vols. I and IV (1967), pp. 654, 3736.

[v] Canada, Canadian Transport Commission, Air Transport Committee, *Decision,* Serial No. 2913, p. 3. The actual losses may be extrapolated from Transair's subsidy request that

Table 4–7. Revenue Earned by Regional Carriers on Unit Toll and Bulk Operations, 1956–1969

Year	*Pacific Western*			*Transair*			*Quebecair*			*Eastern Provincial*		
	Unit Toll ($000)	*Bulk ($000)*	*Bulk As % Of Unit Toll*	*Unit Toll ($000)*	*Bulk ($000)*	*Bulk As % Of Unit Toll*	*Unit Toll ($000)*	*Bulk ($000)*	*Bulk As % Of Unit Toll*	*Unit Toll ($000)*	*Bulk ($000)*	*Bulk As % Of Unit Toll*
1956	2,123	3,545	403	326	3,207	983	1,644	1,050	64	1,164	9,474	814
1957	1,847	4,922	266	919	1,746	189	2,063	44	2	1,431	6,473	452
1958	1,644	5,342	325	1,928	1,090	57	1,957	85	4	1,602	1,101	69
1959	3,066	4,734	154	2,039	739	36	2,957	225	7	2,397	1,167	49
1960	4,352	4,000	92	1,997	772	39	3,479	112	3	3,138	1,360	43
1961	4,045	2,084	52	2,196	1,896	86	3,161	19	1	3,559	1,137	32
1962	4,071	1,526	37	2,478	2,731	113	3,638	17	0.5	3,711	1,324	36
1963	4,396	1,836	42	2,635	2,976	113	3,583	41	1	3,707	1,465	40
1964	5,721	3,121	55	2,426	2,547	105	3,586	36	1	3,631	1,727	48
1965	7,424	4,081	54	2,592	2,375	91	4,638	403	8	3,517	1,150	33
1966	8,850	3,390	38	3,128	2,512	80	5,136	497	10	4,208	1,357	32
1967	10,644	3,719	35	3,571	1,723	48	5,665	825	15	4,637	1,699	36
1968	11,082	6,536	59	4,204	1,899	45	5,472	748	14	5,089	1,586	31
1969	18,096	13,748	74	5,693	2,683	47	8,197	721	9	7,058	1,567	22

Source: Canada, Dominion Bureau of Statistics, *Civil Aviation–Annual,* Cat. No. 51–202, 1956–1969.

Prairies and the Red Lake route into northern Ontario, it initiated a further loss service from Winnipeg through Kenora to Thunder Bay.[26] Table 4–5—the operating results—indicates the effect of the airline's financial position. By 1969, it experienced a deficit in net income of $2 million on operating revenues of $8.5 million. In the midst of this crisis, two Boeing 737's were ordered.[27]

Subsidies had permitted the airline to expand to such an extent that disruption of services would have affected a very wide range of communities. It thereby increased the cost to the Board of any threat of bankruptcy. In addition, the airline could now point to an instrument, which the Board previously did not have, to solve the problem—that is, new entry to more profitable routes, or cross-subsidization. In late 1969, Transair declared it would withdraw all local service west of Winnipeg if this was not granted.[28] Threatened with forced discontinuation of service and an airline that had reduced the effectiveness of subsidies, the Board acted as the model in Chapter Two predicted by substituting an extensive cross-subsidization program for direct subsidies.

Transair was permitted non-stop flights from Regina to Winnipeg. As the model predicts, fares were then increased on the loss services. The previous local stops at Brandon and Yorkton were to be served with a Piper Navajo at higher fares (cf. Winnipeg-Yorkton: $18 in 1967 versus $28 in 1970; Winnipeg-Brandon: $9 in 1967 versus $15 in 1970). In addition, the Winnipeg-Kenora-Dryden route was extended to Sault Ste. Marie and Toronto, while direct flights from Winnipeg to Toronto were implemented. The Board was extremely explicit as to its motivation for implementation of cross-subsidization with this extension when it stated, "This service [Winnipeg-Thunder Bay] . . . is not economically viable and Transair cannot be expected to continue such service unless it can become viable."[29]

Therefore, the introduction of the regional aviation policy resulted initially in the implementation by the regulatory agency of direct subsidies—both because of the decrease in the disutility of this source of funds to the agency and because of the short-run constraints placed upon their increasing the amount of funds that could be generated from cross-subsidization. However, as a result of strategic behavior on the part of Transair—which action decreased the effectiveness of direct subsidies and which expanded its route system until backruptcy and a cessation of service over a large area was threatened—the agency substituted cross-subsidization for direct subsidies. In addition, it permitted the prices charged on the loss sectors to be increased as cross-subsidization was implemented (at least on those segments where competition with Air Canada did not prevent them from doing so).

---

had forecast losses of $2,000,000 over two years if service had been doubled (Canada, Air Transport Board, *Decision,* Serial No. 2550). Thus, actual losses probably were half that amount—or some $1 million over two years.

Eastern Provincial Airways

Eastern Provincial Airways (EPA) reached regional status when it took over Maritime Central Airway's routes in 1963. This network served Fredericton, Moncton, St. John, Charlottetown, New Glasgow, and Halifax in the south, and connected Sept Isles and Labrador to both Moncton, New Brunswick and St. John's, Newfoundland (see Figure 4–2). By 1970, it had expanded this network into a major one by extending its routes into Montreal both from Labrador and from Prince Edward Island, as well as by linking Halifax, Nova Scotia to St. John's, Newfoundland via Deer Lake and Gander. In addition, it was receiving well over $1.4 million in subsidies[w] from the Air Transport Committee[x] to support many of these routes.

Eastern Provincial had long been one of the strongest proponents of direct subsidies. During the formulation of regional policy in the period 1965–66, it persistently argued for subsidization. The operating results reported in Table 4–5 indicate that up to 1967 it had suffered a persistent but steadily decreasing operating deficit.

However, the Board did not face the same initial pressures in the Maritimes as it did in the Prairies. The main trunk carrier in the Maritimes—Air Canada—not only did not appear anxious to suspend its services[y] but claimed to be incurring losses on its overall Maritimes route structure.[z] However, the shift in subsidy availability in 1966 resulted in the introduction of a subsidy program for EPA in 1967.

Backed by these subsidies, EPA, like Transair, proceeded to follow a course of action calculated to break down the barriers it faced to entry on the longer-haul routes. It immediately began to escalate the subsidy cost to the Board of maintaining the financial integrity of EPA. In 1968, the Carvair (a converted DC-4) was used to replace the Dart-Herald EPA had been using on its northern routes. The Dart-Heralds were shifted to the shorter Maritime routes to replace DC-3's. Table 4–8 indicates the resulting rise in costs per available ton-mile from 66¢ in 1965 to 85¢ in 1968.[aa] As a result, subsidies had to be increased from $629,000 to $780,000 between 1967 and 1968.[bb]

Meanwhile EPA applied for route extensions arguing that these would reduce its subsidy requirements. In September 1968, the Board awarded it access to Montreal (Charlottetown-Bathurst-Montreal). In order to emphasize that this

[w]See Appendix A.

[x]The Air Transport Board became the Air Transport Committee under the provisions of the National Transportation Act of 1967. The two names are used interchangeably in this section.

[y]In the 1958 Transcontinental Hearings Air Canada received major support from Maritime groups. See Chapter Nine.

[z]See Chapter Six.

[aa]The average stage-length of unit toll flights held constant at about 145 miles.

[bb]See Appendix A.

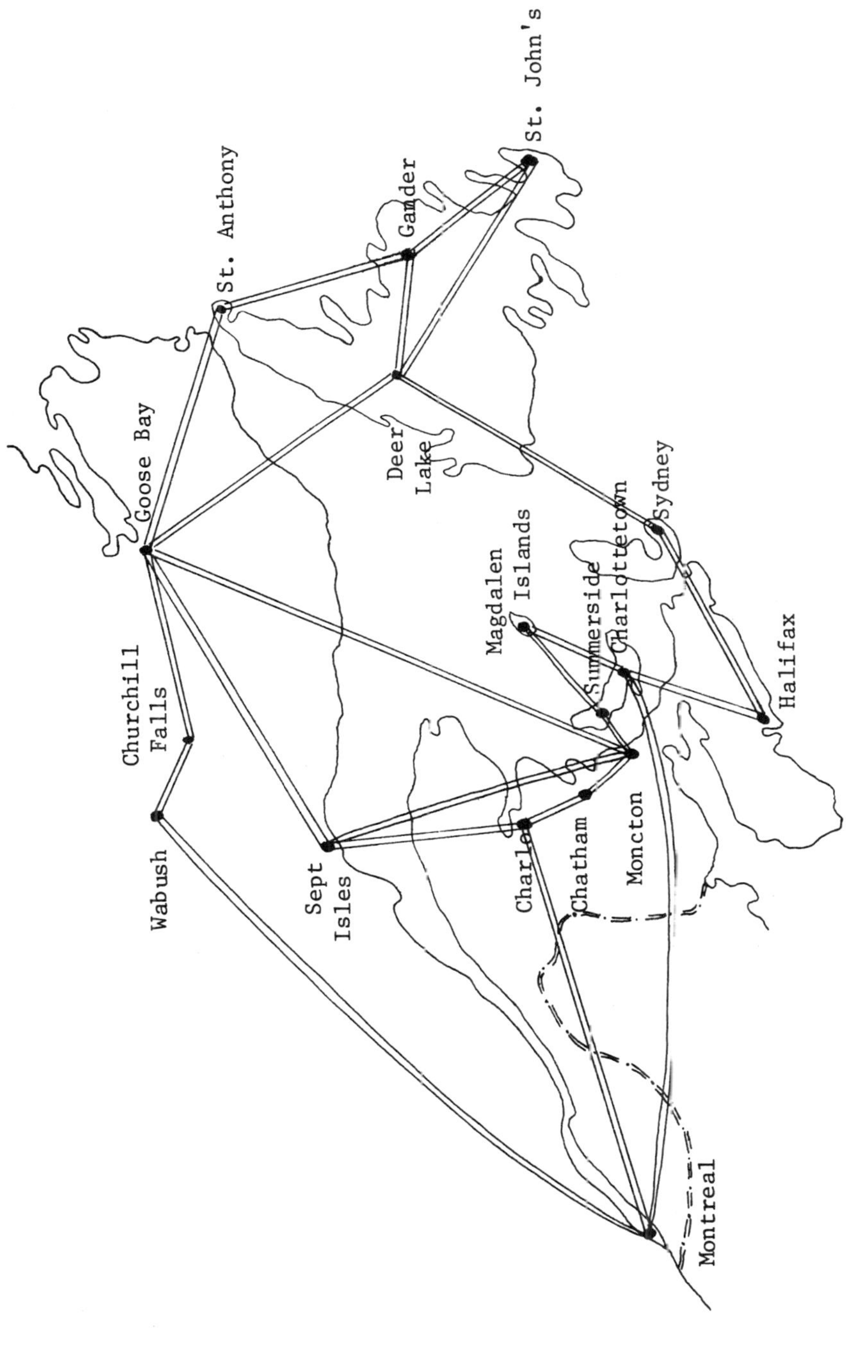

Figure 4-2. Map of Eastern Provincial Airways Route System, 1970.

Table 4–8. Eastern Provincial Airways: System Cost per Available Ton-Mile, 1965–1969 (¢)

Year	*Fly-ing*	*Main-tenance*	*Total*	*Passen-ger Service*	*Aircraft and Traffic Servicing*	*Promo-tion and Sales*	*General Adminis-tration*	*Total*	*Depre-cia-tion*	*Inter-est*	*Total*	*Grand Total*
1965	18.0	21.8	39.8	1.9	12.4	1.2	3.3	18.8	3.7	3.5	7.2	65.8
1966	20.1	21.6	41.7	2.1	14.3	1.2	3.9	21.5	4.3	4.2	8.5	71.7
1967	21.8	23.2	45.0	2.7	14.2	1.8	4.4	23.1	6.2	4.3	10.5	78.6
1968	23.9	25.6	49.5	3.3	14.4	2.7	4.4	24.8	6.0	4.4	10.4	84.7
1969	19.7	15.8	39.5	3.4	8.3	1.8	2.6	16.1	3.5	2.8	6.3	57.9

Source: Canada, Dominion Bureau of Statistics, *Civil Aviation–Annual,* Cat. No. 51–202, various years.

award was an attempt to strengthen EPA via cross-subsidization, the Board deliberately stressed that this route would not be eligible for subsidy.[30] EPA originally implemented service with a Dart-Herald and by May 1969 was achieving load factors of over 60 percent.[31] However, in June, EPA introduced on this route a Boeing 737 that had to overfly the Charlo/Bathurst airport because of inadequate runway facilities. The old route remained serviced by a separate Dart-Herald flight that soon had load factors as low as 16 percent and promised to lead to losses of $500,000 per year.[32] The Air Transport Committee was faced with abandoning a newly implemented service to northeastern New Brunswick or seeing its cross-subsidization policy on this route defeated. In effect, by introducing the larger aircraft the airline was reducing the marginal efficiency of funds derived from that route's operation in providing service to the intermediate point thereon. The Board responded by implementing a subsidy program for this route.

EPA's operating deficit in 1969 increased to $1.7 million as compared to $700 thousand in 1968 (Tables 4–5 and A–1). In the middle of 1969, EPA took delivery of two Boeing 737's. Although their available seat-mile cost was 1.9¢ as compared to 3.6¢ for the Dart-Herald,[33] their extra capacity (117 rather than 44 seats) meant that unless new traffic could be found, the cost per passenger and the amount of subsidies paid would actually increase. This is in fact what happened. Although EPA's costs per available ton-mile were substantially reduced—from 84.7¢ in 1968 to 57.9¢ in 1969—much of this was offset by the system load factor falling from 59.4 to 44.5 percent, leaving only a 9 percent improvement in costs per unit carried. But operating revenues per revenue ton-mile fell from $1.04 to 95¢—some 4.8 percent. The net result was that the gap between costs and revenue per revenue ton-mile only decreased by some 38 percent. However, this occurred in conjunction with a 41 percent increase in revenue ton-miles. The result was an increase in the operating deficit.

In the face of this problem, the Board responded by expanding both routes on which EPA used the 737. The Montreal-Charlottetown flight was extended to St. John's, Newfoundland via Halifax, Sydney, Deer Lake and Gander. Similarly, the Newfoundland-Goose Bay route was extended to Montreal via Churchill Falls and Wabush. Faced with escalating subsidy costs caused by the airline's re-equipment program, the Board chose to expand its cross-subsidization scheme, just as the model in Chapter Two predicted.

As was the case with Transair, subsidies were used by EPA to build up both its route system and the level of service to a stage sufficient to embarrass the regulatory agency if such services were discontinued. As subsidy costs mounted, the agency responded by gradually increasing the amount of cross-subsidization.

Quebecair

Quebecair in 1957 operated routes from Quebec down the St. Lawrence to Forrestville, across the St. Lawrence from the north shore communities of

Forrestville, Baie Comeau, and Sept Isles to Rimouski, Mont Joli, and Matane on the south shore. By 1960, it had developed a scheduled route network into the newly developing areas of Gagnon, Schefferville, and Wabush. In the south, it had added Montreal and created a network stretching from Montreal to Sept Isles both by the introduction of through flights and, in 1961, by the addition of the point Saguenay (see Figure 4–3).

Apart from 1961, the Quebecair system experienced no significant operating deficits before 1965. However, in late 1965, Quebecair absorbed two smaller carriers—Matane Air Services, which had earlier taken over the Cross-River routes, and Northern Wings, which had operated cargo services north from Sept Isles and combined passenger-cargo services east from Sept Isles along the north shore of the Gulf of St. Lawrence. These changes resulted in the shortening of the average stage-length from 140 to 122 miles and in increasing the cost per available ton-mile from 64.9¢ to 77.9¢. As a result of this acquisition, Quebecair's operating deficit in 1966 jumped to $770 thousand on operating revenues of $5.4 million (see Table 4–5). The subsidies that were commenced in 1968 were undoubtedly for the two new unprofitable routes whose acquisition by Quebecair originally led to such large losses.[cc]

As was the case with the other carriers, subsidies failed to place Quebecair in a solvent position. Losses still amounted to almost a million dollars in 1968. Route expansions offered one way of strengthening the airline. In 1969, the Board awarded Quebecair an extension of its northern network and lifted several restrictions requiring intermediate stops on the Montreal to Sept Isles system.[dd] Almost immediately, Quebecair dropped its Cross-River service.[ee]

Pacific Western Airlines

Originally a non-scheduled carrier operating northward out of Vancouver and Edmonton, Pacific Western Airlines (PWA) built up scheduled routes first on Vancouver Island, then on the Prairies from Edmonton through to Regina, and finally by 1960, north from Edmonton up the Mackenzie Valley. All these routes were inherited from CPAir. Its progress during the 1960s was aided by its strong northern routes, by CP Air's expansion into the transcontinental system, and by successful competition with Air Canada on the Calgary-Edmonton segment.

In 1963, PWA linked Calgary to Edmonton when Air Canada moved its

[cc]Proof that these were the two routes receiving subsidies is evidenced by the decrease in subsidies from $700,000 to $400,000 following relinquishment of the Cross-River route in 1969. See Air Transport Committee, *Decision,* Serial No. 2801 (September 4, 1969); see also Appendix A and Studnicki-Gizbert, *The Regional Air Carriers' Problem,* p. 7.

[dd]Air Transport Committee, *Decision,* Serial No. 2803, p. 6. The Air Transport Committee actually invited Quebecair to apply for the lifting of these restrictions.

[ee]Air Transport Committee, *Decision,* Serial No. 2801. The Board did not face discontinuance of service to this point since another lower-level carrier proceeded to take over the route.

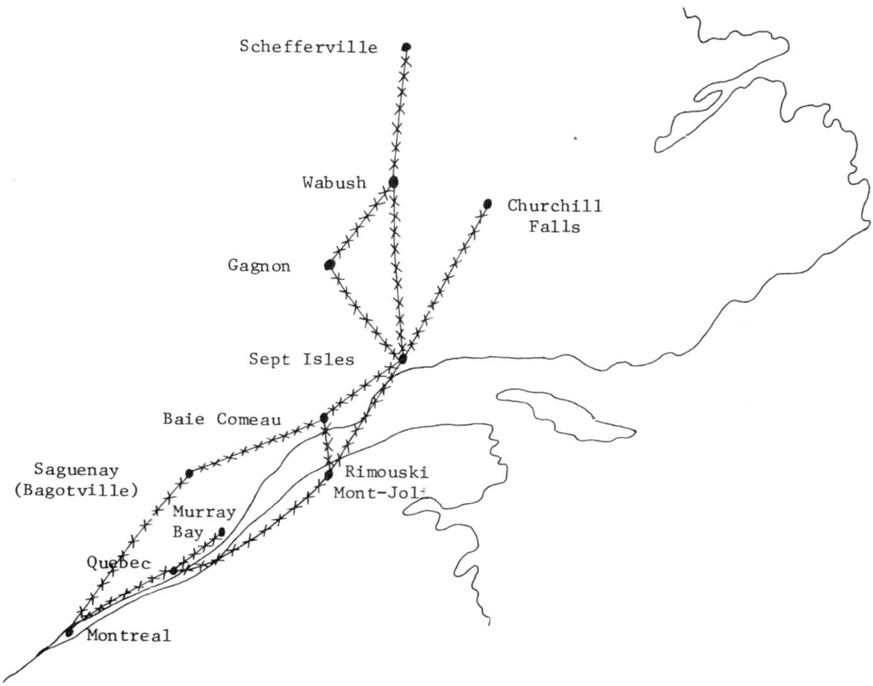

Figure 4-3. Map of Quebecair Route System, 1970.

Calgary operations to the new Calgary international airport, located some distance outside the city. PWA continued the service to the downtown airport. In 1968, PWA was granted access from Vancouver to Calgary with a mandatory stop at Kamloops. In 1969, PWA was also granted a southern link from Vancouver to Calgary via the Okanagan Valley, as well as routes from Vancouver to Prince Rupert, Vancouver to Prince George, and Prince George to Prince Rupert—all of which either replaced CP Air or were competing with CP Air services.[ff] In 1970, Air Canada withdrew from the Calgary-Edmonton route and yielded its Vancouver-Victoria-Seattle short-haul segement to PWA.

PWA was thus able to expand without recourse to subsidies or strategic losses. CP Air no longer required all its regional points to justify entry into the transcontinental market. Air Canada's segments neither fitted into its transcontinental system nor were important enough to maintain for protection of its long-haul market. Most importantly, PWA's network had a north-south orientation from Vancouver and Calgary northwards. With the 1968 boom in northern oil exploration, PWA's bulk revenues grew rapidly from only 35

[ff]PWA was restricted, by intermediate stop provisions on services which paralleled those of CP Air.

percent of unit toll revenues in 1967 to over 70 percent in 1969 and 1970. Because CP Air's and Air Canada's orientation was east-west, their objections to several PWA route extensions, which created east-west links for the two northern systems of PWA, were only perfunctory.

CONSEQUENCES OF THE REGIONAL AVIATION POLICY

The Air Transport Board's objectives were much the same with respect to all the regional carriers. In order to ensure service to outlying communities—the Board's natural constituency—the agency sought to "strengthen" these carriers. Due to a combination of fortuitous circumstances—the passing of a National Transportation Act and the healthy financial state of the two trunk carriers—the government announced a regional aviation policy in 1966 that offered the Air Transport Board a chance to do just this. However, the airlines' own goals were such that, while the regional carriers were "strengthened," the objective of ensuring service to outlying communities was defeated.

The regional carriers did not all face the same barriers in their quest for expansion. Pacific Western operated a strong north-south system that benefited from economic growth in northern Canada. In addition, it found the two trunk carriers willing to allocate it some north-south routes[gg] that did not fit into their east-west transcontinental systems. On the other hand, Transair, Quebecair, and Eastern Provincial Airways had fewer opportunities for northern expansion and faced the opposition of Air Çanada and CP Air since expansion would have to occur in an east-west direction.

The announcement of the regional aviation policy resulted in a series of moves and countermoves of a sequential nature. The agency initiated the sequence with the implementation of a subsidy program. Having successfully altered the constraints facing it, the Air Transport Board set about expanding the services the regionals could provide to outlying areas. Although the new policy offered the Board two sources of funds in order to accomplish this, the agency chose to initiate expansion via subsidies rather than via cross-subsidization because of the short-run constraints it faced in implementing route transfers.

However, the introduction of the subsidy program changed the nature of the strategy available to the regional carriers. The carriers, desirous of entry to longer-haul, mainline routes responded as if they regarded the objective function of the agency as a reaction function. The model predicts that should subsidies become less effective in providing service, then the agency will react by substituting cross-subsidization for direct subsidies.[hh] Following escalation of

[gg]Canadian Pacific gave up its local British Columbia services; Air Canada vacated its Edmonton-Calgary route.

[hh]As is normal for this type of exercise, this prediction depends on a *ceteris paribus* assumption. For instance, should something cause the agency to suddenly place less value on

subsidy costs on the part of the industry, this was indeed the course of action followed by the agency.

This interpretation of the sequence of events assumes that the agency had neither perfect information as to the actions of the industry nor perfect control over the response of the regional airlines. The earlier discussion on the nature of the regulatory institution would support both assumptions. But this explanation of events also assumes that the implementation of the regional aviation program changed the nature of the strategy available to the regional carriers. This assumption needs to be justified.

Prior to 1966, services operated by the regionals that became uneconomic either had to be cancelled or at least rearranged to place them on an economic footing. Subsidies, always on an ad hoc basis during this period, were regarded by both carriers and regulatory agency as strictly temporary. What is more important, since other carriers were not too much smaller in size, bankruptcy of one of the carriers eventually designated as "regional" did not really threaten the agency with a high probability of widespread cessation of service. However, with the new policy, those carriers that were unable to expand via entry to new routes were able to do so with the aid of subsidies. This expansion greatly increased the cost to the Air Transport Board of any disruption of service that might result from bankruptcy of a regional carrier. But the very success of the agency in expanding these carriers also increased the probability that bankruptcy would lead to a cessation of service to many communities. The smaller third-level carriers could not readily be called upon to replace the regional carrier threatening bankruptcy,[ii] and the policy of carving up the country into exclusive areas for each carrier meant the Board could not replace the ailing carrier with another regional carrier without creating a small trunk carrier–an action the government clearly forbade in its statement of regional policy.[34] As a result, when the regional carriers began to escalate their subsidy requirements, the Board was forced to react by replacing subsidies with cross-subsidization.

Even so, this explanation for the course of events essentially treats the objective function of the agency as a static concept. However, Chapter Two demonstrated that the agency can in fact interact with the political process so as to change the constraints placed upon it. Why it did not in fact seek even larger subsidies when faced with escalating subsidy costs must be explained.[jj] The answer lies in the nature of the subsidy program. Each subsidy awarded by the Air Transport Board had, in principle, to be approved by the Treasury Board–the government's central budget-review agency. Any indication that

---

an extra unit of support or should something happen to make it less costly to use subsidies, this result would not follow. But the discussion of the course of regional policy was meant to suggest that there was no obvious change in the agency's environment apart from the behavior of the regional airlines.

[ii]At least not without the chance that a substantial number of routes would lose service.

[jj]Unless we assume the agency had already reached equilibrium in the sense that the first-order conditions were being satisfied.

subsidies were being ineffectively used was a certain invitation to have the whole program cancelled. Thus, with the escalation in subsidy costs and the necessity of having to prevent these carriers from going bankrupt, greater cross-subsidization offered the only short-run alternative available to the regulatory agency.

Ironically, the ultimate result was not an improvement in service to the vast majority of points served by the regional carriers. For once they had gained entry to the denser, longer-haul routes, they began to divest themselves of their low density services to small regional centers. That the agency should have permitted this result is further evidence of the relative impotence of a regulatory agency in the face of recalcitrant industry behavior.[kk]

Using data on the licences issued to the five regional carriers in 1965 and 1972, Table 4–9 illustrates the changing pattern of services. In this table, each city served by one of the regionals in 1965 was classified as to whether or not by 1972 it had been dropped (completely abandoned or transferred to another carrier), whether it had experienced an improvement,[ll] no change, or a reduction in service, or finally whether it was a new point not served previous to the introduction of the regional aviation policy. Table 4–9 indicates that, as a whole, far more centers were dropped than added to the regional network. The difference is most marked when those carriers that faced the greatest entry barriers are compared to those that were not greatly affected by the regional policy. Between Transair and Eastern Provincial Airways, 110 centers were dropped, while only 11 points were added. Quebecair ceased service to 6 points, but only added one. These results should be compared to those of Pacific Western and Nordair. They received no subsidies and thus were unable to play the same bargaining game with the regulatory agency. In both cases, the number of new points added almost equals the number of points that lost regional service.

Table 4–10 compares the size of the centers that were dropped or whose service was downgraded with those whose service was improved.[mm] It is clear that Transair, Eastern Provincial Airways, and Quebecair all dropped their smallest points while implementing service to primarily larger centers. The same pattern is evident for Pacific Western if the points gained by its 1971 purchase of British Columbia Airlines are excluded.[nn] Thus, prior to this merger, Pacific

[kk]We should expect that as a result the regulatory agency will press less diligently for an expansion of the regionals and concentrate in the future on the third-level carriers.

[ll]An upgrading of a licence from class 3 to 2 or to 1, is classified as an improvement in service.

[mm]The difference between the number of centers reported in Table 4–10 and Table 4–9 is the result of a center being recorded more than once in Table 4–9. For instance should a center have one licence suspended and another downgraded it would be recorded in both column 2 and 3 of Table 4–9.

[nn]British Columbia Airlines, had been arguing that it deserved regional status and should replace PWA in British Columbia.

Table 4–9. Changing Pattern of Points Served by Regional Carriers, 1965–1972

Carrier	*Centers Dropped*	*Reduction of Service*	*No Change*	*Improvement of Service*	*New Points Serviced*
Transair	60	3	8	8	8
Eastern Provincial	50	6	5	6	3
Quebecair	6	3	2	5	1
Pacific Western	29	11	5	8	28(10[a])
Nordair	12	1	2	5	11

[a]Without the points Pacific Western acquired when it purchased British Columbia Airlines.

Source: Canada, Air Transport Board, *Directory of Canadian Commercial Air Services* (Ottawa, January 1, 1965); Canada, Canadian Transport Commission, Air Transport Committee, *Directory of Canadian Commercial Air Services* (Ottawa, August 15, 1972).

Western was following a similar pattern. This tends to suggest that regional aviation policy merely strengthened an existing tendency. Finally, Nordair appears to continue to fulfill the role of a local carrier—that is, by actually implementing more new services to local points than it dropped.

The result of Canadian regional aviation policy has not been the creation of a comprehensive network of services to small communities. Instead, four of the five carriers used the opportunity to expand into the scheduled market and to abandon service to isolated low-density points. The one carrier that did not

Table 4–10. Comparison of the Size of Centers Losing Regional Services to Those Receiving a Net Improvement in Service Between 1965 and 1972

Carrier	*Centers*	*Annual Passenger Volume, 1970 (000)*			
		<1	*1 - 50*	*50-100*	*>100*
Transair	Lost	55	2	0	4
	Gained	4	8	1	3
Eastern	Lost	48	1	0	0
Provincial	Gained	0	4	1	3
Quebecair	Lost	5	0	0	0
	Gained	0	5	0	0
Pacific	Lost	27	2	0	0
Western.	Gained	18(5[a])	15(6[a])	4(1[a])	2(1[a])
Nordair.	Lost	2	3	0	0
	Gained	11	2	0	3

[a]Excludes the points gained in the purchase of British Columbia Airlines.

Source: Canada, Air Transport Board, *Directory of Canadian Commercial Air Services* (Ottawa, January 1, 1965); Canada, Canadian Transport Commission, Air Transport Committee, *Directory of Canadian Commercial Air Services* (Ottawa, August 15, 1972); Canada, Statistics Canada, Aviation Statistics Centre, *Air Passenger Origin and Destination, Domestic Report, 1971*, Cat. No. 51–204 (Ottawa: Information Canada, July 1972).

exhibit this tendency–Nordair–was in effect bypassed by the subsidy and major route awards arising from the regional aviation policy. Pacific Western, although receiving no subsidies, appears to exhibit the same general tendencies as the three carriers that received subsidies, if the results of its acquisition of a potential competitor in late 1971 are ignored. The real effect of the regional policy was felt by those carriers that had faced the greatest entry barriers to upward mobility. It is here that the policy helped transform the character of these airlines and indirectly reduce the regional coverage of their services.[oo]

Although this outcome is opposite to that originally posited as the objective of regional aviation policy, this in no way negates treating the regulatory agency as a rational entity attempting to maximize a vector of objectives in order to survive. It merely suggests that any agency does not have perfect information on the likely reaction of the industry to policy instruments under its control. As this chapter demonstrates, three of the firms in the industry formulated courses of action that, given the agency's objective function, were able to break down entry barriers that previously had faced them. What this episode does suggest is the inherent difficulty in obtaining well-defined results from the use of a regulatory institution. The difficulty arises from the uncertainties inherent in the implicit bargains characteristic of the regulatory process. An alternate, apparently more direct form of control over an industry exists–via the direct provision of goods and services by a government-owned corporation. The next section examines the Canadian experience with a state-owned airline.

[oo]Compare this to the effect of American policy in the same area–George C. Eads in *The Local Service Airline Experiment,* Studies in the Regulation of Economic Activity (Washington, D.C.: Brookings, 1972), pp. 1–2, claims that "the primary 'success' of the local experiment has not been the provision of efficient short-haul, low density air service, but the creation of nine relatively weak trunkline carriers."

Part II

The Crown Airline

Chapter Five

A Model of a Government Airline

Governments may influence the performance of an industry not only by regulation but also by the creation of a public or government corporation either to supplement or to supplant the private sector. That government and privately owned corporations may have inherently dissimilar behavioral characteristics, and as a result may perform differently, has been argued by both advocates for and opponents of nationalized corporations. In general, both sides ground their arguments more on vague ideological generalizations than on the type of rigorous analytical framework usually associated with economic models.[1] Only via the development and testing of meaningful models of public behavior can the relative performance of private as compared to public ownership be sensibly discussed. This section treats the public firm as having an objective similar to other organizations, whether they be public or private—that of self-perpetuation. Starting with this behavioral postulate, it develops a model to explain the price and product decisions of a Crown airline.

The literature on firm behavior is far from unanimous as to whether the survival motive forces the management of privately owned firms to maximize profits or whether it merely serves to constrain the pursuit of other goals.[2] Thus, even if the management of the Crown airline can be treated as pursuing the objective of self-perpetuation, it may be improper to regard it as maximizing the probability of its own survival. The management may instead choose to maximize a far more complex function consisting of such things as asset size, rate of growth, sales, or non-pecuniary income that are subject only to the constraint that the probability of survival not fall below a tolerable level. Whether or not tolerable limits to survival can be achieved without maximizing the probability of survival depends upon the nature of the political system. It is not inconceivable that a Crown airline may have some "organizational slack" to play with under certain regimes—for instance, a socialist government—whereas, on other occasions it may be hard pressed to defend itself. For the purposes of this chapter, the Crown airline will be assumed to maximize the probability of its own survival. The relevance of this assumption in the context of the Canadian airline industry can be justified. As we shall see, the Canadian Crown airline has been constantly threatened with major incursions from private interests since its inception.

OBJECTIVES AND INSTRUMENTS

The communality of the survival motive for both public and private firms need not imply similarity of action in pursuit of this goal. In particular, the contrasting nature of property rights in public as compared to private firms suggests each will pursue dissimilar profit objectives. The relative ease involved in the transfer of ownership rights in private corporations leads to the hypothesis that this institution will tend to maximize profits.[3] While the public firm is also susceptible to take-over, its demise must be accomplished via the political process. Thus, the survival of the public corporation like other government organizations will depend upon its demonstrating to the government that the firm's services have elicited significant support from an important sector of the electorate—that is, those members who would be alienated by the demise of the public corporation. As shall be argued, rarely will this lead the public corporation to maximize profits.

Two events threaten the public airline with demise. First, take-over by another firm promises immediate difficulties. Secondly, entry by private firms increases the likelihood that a take-over bid will be successful.[a] But while the probability of take-over for the management of a private firm is inversely proportional to its success in maximizing profits, the public firm's risk of being sold to private interests is not likely to be eliminated as earned profits approach their potential maximum. Take-over pressure should be positively related to the potential earnings to be derived from the acquisition of the public firm. If private interests are to effect such an acquisition, they face two costs. First, certain expenses will have to be incurred in order to influence the political system—to organize a lobby and to influence the outcome of elections. These costs are determined by the nature of the political system and involve a large fixed component unrelated to the amount of profits generated by the Crown airline.[b] In the second place, a price will have to be paid for the Crown

[a]Should the management of a public firm be characterized as following policies that contribute to their own utility, subject to some minor constraints emanating from the political system, both take-over and entry would also be resisted. Therefore, the argument that follows is also consistent with this characterization of the behavior of the management of a public firm.

[b]Although it might be argued that the public will be less likely to want to sell a profitable public enterprise, it might equally well be maintained that it is in precisely such a situation that it is often felt that public enterprises should be turned over to private enterprise. Whatever the effect, it is regarded as of secondary importance compared to the fixed costs of influencing the political system.

company's assets. Again the cost is not likely to reflect completely the earned profits of the Crown corporation since, with no market for its shares, it is difficult to envisage that the book value of the airline will contain the capitalized value of the earnings stream. Therefore, the costs of acquisition of a public firm will not increase dollar for dollar with earned profits. For a Crown corporation, maximizing earned profits may not eliminate the potential gain private interests might anticipate from a take-over. Instead, in a world of imperfect knowledge, earned profits serve to signal to outsiders the potential earnings that could result from just such an acquisition.

While this argument suggests that the maximization of earned profits may do little to eliminate take-over pressure, it does not specify which level of profits will serve to maximize the probability of survival. There are several reasons to expect the level of profits that does so to be low. In the first place, low earned profits may reduce the information available to outsiders as to the potential gain from take-over. However, this only reduces the pressure for take-over. The probability of survival can equally well be increased should the Crown airline develop consumer support sufficiently great to cause the government to resist demands for a take-over. As will be argued, consumer support is most likely to be garnered with policies that tend to result in low earned profits.

Consider the electorate as being divided into two groups—users and non-users of the airline's service. To the extent that non-users will incur noticeable reductions in their tax liabilities as a result of profits earned by a Crown corporation, they would be expected to favor profit maximization on the part of the public firm. However, the impact of the desires of this group on the Crown airline's behavior is not likely to be significant. First, because of the size of this group, benefits to particular members will be small relative to the participation costs they would have to incur if they are to influence the political process. The cost of information to each member regarding the degree to which the Crown corporation falls short of maximizing profits reduces the likelihood that these individuals will actively press for an increase in profits. Users, on the other hand, must balance the benefits they receive from lower prices and higher product quality against the increased tax liabilities they incur as the result of lower profits. Here, too, information costs dictate that this group is likely to appreciate the benefits they receive from low earned profits more readily than the costs.[c] In addition, insofar as the increase in tax liabilities must be shared by users and non-users alike, the benefits to users are likely to be larger than their share of increased tax liabilities. Thus, the survival-minded Crown corporation, if trying to maximize support, will move away from the point of profit maximization.

Losses, on the other hand, cannot be born by the Crown airline without

[c]The additional uncertainty as to whether decreased revenues from the Crown airline's failure to maximize profits imply a change in other programs from which they may not benefit or an increase in taxes reinforces this tendency.

importunity. Contrary to the argument presented above, losses are easily recognized and much more readily deplored by non-users, especially when private firms exist that claim they could perform the same services without cost to the national treasury. In this case, the constraint of a zero level of losses might well be imposed on the public corporation.[d] There is a second reason that a Crown airline will find losses costly. Direct subsidies lead to continuing appraisal and occasional interference from other participants in the political process, whether it be from investigating subcommittees of the legislature or from central budget review agencies. Autonomy from such interference, it has been argued, is important if "consistent" programs aimed at garnering public support are to be developed by a government agency.

It should be noted that this cost is operative at positive as well as negative levels of profits. Interference with the airline's affairs is not guaranteed by the avoidance of losses, although avoidance of losses may substantially reduce such interference. Whether the airline stops short of zero earned profits and adopts a low but positive level of profits depends upon the nature of the financing available to it. The airline may have the option of financing its capital out of internally generated funds or by direct financing from the government. The latter is not costless, especially when as in the Canadian case, this entails annual approval by the government of the airline's capital budget. There may, therefore, be a tendency to use internally generated funds for capital expansion. How important this source of capital will become depends upon the amount of interference exercised by the government in approving the capital budget and upon the cost of using internally generated funds—the loss of support from users and the increased pressure for take-overs. In many instances, the use of internally generated funds may do little to reduce the amount of interference experienced, unless the airline chooses to finance all of its needs internally. For certain ranges of funds requested, interference may be almost unrelated to the amount of funds required. In particular, small increments in previous requests are not likely to upset the bureaucracy; but large ones will, because this will require readjustment of relative budget shares of different programs and a conscious reordering of priorities.[4] There are, however, times when a major expansion in capital is required. In these instances, the airline may turn to internally generated funds. Therefore, it is possible that the profit level chosen by the Crown airline will vary over time.

To this point, the discussion has ignored the possibility that the support of different groups of users may not have equal value to the public airline. The rational public corporation will implicitly weight the value of support it receives in each market. In conjunction with the over-all level of profit chosen for its

[d]Whether a zero level of profits includes a normal rate of return on capital depends upon the method adopted by the government for financing the Crown airline. Should, as in the Canadian case, the government advance all capital requirements at its own long-term interest rate, this rate will determine the zero profit level. Chapter Six discusses this point.

system operations, these weights will determine the profits generated on each route and thus the price and quality of service offered thereon. Therefore, the prices and levels of service in different markets will be interdependent.

It follows equally that the public airline is unlikely to be earning equal marginal rates of return across its route system. Only when each route is treated in isolation would the public airline maximize its support by choosing to move to the same profitability frontier everywhere. For as long as the marginal support of a change in profits is unequal across routes on the frontier that earns the same rate as that chosen for the system, then the airline can increase its support by earning less than this rate on some routes and offset this by earning more than this rate on others. In fact, there is the possibility that losses will actually be incurred on some routes but that these losses will be subsidized by profits earned elsewhere. Thus, the practice of cross-subsidization is a result predicted by this theory of the public firm.

Unfortunately, few additional deductions about behavior can be derived at this level of generality. In deciding whether or not profits in one sector should be used to offset losses in another, the airline must determine the degree to which this action will increase the support accruing to it. The importance of support from any group will be a function not only of the numbers in that group but also of the intensity of feeling exhibited by members of this group on any particular issue. Therefore, it is possible that a small group may be benefited at the expense of a larger group. But the determinants of the trade-off are difficult to specify.

The following example illustrates the problems involved. Consider an airline network as consisting of two sets of routes—those that are short and have light traffic and those that are longer with a greater density of traffic. Because of the nature of airline costs, if served by privately owned firms, the former would be charged relatively higher prices and receive a lower frequency of service than the latter. Will the public airline benefit the users of the former at the expense of the latter? Since users of low density routes are likely to be in the minority, the answer depends upon their importance as a voting block and upon the intensity of emotion they express on this issue. If interpersonal comparisons of utility are possible and it is assumed that the same price-frequency combinations yield equal satisfaction to different individuals, users on the lightly travelled routes will be deriving less total utility than those on the dense routes should the Crown airline adopt the same profit frontier in both cases. If the importance of support (or intensity of emotion engendered) is a function of the marginal loss or gain in utility occasioned by the actions of a Crown airline and it is assumed that diminishing marginal utility yields diminishing degrees of support, then the higher intensity of support of users on shorter distance routes may be sufficient to outweigh their lower numbers. Small decreases in price to these users offset by increases in price to users on the mainline routes could result in a net increase in the support offered to the Crown airline.

This approach treats support as a function of the absolute price level—or some measure of the quality of service. As illustrated above, difficulties in comparing inter-route marginal utilities and in balancing the size of the gain to each group against relative numbers yield vague predictions as to the public airline's behavior. But a more serious criticism can be made of this approach. It ignores certain implications of the fact that the impact of the public airline must be measured from some starting point—that is, from the situation that would have existed in the absence of the public corporation. Choosing to treat support generated on each route as a function of profits is one way to handle this. However, since data on route profits is typically either unavailable or unreliable, treating consumers as if they had access to this information is unrealistic. A second approach argues that support should be a function of the difference between the profit-maximizing price and that charged by the public corporation.[5] It is this difference that is commonly used to justify the existence of a Crown corporation. However, the costs of information make it as difficult for consumers to evaluate the existence and magnitude of this difference as to judge the size of the profits being earned on each route. A different benchmark has received more attention in public debate over the performance of public corporations.

Instead of concentrating upon the absolute level of fares, public debate often centers upon the relative level of different fares. The fact that debate should focus on relative fares is important because it indicates that the public corporation's success in dealing with this issue is relatively easy for the public to evaluate. In the case of transportation systems, debate on the rate structure inevitably leads to the question of fairness and an attempt to define an acceptable standard of equality. The standard of comparison for different fares—in effect, the demand for equity—will vary. When the service is readily comparable, such as the case of traffic on the same route, equality of absolute fares will be important. The Australian Crown airline successfully implemented service against established private airlines with a "one fare for all" campaign—a program that eliminated differential prices for business and personal travel on the same route.[6] In other cases, when the service is not similar but the distinguishing characteristics may be sufficiently subtle, equality of fares is also demanded. The early history of the street railroads in the United States was marked by a flat fee structure independent of mileage.[7] Although it was true that long-distance riders received a different service than short-distance riders, the linearly continuous nature of the systems made it difficult to separate the nature of the service to each class. In the same vein, Coase reports that even though a two part tariff—one for primary and one for secondary distribution—for the British postal service was strongly recommended by one of the system's chief architects, this was politically unacceptable.[8] Delivering a letter in a small town was not sufficiently differentiable from delivery in a large town to permit differences in fees charged. On the other hand, transportation service on different routes is a readily differentiated product. Here the standard of comparison has been not the absolute fare but the fare standardized for mileage travelled—that is, the fare per mile. Communities have often argued that they were unfairly penalized should their transportation rates, calculated on a per-mile basis, be higher than the rates charged others.[e]

Fares are only one of the characteristics of performance that are compared across routes. The quality of service receives equal attention. Outlying communities both in Canada and the United States have long argued that it was the government's responsibility to provide them with transportation service comparable to that existing elsewhere. Such pressure has taken the form of demanding that service by a mode not serving the community be implemented or that existing service not cease. The airline industry has also faced demands from outlying areas that service be upgraded either to provide the same quality of aircraft serving mainline routes or a frequency of service comparable to that existing elsewhere.

Thus, in the case of an airline system, two issues appear to be highly visible and to excite public interest: (1) the prevention of "discriminatory" pricing and (2) the provision of service. In dealing with both issues, the public airline can be expected to generate goodwill on local or regional routes.[f] Because of the short-haul nature of many of these routes, the distance-related taper in the cost function would ordinarily result in higher fares per mile thereon than on the longer or denser mainline routes. It is these communities that will support the Crown airline should it reduce the fare taper that would otherwise occur. Moreover, many such communities, by their very nature, tend to have fewer transportation alternatives and thus have a greater ability both to recognize and appreciate any improvement in their transportation services. Therefore, the Crown airline might also be expected to offer them a greater frequency of service or a better quality of aircraft than the fare level would justify. These policies will be accomplished at a cost. Fares in other areas will be higher and the quality of service lower than would be the case if a competitive market were allowed to function freely. In summary, an airline route system dominated by the existence of a Crown airline should be characterized by less of a distance-related taper in the fare per mile charged and greater comparability in the quality of service provided than would be found in a competitive airline market.

This argument by itself might suggest that the public firm merely acts as a profit-maximizer on longer distance routes—by increasing fares thereon and thereby decreasing the fare taper. But the airline should also be expected to reduce prices on shorter routes below costs, thereby establishing losses in its

[e]For one of the most recent examples of this argument, see Canada, Province of Manitoba, Royal Commission Inquiry into Northern Transportation, *Report* (Winnipeg: Queen's Printer, 1969), pp. 235–6.

[f]It may also concentrate its attention on a subset of these regional constituencies that for some reason may be politically more important for the party in power.

pattern of cross-subsidization. The reason that this pattern will result lies not just in the support thereby generated but also in the effect this policy will have on the potential return the private sector could earn from a take-over or from entry. The incentive for a take-over is provided by the potential profits that would result. If the public firm merely maximized profits on mainline routes, the private firm could hope to earn these from either a take-over or entry. However, to the extent that the public firm uses these profits to support loss services that the government comes to regard as essential, then the private firm will have to guarantee continuance of these services. This, in turn, lowers the rate of return the private firm could expect to earn. This particular pattern of cross-subsidization increases the probability of survial not only by increasing support from consumers, but also by decreasing the pressure from outsiders for take-over or entry.

All this suggests that in order to reduce disparities in the fare charged different routes, prices that exceed costs will be set on those routes that might ordinarily have the lowest fare per mile—that is, the longer and more heavily travelled city-pairs. But it should be recognized that this does not imply the profit-maximizing price will be charged on these routes. Although the Crown airline can hope to reduce the likelihood of entry, it cannot ignore its possibility. The greater the profits generated on the long distance or dense routes, the greater is the possibility that private carriers will try to enter hoping that they will not face the "burdens" borne by the Crown airline. Thus, the degree to which prices on these routes exceed the competitive equilibrium will depend upon the relative importance of two offsetting forces: the one stemming from demands for policies which lead to cross-subsidization; the other stemming from pressures for entry.

RATIONALE FOR A PUBLIC CORPORATION

If a public corporation is likely to choose a price-frequency combination so as to yield itself maximum support, and if the primary way it accomplishes this is via cross-subsidization of regional sectors, a relevant question to ask is whether this is sufficient reason for the creation of a Crown airline. Since the results of regulatory agency behavior were found to be similar to that just described, why is it that the institutional framework of a public corporation might be preferred to that of regulation?

The answer to this question revolves on the difference in the nature of the property rights characterizing the firms in each case. Recall that a regulatory agency offered the private firms in an industry either protection from entry or higher profits in return for services or a price structure that might not otherwise have existed. But the airlines remained under private ownership, still more or less pursuing maximum profits. For the regulated firm, a promising avenue for increased profits lay in the pursuit of strategic bargaining with the agency—an occurrence documented in the previous section. The incentive to use profits not only to cross-subsidize or to price discriminate in a fashion desired by the regulatory agency but also to reward shareholders persisted in this institutional framework. The change in property rights associated with the creation of a public corporation reduces these bargaining costs and releases those resources, which the firm had previously used to forestall take-overs, for use in such vote-garnering policies as cross-subsidization. In effect, the public corporation becomes the more efficient vehicle for the creation of government support.

Failure to universally adopt the institution of a public corporation is understood when the pressures to create a regulatory agency are recalled. The government, in establishing such agencies, was not attempting to maximize user support. Rather, it was attempting to arbitrate between producers and consumers, each of whom had a conflicting opinion as to the type of service that should be offered. The public corporation is likely to be adopted where either private firms do not exist, or where government expense in providing infrastructure is so large that it has the added incentive to obtain as much user support as possible because of the marginal disutility likely to be suffered by taxpayers in financing the project.

THE EFFECT OF EXOGENOUS CHANGES IN THE CROWN AIRLINE'S ENVIRONMENT

A formal behavioral model of the public airline permits hypotheses to be formulated concerning the response of a Crown airline to events beyond its control. The public airline has been portrayed as having an objective function containing such variables as the rate structure, a measure of the relative quality of service on different routes, and the level of profits earned on mainline routes. The state-owned airline was characterized as choosing values for these variables so as to maximize its utility—subject only to the constraint that the sum of profits earned on mainline routes and losses incurred on regional routes equal the overall level of profitability chosen by the airline.

Several events have affected the level of net revenues earned by the Canadian Crown airline on different sectors of its route system. First, the introduction of new aircraft has increased the profits earned on mainline or trunk routes without significantly affecting net revenues on the loss sector. Secondly, the government has introduced competitors to the Crown airline on both sectors, though not simultaneously. Again this had the effect of changing net revenues in one sector but not the other. Predictions as to the effect these events should have had on the level of the Crown airline's decision variables provide a frame of reference for the subsequent discussion of the actual behavior of the Canadian airline.

Let P_2 and P_1 stand for the prices charged on the regional and mainline sectors, respectively; and $L(P_2)$ and $R(P_1)$ represent the net revenues earned in each. As argued previously, there is reason to believe $L(P_2)$ may be negative. Then the rate structure can be represented by $P_2 - P_1$, where each price is suitably standardized by dividing by length of trip. It has been argued that decreasing the value of this variable increases the public airline's support or decreases the pressures placed upon it. In addition to this proxy for the fare structure, profits earned on mainline routes $R(P_1)$ also enter the airline's utility function. The efforts required by the Crown airline to protect itself from new entrants will be a function of these profits.[g] Then by letting K stand for the overall or system level of profitability the airline chooses to earn,[h] the public airline is hypothesized to choose prices in both sectors P_1, P_2 so as to maximize:

$$U\,[P_2 - P_1; R(P_1)] + \lambda\,[L(P_2) + R(P_1) - K]. \tag{5–1}$$

For simplicity of exposition, measures of the relative quality of service have been excluded from this formulation. They may be included without changing the qualitative nature of the predictions that follow.

The geometrical representation of the maximization procedure is depicted in Figures 5–1 and 5–2. In Figure 5–1, the utility isoquants, drawn in $R(P_1), P_2 - P_1$ space in quadrant 3, are translated into isoquants in P_2, P_1 space in the first quadrant making use of the relationship between R and P_1 as depicted in the second quadrant. The $U_i\ [P_2 - P_1, R(P_1)]$ shall be interpreted as constant support curves faced by the airline. Since support increases as the arguments of this function decrease, the concavity of these U_i is just the reverse of the normal quantity indifference curves used in demand theory. However, the $U_i(P_2,P_1)$ need not be as drawn. Whether they are concave or convex depends on the relative concavity of $R(P_1)$ and the $U_i[P_2 - P_1, R(P_1)]$.

The support isoquants $U_i(P_2,P_1)$ derived in Figure 5–1 are transposed to quadrant 1 of Figure 5–2. The profit constraint facing the airline (C), is drawn in the same quadrant. It is derived from the net profit curve of sector 1 (R_1) drawn in quadrant 2 and the net loss curve of sector 2 (L_1) drawn in quadrant 4. C_1 is drawn here on the assumption that the public airline will utilize all profits generated on the mainline routes to subsidize losses on the regional routes. As long as the two net revenue functions exhibit the concavity depicted in Figure 5–2 the profit constraint will be concave upwards. With profit constraint C_1, the support-maximizing public airline will choose position A, setting prices at P_2', P_1'.

[g]Consumer opposition on mainline routes may also develop in response to this variable.

[h]Including system-wide profitability in this manner ignores the previous discussion that treated it as one of the decision variables of the airline, rather than a rigid constraint imposed by government policy. For our purposes, the approach adopted here is regarded as a reasonable approximation to the decision process. Essentially, the variation in overall profitability chosen by the airline is being regarded as of lesser magnitude than the response of prices and quality of service to these events. Chapter Six tends to confirm the reasonableness of this assumption. Use of the profitability constraint in this fashion is no different than regarding income as fixed in standard demand analysis.

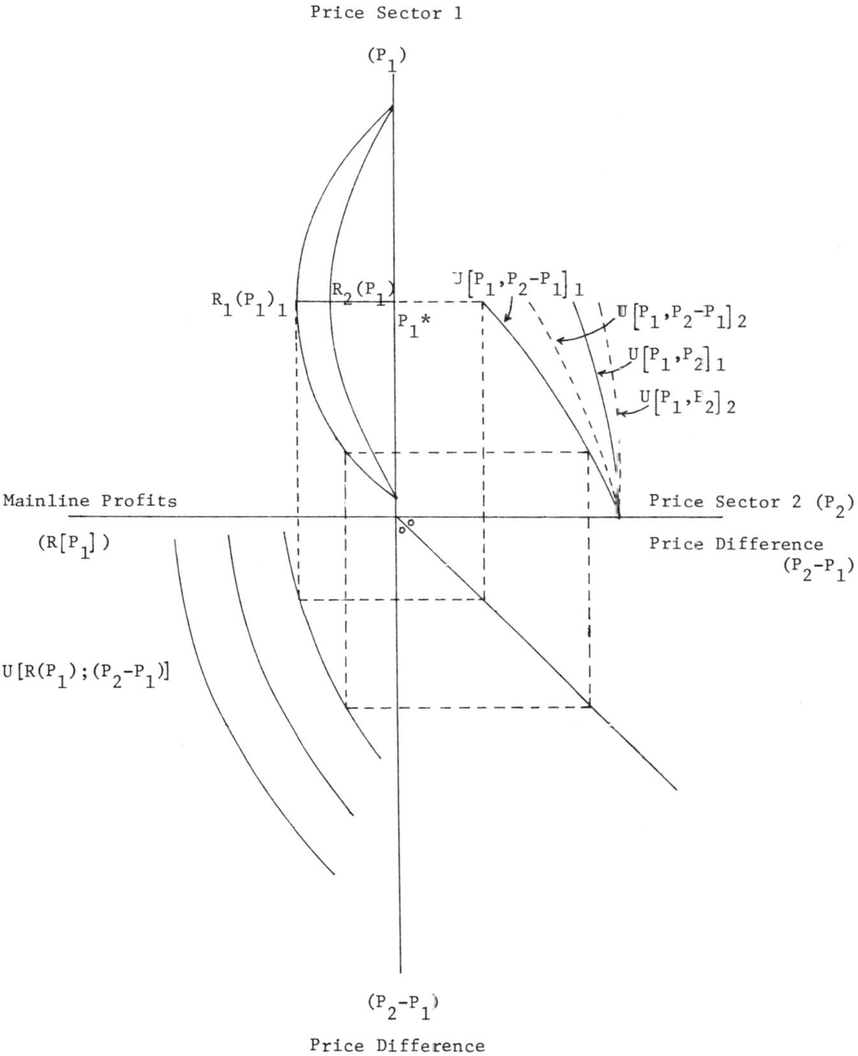

Figure 5–1. The Transformation of Utility Isoquants Drawn for Price Differences and Mainline Profits into Isoquants Drawn for Prices in Two Sectors.

Now consider the effect of entry of a private carrier to the mainline routes on the behavior of the Crown airline. In the Canadian case, entry was accompanied by a government restriction on the private carrier that relegated to this airline a pre-determined percentage of the market. Entry has the effect of shifting the net revenue curve of the mainline sector (R_1 in quadrant 2 of Figure 5–2) downward.

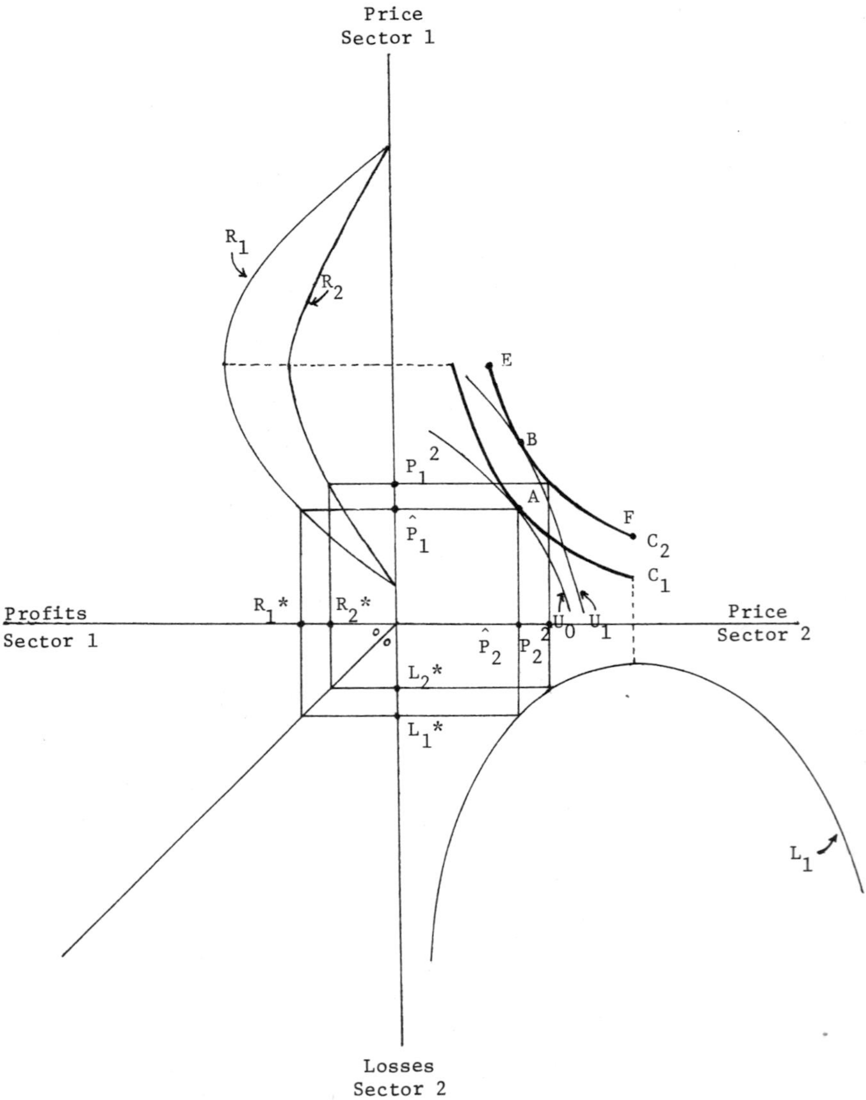

Figure 5–2. The Effect of a Shift in the Potential Profits Available on the Degree of Cross-Subsidization and Prices in the Profit and Loss Sectors.

Whereas $R_1(P)$ is the relevant profit curve for a monopolist, $R_2(P)$ is the profit curve for a dominant firm whose demand is K times the market demand—where $1-K$ *is the share of the market guaranteed the new entrant.*[i] The slope of $R_2(P)$ will generally be lower than for $R_1(P)$.[j] As a result, the new constraint C_1 drawn in Figure 5–2 not only shifts outwards but becomes steeper.[k] The rotation of $R(P_1)$ will also cause each $U_i(P_2,P_1)$ to become steeper as Figure 5–1 shows. In Figure 5–2, the tangency point between the new constraint C_1 and an iso-support curve is represented by point B.

While Figure 5–2 is drawn in such a way that both prices increase, the necessity of this outcome is not obvious. Abstract for the moment from the rotation in the support curves and consider the movement from A to B as resulting only from a change in the profit constraint. Such a movement may be divided into an income and price effect. The income effect taken alone would lead to an increase in the price of both sectors. However, because of the twisting of the constraint, the price effect operates in opposite directions. It is now more expensive to obtain a reduction in the loss sector's price by increasing the price in sector 1. This substitution effect will tend to increase the price in sector 2 and decrease it in sector 1. Only in sector 2 is the sign of the change resulting from both these factors unambiguous. But even this conclusion is tenuous because the support curves have rotated in the same direction as the budget constraint. This would tend to decrease prices on the loss sector and increase them on the mainline route.[l]

The relative magnitude of these offsetting effects can be better examined by totally differentiating the first order conditions of equation (5–1). The first order equations are:

$$
\begin{aligned}
U_1 + \lambda L_{P_2} &= 0 \\
-U_1 + U_2 R_{P_1} + \lambda R_{P_1} &= 0 \\
R(P_1) + L(P_2) - K &= 0
\end{aligned}
\qquad (5\text{–}2)
$$

[i]This assumes that the new entrant will fully utilize its guaranteed share and follow the pricing leadership of the established public firm. Both assumptions are realistic in light of the Canadian experience to be discussed later.

[j]If net revenues $(R) = KP_1Q_1(P_1) - C[KQ_1(P_1)]$ where K is market share, then a sufficient condition for $\partial(\partial R/\partial P)\ \partial K > 0$ is $\partial^2 C/\partial Q^2 \geqslant 0$ providing $\partial R/\partial P > 0$. Whether the zero-profit point $[R(P_1) = 0]$ remains the same as is drawn in Figure 5–2 depends upon the existence of constant average costs.

[k]In Figure 5–2, the same price maximizes both profit curves. This assumes that the new entrant shares the same cost curves as the public airline and that profits are jointly maximized. As John T. Wenders, "Collusion and Entry," *Journal of Political Economy* LXXIX, no. 6 (1971):1258–77, has shown, the rational profit-maximizing monopolist faced with entry will generally choose to lower market price. In this case, R_2 in Figure 5–2 should be drawn so as to be maximized at a lower price than R_1.

[l]Not only will they rotate but they will become less concave if $|R_{P_1P_1}|$ falls. This could result in the corner points E or F suddenly being sought by the Crown airline.

Then differentiating each equation yields:

$$\begin{bmatrix} U_{11}+L_{P_2P_2} ; & -U_{11}+R_{P_1}U_{12} & ; L_{P_2} \\ -U_{11}+U_{12}R_{P_1} ; & U_{11}-2U_{12}R_{P_1}+U_2R_{P_1P_1}+R_{P_1}{}^2U_{22}+R_{P_1P_1} & ; R_{P_1} \\ L_{P_2} ; & R_{P_1} & ; 0 \end{bmatrix} \begin{bmatrix} dP_2 \\ dP_1 \\ d\lambda \end{bmatrix} = 0 .$$

Let this matrix be represented by A and its determinant by D. The effect of an event that changes the profitability of the mainline routes can be examined by introducing a shift parameter α into both the profit function R and its slope R_{P_1}.[m] Then,

$$\begin{bmatrix} \\ A \\ \\ \end{bmatrix} \begin{bmatrix} dP_2 \\ dP_1 \\ d\lambda \end{bmatrix} = \begin{bmatrix} -U_{12}R_\alpha d\alpha \\ +(U_{12}-R_{P_1}U_{22})R_\alpha d\alpha-(U_2+\lambda)R_{P_1\alpha}d\alpha \\ -R_\alpha d\alpha \end{bmatrix}$$

and

$$\frac{dP_2}{d\alpha} = \left\{ \left[-(U_2+\lambda)R_{P_1}L_{P_2}\right] R_{P_1\alpha} + \left[(R_{P_1}+L_{P_2})U_{11}+R_{P_1P_1}(U_2+\lambda)L_{P_2}-L_{P_2}R_{P_1}U_{12}\right] R_\alpha \right\} \Big/ D$$

$$\frac{dP_1}{d\alpha} = \left\{ L_{P_2}{}^2(U_2+\lambda)R_{P_1\alpha} + \left[(U_{11}+L_{P_2P_2})R_{P_1}+L_{P_2}(U_{11}-U_{12}R_{P_1})-L_{P_2}(R_{P_1}U_{12}+L_{P_2}[U_{12}-R_{P_1}U_{22}])\right] R_\alpha \right\} \Big/ D .$$

Using the second order conditions and assuming both arguments in the utility function are normal—that is, $\delta(P_2-P_1)/\delta K,\ \delta R/\delta K > 0$—it can be shown that:

$$\frac{dP_2}{d\alpha} = \quad sgn\ R_{P_1\alpha} - sgn\ R_\alpha$$

$$\frac{dP_1}{d\alpha} = \quad -sgn\ R_{P_1\alpha} - sgn\ R_\alpha \tag{5–3}$$

$$\frac{dP_2}{d\alpha} - \frac{dP_1}{d\alpha} = sgn\ R_{P_1\alpha} + sgn\ R_\alpha .$$

[m]As in the section on regulation, it will be assumed that the airline always lies in the region where $R_{P_1}, L_{P_2} > 0$.

The effects of an event that causes a change in the revenue function on the unprofitable routes (L) can also be examined by including a shift parameter α in L and L_{P_2}. If the first order conditions (5–2) are differentiated totally, and if the same assumptions about the second order conditions and about the normality of $P_2 - P_1$, and R are made, then it can be shown that:

$$\frac{dP_2}{d\alpha} = \quad sgn\ L_{P_2\alpha} - sgn\ L_\alpha$$

$$\frac{dP_1}{d\alpha} = -sgn\ L_{P_2\alpha} - sgn\ L_\alpha \tag{5–4}$$

$$\frac{dP_2}{d\alpha} - \frac{dP_1}{d\alpha} = sgn\ L_{P_2\alpha} - sgn\ L_\alpha \ .$$

Once the effect of exogenous events upon the net revenue curves (R_α, L_α) and their slopes ($R_{P_1\alpha}$ and $L_{P_2\alpha}$) is determined, equation sets (5–3) and (5–4) can be used to predict how the airline's decision variables (P_2 and P_1) will change in response to these events. An upward shift in the demand for air travel on the mainline route will cause profits to increase thereon ($R_\alpha > 0$). It should also increase the slope of the net revenue function ($R_{P_1\alpha} > 0$).[n] A decrease in costs unique to the mainline routes will also cause R to increase but will cause R_{P_1} to fall. The effect of entry to either route will be to cause the net revenue function to fall. The effect of entry to either route will be to cause the net revenue function to fall. To the extent that it also causes the demand curve to become more elastic, entry will reduce the slope of the net revenue function ($R_{P_1\alpha} < 0$, $L_{P_2\alpha} < 0$). Should the entrant be guaranteed a set share of the market, it can also be shown that entry in this case reduces R_{P_1}.[o]

The results of substituting these values for the signs of R_α, L_α, $R_{P_1\alpha}$ and $L_{P_2\alpha}$ into equation sets (5–3) and (5–4) are summarized in columns 2 through 5 of Table 5–1. An increase in demand engendered by the introduction on the mainline routes of new equipment that is faster but not less costly should decrease price thereon and increase the price spread between the two sectors. The sign of the price change on the regional routes is ambiguous. A cost reduction on the mainline routes should decrease prices on the regional routes. Observation of falling prices on the mainline routes and an increased price differential between sectors in response to this event would be compatible with this model. Entry to mainline routes should increase prices thereon but decrease the spread between the sectors. Prices could increase or decrease on the regional routes. Entry to the regional routes is predicted to increase the price on the

[n]Writing $Q = F(P+T)$ where T is time cost, it then follows that if the new aircraft reduces time cost and $R_{P_1P_1} < 0$, that $R_{P_1\alpha} > 0$.

[o]See footnote j in this chapter.

Table 5–1. The Effect of Exogenous Events upon the Airline's Decision Variables, Model I

	Demand Increases	*Costs Fall*	*Entry Occurs on Mainline Model I(A)*	*Entry Occurs on Regional*	*Entry Mainline Model I(B)*
	$R_\alpha > 0$	$R_\alpha > 0$	$R_\alpha < 0$	$L_\alpha < 0$	$R'_\alpha < 0$
	$R_{P_1\alpha} > 0$	$R_{P_1\alpha} < 0$	$R_{P_1\alpha} < 0$	$L_{P_1\alpha} < 0$	$R'_{R\alpha} < 0$
dP_2	?	–	?	?	+
dP_1	–	?	+	+	?
dP_2-dP_1	+	?	–	?	+

mainline routes. However, the predicted sign of the change in prices on the regional routes and the price spread between sectors is indeterminate.

This derivation of the effects of entry on the mainline routes is based upon a questionable assumption. Equation (5–1) implies both that public opprobrium and that pressure for entry are functions not of total profits earned but only of the share of this variable accruing to the Crown airline. Suppose instead that the pressure placed upon the political system that creates difficulties for the Crown airline is a function of total profits earned on mainline routes by both the Crown airline and the newly introduced competitor. Then the effect of entry to the mainline routes may be examined by rewriting equation (5–1) as:

$$U\,[P_2 - P_1\,;R(P_1)] + \lambda\,[R'\,(R[P_1]) + L(P_2) - K] \qquad (5\text{–}5)$$

R' is the portion of the total mainline profits accruing to the Crown airline. The effect of entry can be examined by introducing a shift parameter α in R' and its slope $\delta R'/\delta R$. Entry will reduce the profits accruing to the Crown airline—that is, $R'_\alpha < 0$. Whereas $R'_R = 1$ when the Crown airline is the sole carrier, it will fall as the result of entry—that is $R'_{R\alpha} < 1$. Then differentiating the first order conditions of (5–3) yields:

$$\frac{dP_2}{d\alpha} = -sgn\ R'_{R\alpha} - sgn\ R'_\alpha > 0$$

$$\frac{dP_1}{d\alpha} = +sgn\ R'_{R\alpha} - sgn\ R'_\alpha = ? \qquad \because\ R'_{R\alpha} < 0\ ;\ R'_\alpha < 0$$

$$\frac{dP_2}{d\alpha} - \frac{dP_1}{d\alpha} = -sgn\ R'_{R\alpha} - sgn\ R'_\alpha > 0\,.$$

The results are reported in column 6 of Table 5–1. This variant of the model predicts that entry to the profitable routes should result in an increase in prices

Table 5–2. The Effect of Exogenous Events upon the Airline's Decision Variables, Model II

	Demand Increases	*Costs Fall*	*Entry to Mainline Routes*	*Entry to Regional Routes*
	$R_\alpha > 0$ $R_{P_1\alpha} > 0$	$R_\alpha > 0$ $R_{P_1\alpha} < 0$	$R_\alpha < 0$ $R_{P_1\alpha} < 0$	$L_\alpha < 0$ $L_{P_2\alpha} < 0$
dP_2	–	?	+	?
dP_1	?	–	?	+
$d(P_2\text{-}P_1)$ (a)	?	+	?	–
(b)	–	?	+	?

Note: (a) assumes $d(P_2\text{-}P_1)dK < 0$; (b) assumes $d(P_2\text{-}P_1)/dK > 0$.

on the loss sector, and an increase in the spread between the prices in the two sectors. The sign of the price change on the mainline routes is ambiguous.[p]

Whether this variant of the model or a straightforward application of the original model is correct can be adjudicated on grounds other than the realism of the underlying assumptions. The original version—model I(A)—predicts that the price on the mainline routes should increase in response to entry thereon but is ambiguous as to the price in sector 2. Therefore, observation of a price decrease on the mainline routes would rule out this model. On the other hand, discovery that prices fell on the loss sector would rule out the alternative—model I(B). Prices generally moved up in response to entry. However, when entry first occurred prices on several of the longest mainline routes did not change or fell slightly. The two models also differ in their predictions as to the change in the price spread that should be observed. The modified model predicts that the price spread should increase in response to entry on the mainline routes. The first version—model I(A)—predicts it should fall. Chapter Nine indicates the price spread increases in response to entry on the mainline routes. Therefore, the alternative model, which enters only the profits accruing to the Crown airline in its utility function, is rejected.

There is an alternative more general way of formulating the Crown airline's decision process. The airline might be treated as maximizing $U[P_2, P_1]$ subject to $R(P_1) + L(P_2) = K$. It is the absolute price level that is regarded as generating support rather than the relative price levels. The effects of the introduction of aircraft which either generate new demand or decrease costs and the effect of entry to the industry can be investigated in the same manner as was used previously. Table 5–2 presents the signs of the predicted changes in the airline's decision variables. These results are generally consistent with a system-wide price

[p]All of the other predictions reported in columns 2, 3 and 5 for model I(A) apply in the case of model I(B).

decline resulting from an increase in demand or cost reductions and with system-wide price increases in response to entry on either sector. Comparison of Table 5–1 and 5–2 reveals that there are two major differences between this model and the one previously adopted. Should regional prices not fall in response to new demand-generating technology, the second model can be rejected. Should regional prices not fall in response to cost-reducing technology the first model is contradicted. As we shall see, not all regional routes received price reductions in response to the introduction of the aircraft that increased demand. On the other hand, all received some benefit—either in the form of a price decrease or service improvements[q]—in response to the introduction of lower cost aircraft. This is the first reason for rejection model II. The second reason for doing so is that it tells us nothing about movements in the price differential likely to be occasioned by these events. To obtain results similar to those produced by model I, it must be assumed that $d(P_2-P_1)/dK < 0$. But this adds a new dimension to the model—a dimension directly incorporated into model I. It is better to incorporate one's assumptions directly rather than in this ad hoc manner. For both reasons, model I—or more properly I(A)—will be adopted.

This exercise in comparative statics yields several testable hypotheses. First, a change, either in technology or competition policy, which pertains to one only of the profit or loss sectors, will be felt throughout the route system. The introduction of new equipment on mainline routes, which does not change costs but reduces time of travel, should decrease the price thereon and increase the price spread between the regions. Cost-reducing technology on mainline routes should decrease prices or increase the quality of service on the regional routes. Entry to mainline routes should increase the price on the regional routes and increase the price spread between the sectors. Entry to regional routes should increase the price on at least the mainline sector. Thus evidence that these responses were in fact observed will lend support to the model proposed herein.

Of course, corroborating evidence of this kind does not in and by itself rule out alternative explanations of these events—that is, explanations based upon a profit-maximizing theory of the firm. But then, the occasion is rare when a set of events is compatible with only one underlying model. No attempt will be made here to eliminate all such competing models. Nevertheless, this issue cannot be completely ignored. In the final chapter, it will be suggested that certain of the more obvious alternate rationalizations can be eliminated.

The next chapters are devoted to an examination of the behavior of Air Canada—the Canadian Crown airline. In particular, evidence substantiating the model of the public firm will be sought—that is, evidence as to the profit

[q]While the comparative statics exercise has been conducted in terms of price, it was implicitly understood that P represents a joint good—benefits to that sector. As such, it should be regarded as a combination of the price differential and the service quality.

constraint chosen by Air Canada, as well as evidence that it developed a system of internal cross-subsidization, that it equalized the treatment received by different routes both in terms of fare per mile charged and quality of service, that it responded to cost-reducing innovations on specific routes by decreasing prices across its route system, and that the result of new entry was a perverse movement in prices upward across its route system.

Chapter Six

The Canadian Crown Airline: The Level of System Profitability and the Practice of Cross-Subsidization

Air Canada (Trans-Canada Air Lines until 1964) was formally incorporated as a Crown corporation in 1937. The federal government had initially proposed joint ownership with the two national railways and itself, each owning one-third of the airline. When the Canadian Pacific Railway Company—the privately owned carrier—refused to accept this arrangement, the federal government created the airline as a wholly owned Crown corporation.[a] The government envisioned Air Canada's major domestic function to be the provision of transcontinental service between urban points of "mainline" character.[1] Enabling legislation specifically instructed the airline to set fares that were "competitive with other similar transportation services in North America."[2] Initially, the airline was also designated as sole operator of Canada's international air services. The emphasis that was placed on the trunkline nature of the airline was apparently meant to allay fears that the government airline would compete with the "bush" or frontier air services.[3] However, with the passage of time, its role was broadened to include "regional and feeder lines as well as the main transcontinental runs."[4]

This chapter begins to examine the extent to which the Crown airline's behavior conformed to the predictions developed in the previous chapter. Although initially given a monopoly of transcontinental service between St. John's, Newfoundland, and Victoria, British Columbia, it should not have been expected to earn monopoly profits. A level of profits close to zero, possibly varying over time, should have been chosen by the airline. Concomitant

[a]That the government had not entirely despaired of some accomodation with the CPR is evidenced by the peculiar ownership arrangement adopted for Air Canada. The government-owned railway (CNR) was given control over the shares of Air Canada with the power to dispose of 49.8 percent of them to a private party upon approval of the Minister of Transport.

with this system-wide constraint should have been the development of cross-subsidization within the route system.

PROFITABILITY OF THE CROWN AIRLINE

An integral part of the theory of the public corporation concerned the level of profits the Crown airline would choose to earn—what will be referred to as the public airline's overall profit constraint. It was argued that the constraint could take on either positive or negative values. *Ceteris paribus,* the less government interference in the airline's budget procedure, the greater the government's acceptance of operating losses; and the less vociferous public complaints about deficits incurred by government corporations, the lower would be the level of earned profits chosen. Since none of these factors was fixed, it is quite possible that the profit constraint chosen by the Crown airline varied over time.

The development period of the airline between 1937 and 1945 was characterized by an incentive system entirely different from the one that followed. During this period, the government continuously underwrote the operating losses of the Crown airline. Even so, it did this with some reluctance, thereby emphasizing to the airline the political costs of deficit operations. The 1937 legislation, which had created the airline, stipulated that over an initial period lasting until January 1, 1940,[b] mail rates were to be fixed and deficits would be paid annually out of monies to be appropriated by Parliament.[5] Thereafter, the mail rate, calculated on a plane-mile basis, was to be adjusted annually, so as in the case of a surplus to decrease it by half. Recognition of the incentive that this type of adjustable subsidy would give the airline to expand its services led the government to require that both the Minister of Transport and the Postmaster-General approve new services. The importance of the carriage of mail during this period is illustrated in Table 6–1. Although its relative magnitude was decreasing during this period, mail revenues still accounted for almost 40 percent of total revenues by the end of the Second World War.[c]

Although unique because of the degree of direct government support for operations, this period effectively demonstrates the political costs to a survival-conscious public airline of earning either deficits or profits. First, the automatic adjustment mechanism embodied in the subsidy program emphasized the government's dislike of deficits, for although an initial subsidy was recognized as inevitable, it was implemented in a way calculated to minimize the government's risk of political embarrassment. Annual appropriations aimed directly at supporting Air Canada would have been subject to far greater opposition scrutiny than mail payments buried in the Post Office budget. On the other hand, the emergence of profits in 1940 led the government to indicate its

[b]This was later extended for two years to December 1942.
[c]By 1951, mail only accounted for 15 percent of total revenues.

Table 6–1. Air Canada Operating Revenues by Category, 1938–1944 ($000)

Year	*Passengers*	*Goods*	*Other*	*Mail*	*Total*	*Mail as % of Total*
1938	15.2	3.9	15.5	556.2	590.8	94%
1939	643.9	27.6	46.1	1,632.9	2,350.5	70%
1940	1,574.2	39.5	146.3	2,832.4	4,592.4	62%
1941	2,366.8	78.8	304.1	3,058.1	5,807.8	53%
1942	3,094.9	173.0	857.5	3,211.9	7,337.3	44%
1943	4,273.7	330.0	1,259.9	3,515.8	9,379.5	37%
1944	4,507.0	326.2	1,679.3	3,802.4	10,314.9	37%

Source: Canada, Department of Reconstruction and Supply, Directorate of Air Development, "Development of Commercial Air Services in Canada, 1919–1944" (unpublished paper prepared by H. Cunningham, Ottawa, 1946, mimeographed).

displeasure with this state of affairs. Since the Air Canada "contract" had been extended to 1943, mail rates were not due to be adjusted until then. With the emergence of profits in 1940, the mail rates were reduced in early 1941. Even though the Crown airline's profits amounted to less than $500,000,[d] the temptation to utilize these funds to bolster the government's own cash position was overriding.[6] In taking this action, a statement was issued by C.D. Howe—which pronouncement, coming from the Minister for Civil Aviation and the founder of the airline, was certain to influence the airline's behavior: "The view of the government was that we would set up this company so that it would never earn much profit."[7]

Anticipating postwar expansion of the airline system and wanting to avoid conflicts with the Postmaster-General, Air Canada was successful in obtaining a 1945 amendment to the Air Lines Act that permitted the mail contract to be amended at will by Order-in-Council.[8] As a result, the contract was changed so that the airline was remunerated for mail carried on a pound-mile basis rather than according to the number of plane-miles flown.[e] Although this change removed most of the anxiety the Post Office might have had about undue expansion of service, it also eliminated the automaticity with which deficits were covered. Mail rates were no longer adjusted, albeit with a lag, so as to cover deficits. Deficits were now to require annual votes by Parliament and therefore rather close scrutiny by friend and foe alike.

Between 1946 and 1950, the airline's losses amounted to $11.5 million.[9]

[d] Not only did this episode serve to elicit a clear government statement on the desired profit position of the public airline, but since mail payments exceeded net profits, this episode also indicated the emphasis the government placed on reducing the airline's net drain on the treasury.

[e] The mail contract was changed in 1948 to a flat monthly fee in return for "all up" service, but reverted in 1951 to a ton-mile basis.

Table 6–2. Air Canada Profits, Interest Charges, and Net Income, 1950–1970 ($000)

Year	*Total Profits Operating and Non-Operating*	*Interest Charges*	*Net Income*[a]
1950	–(575)	751	–(1,325)
1951	4,641	751	3,891
1952	2,756	751	1,284[b]
1953	1,322	765	375[b]
1954	1,290	794	496
1955	1,185	996	190
1956	2,843	1,287	1,556
1957	2,095	1,690	404
1958	3,043	2,495	547
1959	4,143	2,988	153
1960	5,491	8,097	–(2,607)
1961	4,061	10,511	–(6,450)
1962	7,978	11,519	–(3,541)
1963	12,147	11,619	528
1964	12,897	11,491	1,406
1965	15,288	11,298	3,990
1966	17,399	11,580	2,910
1967	20,954	13,857	3,547
1968	34,611	18,247	8,184
1969	38,339	25,246	1,548
1970	29,776	31,920	–(1,072)

[a]After taxes and provision for deferred taxes.
[b]Corrected for taxes later refunded.
Source: Air Canada, *Annual Report,* various years.

While the government appeared willing to finance the losses incurred during this expansionary period, it did so only after forcing the airline to first draw down the $1.5 million it had accumulated in retained earnings during the war years.[10] Deficits were thus met first out of internally generated funds, then out of general government revenues.

Athough this policy was never officially formalized, it appears to have persisted in practice. Table 6–2 and Table 6–3 present the financial results and capital structure of the airline for the period 1950 to 1970. Only two periods of deficits have occurred since 1950: the first at the time of the introduction of long-range jet aircraft in 1960, the second during the jumbo jet re-equipment phase in 1970. It is probably not a coincidence that in 1960 the airline shifted all of its retained earnings (see Table 6–3) to a special account for overhaul and maintenance, thereby leaving it with exactly the amount of subscribed capital in its equity account–$5 million.[f] During these three years, deficits were covered

[f]The airline argued this was needed to cover the losses that would be incurred upon the sale of its fleet of Super Constellations. These had become obsolete with the introduction of the long-range jet aircraft.

Table 6–3. Capital Structure of Air Canada, 1948–1970 ($000)

Year	*Equity*	*Notes and Debentures*	*Insurance Reserves*	*Overhaul and other Reserves*	*Deferred Taxes*
1948	25,000	1,500	3,113	499	......
1949	25,000	....	3,659	581	......
1950	25,000	....	4,079	861	......
1951	28,891	....	4,571	861	......
1952	29,698	......	5,164	861	......
1953	9,955	20,000	5,782	861	......
1954	8,819	23,100	6,000	837	......
1955	9,711	33,500	6,000	468	......
1956	11,267	40,000	6,000	394	......
1957	11,471	52,000	5,671	392	......
1958	11,689	83,100	6,000	.....	......
1959	11,842	135,100	5,846	.....	......
1960	5,000	209,100	5,690	6,841	......
1961	5,000	227,671	8,362	4,238	......
1962	5,000	237,471	8,817	.....	......
1963	5,528	237,471	5,982	.....	......
1964	6,783	235,820	3,218	.....	......
1965	10,573	235,820	5,289	.....	......
1966	13,283	235,820	10,000	.....	2,910
1967	16,630	302,820	6,249	.....	6,460
1968	24,614	392,820	6,463	.....	14,640
1969	32,725	467,602	......	.....	15,885
1970	37,689	547,602	......	.....	19,096

Source: Air Canada, *Annual Report,* various years.

entirely by parliamentary appropriations. However, with ample retained earnings available in 1970, the loss appears to have been borne by these internally generated funds, since no special parliamentary appropriations were ever made.

Thus, the government, while meeting the deficit in the early years, devised several ways of signalling its disapproval of deficits. Moreover, its tendency to draw on the airline's retained earnings prior to covering operating deficits meant the airline could not expect to build up retained earnings and run the occasional deficit without losing these funds. To the extent that internally generated funds bore some utility to the corporation for purposes other than meeting unexpected deficits, the airline would be less likely to carelessly incur the occasional deficit.

In contrast to the United Kingdom, where recent guidelines as to the financial performance expected of Crown corporations have been issued,[11] the Canadian government has not set explicit rules regarding the financial results demanded of its Crown airline. Instead, implicit constraints have gradually evolved which require Air Canada to earn at least the cost of funds advanced to it—the government long-term bond rate. Initially, the 1937 legislation required the Crown airline to pay 5 percent on the capital that had been subscribed to it by Canadian National Railways (CNR).[g] Following a 1945 amendment to this legislation, Air Canada instead began to pay the same rate as did the CNR on its advances from the government. Thus, even during the early period when deficits were almost continuously incurred, the government established the principle that capital was not to be regarded as a free good. That it should have engaged in what was essentially a bookkeeping operation is significant. Since operating costs were not even being covered at this time, this action did not serve to reduce the amount of government revenues required to support the airline. In serving to emphasize the true size of the deficit, this action ensured that maximum pressure was brought to bear on the airline to reduce the deficit. This policy served as an additional signal to the airline that the government was not willing to tolerate deficits in the long run.

In 1953, Air Canada's $25 million in capital was divided into $5 million equity and a $20 million debenture. Subsequent capital subscriptions were met entirely by debt issues—notes and debentures generally bearing interest rates of 1/8 of 1 percent above the long-term bond rate.[h] Table 6–3 indicates that as a result of this reliance on debt instruments, equity as a percentage of total capital invested fell from 33 percent in 1953 to 6 percent by 1970. Providing the airline found deficits too costly, this would have effectively constrained the Crown airline to earn at least the government's opportunity cost of capital—the long-term bond rate.

In the post-1950 period, the airline itself recognized that deficits were not acceptable by acknowledging publicly that it was not to be "a drain upon the national purse." [12] Thus, the airline should over this period have earned a rate of return equal to or greater than the long-term government bond rate. Table 6–4 presents a comparison of the return earned by the airline and the government long-term bond rate. Column 2 represents the airline's own estimates of its profitability. Column 1 is calculated from Tables 6–2 and 6–3 as the ratio of total profit[i] to the sum of equity, debt, and deferred taxes. Contrary to Air Canada's calculations, it uses year-end capital invested rather than a yearly average. It also differs because it includes deferred but unpaid taxes as part of both earnings and equity. This accounts for the difference in the two series during the profitable years of the late 1960s. Excluding the unusually profitable year of 1951, a test of the difference in the means of the revised rate of return series and the long-term bond rate for the period 1952 to 1970 reveals no significant[j] difference in the time series.[k]

[g]See footnote a of this chapter for an explanation as to why this indirect route for capital financing was adopted.

[h]The original debenture ($20 million in 1953) bore the rate of 3.88 percent as compared to the government's bond rate of 3.65 percent for that year (see Table 6–4).

[i]Total profit excludes taxes paid but includes deferred taxes which are not paid to the government.

[j]The t statistic becomes significant only at the 25 percent level.

[k]The same test was run on two variants of the airline's rate of return. First, deferred

Table 6–4. Comparison of Rates of Return for Air Canada, Canadian Long-Term Government Bonds, and U.S. Domestic Trunk Carriers, 1951–1970 (%)

Year	*Air Canada* *(1)*	*(2)*	*Government Long-Term Bond (3)*	*Return on Investment U.S. Carriers (4)*
1951	16.06	n.a.	3.50	13.44
1952	6.85	7.9	3.72	14.19
1953	3.81	3.4	3.65	11.22
1954	4.04	4.2	3.21	11.21
1955	2.74	3.2	3.41	11.35
1956	5.55	6.0	4.00	9.57
1957	3.30	3.7	4.11	4.80
1958	3.21	3.8	4.15	6.49
1959	2.64	2.7	5.07	7.12
1960	2.56	1.8	5.19	2.79
1961	1.75	1.5	5.05	1.00
1962	3.29	3.1	5.11	3.72
1963	5.00	4.8	5.09	4.02
1964	5.32	5.2	5.18	9.62
1965	6.20	6.1	5.21	12.95
1966	6.90	5.4	5.77	11.25
1967	6.43	5.2	6.01	8.21
1968	8.01	6.3	6.67	4.93
1969	5.49	4.8	7.59	3.88
1970	4.93	4.5	7.91	4.12

Sources:

(1) Calculated from *Annual Reports* as Net Income after taxes paid over equity plus debt plus deferred tax reserve.

(2) Air Canada's own calculations: 1952–1958–Canada, Parliament, House of Commons, Sessional Committee on Railways, Airlines and Shipping, *Minutes of Proceedings and Evidence,* No. 3 (May 7, 1959), p. 29; 1959–1970–Air Canada, *Annual Report, 1971.*

(3) Bank of Canada, *Statistical Summary* (Ottawa: the Bank), various years, the MacLeod, Young, Weir Index.

(4) U.S., Civil Aeronautics Board, *Handbook of Airline Statistics* (Washington, D.C.: 1965 [for 1951–1959], 1967 [for 1960–1963], 1971 [for 1964–1970]). This index is not consistent either as to coverage or to definition, but generally includes domestic trunk carriers' operations.

But this does not mean the chosen rate of return never varied. The airline has earned deficits on two occasions in the post-1950 period–though, this might merely be interpreted as the result of imperfect knowledge in a world of uncertainty. What is of greater interest is the difference in the behavior of the airline in the 1950s as compared to the 1960s. Tables 6–3 and 6–4 show that in the 1950s the airline just earned the government long-term bond rate and

taxes were excluded to accord with Air Canada's own definition. Secondly, to correct for any manipulation that might have occurred in the reserve categories, both overhaul and insurance reserves were included in the capital account with appropriate corresponding changes made in the net income. The means of both these series were not significantly different from that of the government long-term rate.

accumulated very little in the way of retained earnings. In the mid-1960s, the reverse was true. The airline thus chose to earn more than the minimum constraint imposed by a no-loss criterion in the latter period. The difference in its behavior accords with the earlier suggestion that the profit "constraint" might become positive if the demands the airline was placing on the treasury for capital expansion increased markedly, for between 1952 and 1957, Air Canada's assets increased by only $46 million; between 1963 and 1969, they jumped by over $319 million.

Therefore, the history of the airline can be divided into three periods according to the level of profit "constraint" operative. In the initial period, the government for the purpose of development willingly met the airline's losses while emphasizing both directly and indirectly that this could not continue indefinitely. For the whole of the post-1950 period, the airline averaged a rate of return approximately equal to the government's cost of capital. However, within this period, the profit "constraint" appeared higher during the period of rapid asset growth in the mid-1960s.

CROSS-SUBSIDIZATION

The public airline has been hypothesized to act so as to maximize a function of the service frequencies and relative prices on the different routes of its system subject to a profit constraint. It has been argued that, as a result, the airline will adopt a price-product mix that results in a policy of cross-subsidization.

The applicability of the positive model has already been suggested by Air Canada's choice of overall system profitability. Since cross-subsidization is one of the major implications derived from the model, evidence of dissimilar marginal rates of return earned on different parts of the route system would further corroborate the theory of the public firm.

Evidence as to the exact marginal rates earned in different sectors is unavailable. However, data on the profits earned by Air Canada, by route sector, does exist. Table 6–5 provides a breakdown of these profits for 1957. Profits were apparently generated on the Transcontinental and International sectors. Losses were incurred on the Vancouver-Victoria route, on certain Prairie short-haul routes, on the local route from Winnipeg through Thunder Bay and Sault Ste. Marie to Toronto, in Northern Ontario, in Eastern Quebec, and throughout the Maritimes.[1] Table 6–6 shows that the same pattern persisted throughout the early 1960s.

Because of the difficulty of allocating costs amongst routes, these tables offer somewhat less than definitive proof of the existence of losses. However, other pieces of evidence may be adduced to suggest the existence of the practice of

[1]The classification of the loss routes in Table 6–5 into those that might potentially be profitable and those that were regarded as social obligations was made by the Crown airline.

Table 6–5. Pattern of Cross-Subsidization for Air Canada, 1957 ($ millions)

Route	*Profit*	*Loss*
Profitable routes:		
Trans-Atlantic and Southern combined.......	3.7	
Transcontinental	5.7	
Potentially profitable:		
Transborder		–1.5
Quebec and Sept Isles		–0.9
Newfoundland		–0.2
Subtotal		–2.6
Profitable long term:		
Pacific Coast		–1.3
Maritimes		–1.7
Subtotal		–3.0
Social routes:		
Prairies and Foothills		–1.4
Great Lakes		–0.1
N. Ontario and Quebec		–1.2
Subtotal		–2.7
Total	9.4	–8.3

Source: Canada, Department of Transport, *Airline Competition in Canada: A Study of the Desirability and Economic Consequences of Competition in Canadian Transcontinental Air Service,* prepared by Stephen Wheatcroft (Ottawa, May 1958), p. 31.

cross-subsidization. Chapters Eight and Nine indicate that in what have here been denoted as loss sectors are routes that have been charged lower fares than comparable routes elsewhere. In addition, Chapter Nine recounts how the transfer of Prairie routes from Air Canada to Transair was accomplished only after the payment of a subsidy to the regional carrier. Equally revealing is a comparison of the fares of the two Eastern regional carriers to those of the

Table 6–6. Air Canada Operating Income, by Sector, 1959–1965 ($000)

Sector	*1959*	*1960*	*1961*	*1962*	*1963*	*1964*	*1965*
International	2,000	4,603	5,872	9,030	10,493	11,033	13,124
Transcontinental	5,420	5,008	8,132	10,873	11,412	10,740	15,900
Montreal-Toronto	–2,306	–3,877	–3,047	–2,273	–1,783	–2,248	–4,485
Transborder	1,173	346	–1,872	–1,827	–1,018	–973	–2,955
Other Domestic	–5,233	–6,683	–8,517	–9,601	–9,478	–9,139	–10,796
Charter	188	104	289	444	449	1,037	1,206
System	1,243	–497	857	6,646	10,075	10,450	11,993

Note: Operating income exludes revenues from incidental services and deferred expenses, interest, and other non-operating items.

Source: Canada, Department of Transport, "Further Airline Competition in Canada: A Study of the Consequences of any Further Development of Domestic Mainline Competition in Canada" (unpublished paper prepared by Stephen Wheatcroft, Ottawa, February 1966, mimeographed), Appendix 3.

Crown airline, for according to the evidence on sector profitability and that, which is to come, on price structure, routes in Quebec and the Maritimes generally benefited from the Crown airline's pricing policy.

Tables 6–7 and 6–8 compare the fare per mile on those routes of Quebecair and Eastern Provincial Airways that in 1970 faced competition from Air Canada to the fare per mile on those routes that were not competitive with the Crown airline. The routes are arranged by stage-length since cost per mile declines with distance flown. The routes are also divided by number of intermediate stops, since a six-hundred-mile flight involving no intermediate stops is not comparable to one with three. Both tables indicate that the prices charged by the Crown airline in these regions were well below those on comparable non-competitive routes of these two regional carriers.[m]

These results are compatible either with the contention that the Crown airline charged fares on routes in these regions that were often below costs or the possibility that the regional carrier exacted monopoly prices on those routes where it was the sole carrier.[n] Both interpretations are compatible with the positive models presented in this book. The latter follows from the model of regulation; the former from the model of the public corporation. But Chapter Four described the extent to which Eastern Provincial Airways had to rely upon subsidies during this period—on routes that paralleled those of Air Canada. In particular, EPA's Montreal-Charlo-Chatham-Moncton route was heavily subsidized. This EPA route contained segments of 400, 76, and 72 miles in length. The corresponding fare per mile was 8.25¢, 10.53¢, and 11.11¢, respectively. The Montreal-Charlo segment carried at least 8,000 passengers in 1970, the Charlo-Chatham segment at least 2,000.[13] Two of Air Canada's routes possessed similar characteristics to this subsidized segment and were charged similar fares. Its Quebec-Fredericton route was some 277 miles long, carried around 10,000 passengers and was charged a fare of only 8.66¢ per mile. Its Montreal-Trois Rivières segment was 92 miles long, carried less than 2400 passengers, and was charged a fare of 11.96¢ per mile in 1970.[o] Therefore, while some of the fare differential exhibited in Tables 6–7 and 6–8 is no doubt due to cross-subsidization within the regional system, part must be attributed to the existence of losses on some of the Crown airline's routes in this region.

Of course, there are alternative explanations for the pattern of route profitability observed. A price discriminating monopolist, part of whose production process is joint and is characterized by significant economies of scale, could exhibit losses on some routes. Or the interdependence of demand curves may provide a rationale for loss-leader selling. The airline, it might be claimed,

[m] To test whether volume of traffic alone might account for the differences in regional prices, a regression of fare on distance, volume, and a dummy variable for competitive routes was performed. The volume variable was not significant.

[n] The possibility of economies of scale providing an explanation is ruled out by footnote m.

[o] That Air Canada claimed this was one route in particular where it incurred losses became evident when the Crown airline applied to abandon this route in the early 1970s.

Table 6–7. Comparison of Quebecair Fares on Competitive and Non-Competitive Routes, April 1970

	Competitive			Non-Competitive		
Number of Stops	*Route*	*Distance*	*Fare per Mile (¢)*	*Fare per Mile (¢)*	*Distance*	*Route*
	Quebec-Saguenay	107	12.15	16.67	114	Sept Isles-Baie Comeau
1				15.83	139	Saguenay-Baie Comeau
	Quebec-Montreal	146	10.27	14.86	148	Sept Isles-Gagnon
				14.56	158	Sept Isles-Rimouski
				13.41	179	Quebec-Rimouski
				12.70	189	Sept Isles-Wabush
	Saguenay-Montreal	234	9.83	13.01	246	Sept Isles-Churchill Falls
	Saguenay-Sept Isles	253	9.49			
	Quebec-Sept Isles	336	9.23			
				12.54	319	Sept Isles-Schefferville
				10.15	325	Montreal-Rimouski[a]
	Montreal-Sept Isles	483	7.87	9.24	368	Montreal-Baie Comeau[a]
				9.35	631	Montreal-Gagnon[a]
2				8.37	672	Montreal-Wabush[a]
				9.33	729	Montreal-Churchill Falls[a]
				8.60	802	Montreal-Schefferville[a]

[a]It is probably misleading to classify these routes as wholly non-competitive. Although the destination on these routes was not served by Air Canada, part of the journey could have been made on the Crown carrier.

Table 6–8. Comparison of Eastern Provincial Airways' Fares on Competitive and Non-Competitive Routes, April 1970

	Competitive			*Non-Competitive*		
Number of stops	*Route*	*Distance*	*Fare per Mile (¢)*	*Fare per Mile (¢)*	*Distance*	*Route*
	St. John's-Gander	125	10.40	15.00	100	Halifax-Charlottetown
	Deer Lake-Gander	133	12.03	13.71	124	Wabush-Churchill Falls
0				12.50	152	Charlo-Sept Isles
				13.75	160	Churchill Falls-Goose Bay
	Sydney-Halifax	184	10.34	16.93	189	Gander-St. Anthony
	Sydney-Deer Lake	251	7.57	16.08	255	Goose Bay-St. Anthony
				12.78	313	Goose Bay-Deer Lake
				11.21	330	Goose Bay-Sept Isles
	Montreal-Charlottetown	527	7.02			
	St. John's-Deer Lake	258	9.69	11.97	284	Goose Bay-Wabush
1				11.97	284	Sydney-Charlottetown
	Gander-Sydney	384	7.55	11.48	444	Gander-Goose Bay
	Deer Lake-Halifax	435	8.50	13.10	473	Deer Lake-Churchill Falls
				11.61	482	Charlo-Goose Bay
	Montreal-Halifax	627	5.90	10.67	731	Montreal-Churchill Falls
	St. John's-Sydney	509	5.70	9.80	571	St. John's-Goose Bay
2	Gander-Halifax	568	7.25	10.59	597	Deer Lake-Wabush
	Montreal-Sydney	811	6.41	10.43	604	Gander-Churchill Falls
	Montreal-Goose Bay	1104	6.16			
3	St. John's-Halifax	540	7.59	10.67	731	St. John's-Churchill Falls
4	Montreal-Gander	1195	5.52	9.80	855	St. John's-Wabush

Note: Two sets of routes were omitted from this comparison—the Moncton-Chatham-Charlo-Montreal system and the routes from Moncton to the Magdalen Islands. The latter were extremely short with very high fares per mile. The former were heavily subsidized and since they coincide with the Air Canada route at origin and destination were neither clearly competitive nor non-competitive. Their fares per mile fell between the competitive and non-competitive results reported above.

willingly incurs losses on some routes because of the contribution passengers, who originate thereon but who continue beyond, make to the profits earned on the rest of the system. The issue of the relevance of both of these alternative explanations is left to the concluding chapter. If they are to be taken seriously, they must be compatible with the whole range of public airline behavior that will be set fourth in subsequent chapters.

However, interdependence of markets along with the possible existence of economies of scale within each market does make it difficult to draw inferences about unequal rates of return from the existence of deficits. If the effect of the overlap of markets is disregarded, it may be concluded that the average profit per passenger from operating loss routes[p] is less than that earned on the mainline routes. The latter were all long or intermediate range routes requiring lower capital-output ratios because of the high utilization obtained from aircraft on longer routes.[14] (Approximately 80 percent of capital is accounted for by investment in aircraft.[15]) Thus, the Crown airline, it could be argued, earned higher than average rates of return on the trunk than on the regional routes. But the overlap of markets obscures the validity of this conclusion. For, to the extent that economies of scale on the mainline exist, operating the loss route leads to greater traffic on the mainline and lower average costs. Therefore, the marginal rate of return from operating loss services may be equal to that earned on the mainline.

On the other hand, it should be emphasized that the model of the public airline stands not on one event, but on the confluence of a set of events, all of which accord with the predictions of the public enterprise model. Some aspects of the Crown airline's behavior are likely, as in this case, to be compatible with alternate explanations. However, as we shall see, the alternate explanation—in this instance, the interdependence of markets—fails to explain the response of the Crown airline to entry and to the introduction of new technology. What is important here is that the existence of deficits is at least *prima facie* evidence that the Crown airline was following a policy of internal cross-subsidization.

More persuasive evidence as to the existence of cross-subsidization exists, for the airline in attempting to develop support for itself acted as if it were cross-subsidizing one segment of its route system with another. Cross-subsidization by itself is not the ultimate objective of the Crown airline. Cross-subsidization results from providing a highly visible form of benefit to specific groups of consumers—via a policy of fare or service equalization.[q] The

[p]Even if it is positive because of the profit contributed by passengers who continue elsewhere.

[q]In reply to a query as to how the airline became involved in social routes, the President of TCA replied, "The most famous of these was the so-called milk route. We were overflying all these areas in our Winnipeg-Regina-Lethbridge-Calgary route and there were six or seven small towns—and there is no other word for them—which were directly under the airway, all of which had airports built in connection with the Empire training plan, and it was too easy to say: 'The planes are going overhead; the airport is there and here we are, so why not have

airline though readily admitting the existence of the practice has not emphasized the transfer elements inherent in cross-subsidization.[16] There is no reason to unnecessarily risk antagonizing passengers on the profitable sectors. Rather, it has stressed the benefits to the loss sectors resulting from such a policy. Annual reports emphasize that "T.C.A. [Air Canada] has from the outset recognized a responsibility to provide a balanced service to communities both large and small."[17] More emphatically, it was pointed out, it "operated to a large number of communities of relatively small population that would not normally be served by an enterprise concerned solely with profit potential."[18]

The success of this policy must be assessed by the degree of support thereby engendered. Perusal of Hansard reveals that at least some Members of Parliament felt their constituencies had benefited from the Crown airline's policies.[r] For instance, a Prairie M.P. stated that "I realize if we had to depend upon competitive service only without the operation of a public company like Trans-Canada Air Lines which considers the welfare of the general public, we might have much less service."[19] Support was forthcoming not only because of recognition of service benefits, but also because its continued provision was associated with the existence of the Crown airline. For, the Maritime Transport Commission argued that "internal cross-subsidization affords a better assurance of a high overall standard of airline service on unprofitable or marginally profitable routes than . . . direct subsidy . . ."[20] The public, the regulatory agency, and the Crown airline all regarded cross-subsidization as more reliable than direct subsidies.

Although relatively free from threat of take-over because of its institutional nature, the public firm may still be susceptible to erosion of its market by competitors. There is evidence to indicate that in the airline industry economic barriers to entry are insufficient to guarantee most operators a monopoly position.[21] Thus, the public airline is likely to utilize its support to bolster the only barrier of any importance—legal restrictions upon entry enforced by the power of the state. That this was its strategy is evidenced by the following statement made by the airline:

> We have a responsibility for the so-called social routes. If Canadian aviation is going to be required to operate in several so-called social routes, then it has to be kept financially sound by at least a very strict curtailment of competition.[22]

Thus, not only are the route results compatible with the existence of cross-

---

service?' And I think TCA answered at the time: 'Why not?'" See Canada, Parliament, House of Commons, Sessional Committee on Railways, Airlines and Shipping, owned and controlled by the Government, *Minutes of Proceedings and Evidence,* No. 4(November 27, 28, 1962), p. 334.

[r] A much more striking example will be developed in the chapter on transcontinental competition.

subsidization, but the manner in which the Crown airline has used the practice to garner support also accords well with the purposive survival-oriented behavior postulated for the public airline. As we shall see, through the selective development of social routes, the airline has been able to develop enough support to protect its predominant position in the Canadian airline industry.

Chapter Seven

Equipment, Efficiency, and the Public Airline

INTRODUCTION

Until now, the model has stressed the divergence of the public airline's price and product decisions from those of a privately owned firm. Yet, debate concerning the desirability of public ownership often revolves around the relative efficiency of private, as opposed to public, enterprise.[1] The inconclusive nature of this controversy owes much to the failure of either side to adopt a consistent framework within which the actions of the public firm can be analyzed. Expanding upon the model previously adopted, this chapter examines the extent to which the Canadian airline was governed in its equipment decisions by efficiency criteria.

Nothing in the model of the public firm leads necessarily to the conclusion that this institution need be as efficient as the profit-maximizing private corporation. In the private sector, the maximization of profits necessarily requires operation of the firm at minimum costs. A bureaucracy, on the other hand, in striving to maximize the probability of its survival, need neither maximize profits nor minimize costs. It is conceivable that the use of an excessive number of factors of production might yield an agency support equal to that generated by its manipulation of the rate structure. The public firm can be expected to trade off support from one source against another until the ratio of the marginal value of support from one more passenger versus one less factor is equal to the ratio at which the firm can transform one unit of support into another. There is ample evidence that public corporations have found factor support to be important. It has been noted that state railways in underdeveloped countries tend to employ more labor than necessary.[2] The British Crown airlines have been burdened with a succession of inefficient domestic aircraft that were forced on them by government policy.[3]

The support forthcoming from an employed factor should be a function of the excess of its remuneration over its opportunity costs as well as the likelihood that this surplus depends upon the perpetuation of specific government policies—in this case, the continued existence of the public corporation. While any factor will appreciate receipt of such a benefit, there may be certain groups that because they are more powerful and because they exhibit more intense preferences for these benefits tend to be favored by government policy. Declining industries that contain particularly large groups, most of whom have special skills not readily transferable to other industries, satisfy both these conditions. The success of North American railway unions in preventing the abandonment of railway passenger service when faced with an expanding highway system illustrates the power of one such group.

A government interested in building factor support need not do it via the creation of a public corporation. Direct payment to specific groups, the erection of barriers to entry, and the imposition of tariffs can and have been used to serve the same purpose. The creation of a state-owned monopoly essentially promises factors of production higher payments because of the entry restrictions that usually accompany the creation of public firms. As such, factor support is likely to be directed to the entry restrictions rather than to the public corporation per se. This implies that the support the Crown airline may expect from its factors of production will vary with the type of threat posed to the Crown airline's existence. When a public monopoly is threatened with displacement by a private monopoly, most of the labor force is unlikely to feel its surplus to be dependent upon the continued existence of the Crown corporation. To a strong labor union, a private monopoly offers equally good opportunities for extracting part of the earned surplus. However, the labor force is likely to oppose changes in market structure that lead to greater competition and reduce both industry profits and the surplus available to the labor force. That the reaction of the labor force will vary in these two situations is borne out by Canadian experience. Whereas the Canadian public airline's pilots have publicly opposed the expansion of the "regionals,"[4] there appears to be no evidence of their taking a public stand on the demands of CP Air for an increased share of the domestic market. The former event promised a much more radical change in the market structure of the Canadian airline industry than the latter. Since the major threat to Air Canada during the postwar period was from one large privately owned firm (CP Air), whose entry would only have transformed the industry into a duopoly, this suggests the Crown airline was unlikely to be very successful in building support for itself from its employees.[a]

[a]This does not imply the public firm will neither hire an excessive number of factors nor pay them more than competitive wage rates. It does imply there should be no difference between a public and private firm in this regard as long as entry is tightly controlled. David G. Davies, "The Efficiency of Public versus Private Firms: The Case of Australia's Two Airlines," *Journal of Law and Economics* XIV, no. 1 (1971), tests this proposition for Australia. Unfortunately he fails to standardize for differing outputs. If this is done, it is difficult to distinguish between the efficiency of the private and the government-owned airline.

The Crown airline may also serve as a vehicle by which the government generates support from domestic aircraft producers. The dislocations associated with the dismemberment of an aircraft manufacturing industry imply that its labor force is likely to regard itself as earning substantial rents and, therefore, to actively support the use of domestic aircraft. However, the reluctance of the British Crown airlines to purchase domestic equipment[b] suggests that initially the net benefits from doing so are likely to be overestimated by the government. That the public airlines should have resisted the government's request is not incompatible with our characterization of them as agents of the government. As agents they are responsible for evaluating the repercussions of the purchase of inefficient equipment. Such a policy will reduce the future surplus available for support-generating purposes by an amount that may not have been readily appreciated by the government. More important, the support generated by the choice of domestic capital equipment is a contingent asset whose lifetime is so short that it is likely to be virtually worthless to the airline when required. It is significant that when the British government finally required BOAC to purchase the VC-10, it excused the airline from paying interest and dividends on a substantial proportion of its capital stock.[5] As a result, the tax required to generate this factor support was shifted from airline users to the general treasury.[c]

The next section discusses the equipment choice of the Crown airline. Although ultimately efficiency can only be judged by considering relative factor prices, the appropriateness of the technology adopted, and the proximity of total costs to the minimum cost envelope,[d] at least an analysis of equipment chosen should reveal any tendencies toward inefficient operations. Since such a study must utilize the wealth of data collected for the United States, it indirectly provides a comparison of the effect two differing public control structures—regulation versus public ownership—had upon the product performance of the industry.

PISTON AIRCRAFT PRIOR TO 1950

At its inception, the set of aircraft available to Air Canada consisted of the Douglas DC-2, DC-3, the Boeing 247, and the Lockheed L-10, L-14 series. The

[b] David C. Corbett in *Politics and the Airlines* (London: Allen and Unwin, 1965), pp. 261–3, recounts BEA's battles to avoid first the "Marathon" and then the "Trident," although it claimed to accept "an obligation to foster the development of British transport aircraft." Graham L. Reid and Kevin Allen in *Nationalized Industries,* Penguin Modern Economics Texts (Harmondsworth, Middlesex: Penguin, 1970), pp. 177–8, recount BOAC's attempts to purchase the Boeing 707 rather than the British Aircraft Corporation's VC-10.

[c] With entry controls the private airline is also susceptible to such lump-sum political extractions. In return for being awarded the international routes across the Pacific in the late 1940s, CP Air agreed to purchase the Canadian-made North Star.

[d] A much more ambitious attempt to rank airlines by their efficiency can be found in Mahlon R. Straszheim, *The International Airline Industry,* Transport Research Program (Washington, D.C.: Brookings, 1969).

DC-3 was the least expensive to operate on a seat-mile basis,[6] but with 21 seats, was also the largest. For a load of less than 10 passengers, the Lockheed aircraft appears to have had the lowest costs per passenger.[7] Table 7–1 outlines the composition of the Air Canada fleet from 1937 to 1971. Beginning with the Lockheed L-10A in 1937, the airline proceeded to expand with subsequent versions of this aircraft (the L-14 and L-18)[e] until the end of the Second World War. In view of the fact that the average number of passengers per flight was well below 10 (1.27 in 1938, 5.65 in 1939, 5.82 in 1940, 6.33 in 1941) the airline's choice was not inappropriate from a cost standpoint.[f] In addition, this equipment had the advantage of greater speed than the DC-3. As Table 7-2 indicates, the latter only had a maximum cruising speed of 190 m.p.h., while the L-18 was capable of some 230 m.p.h.

Wartime traffic growth rapidly strained capacity. The average load in 1943 and 1944 reached 9.62 and 9.37 passengers per flight, respectively. With the end of the war, a surplus of DC-3's materialized and Air Canada re-equipped itself with this aircraft.[g] Although slightly slower and with somewhat shorter range than the Lockheed L-18's, their passenger capacity was at least 50 percent greater (Table 7–2). As Table 7–1 indicates, these were to serve as the sole short-haul aircraft used by the airline until the advent of the Viscounts in 1955.

Although Air Canada initially regarded the adoption of the DC-3 as temporary,[8] the airline failed to re-equip with any of the aircraft specifically designed and adopted for short-haul service in the United States. The Martin 202 (1947), the Martin 404 (1951), the Convair 240 (1948), and the Convair 340 (1952) were not only less expensive to operate on a seat-mile basis than the DC-3, [9] but had a maximum cruise speed between 250 and 280 m.p.h., [10] and apart from the Martin 202 were all pressurized. However, technical shortcomings remove both of the first two models from consideration as viable alternatives. The Martin 202 had structural faults in the wings [11] that led to intermittent grounding between 1948 and 1951.[h] The Convair 240 not only could not carry its full payload over short distances because of inadequate

[e]The L-14-08 was the L-14H stretched slightly, but with the same engine as the L-18–effectively the same aircraft. This arrangement was brought about by wartime shortages.

[f]Even when equipped with DC-3's, Air Canada kept the L-18 for the mountain section from Alberta to Vancouver because of its superior single engine performance. See Peter Brannon et al., "TCA's First Quarter Century of Service," *Canadian Aviation* XXV, no. 9 (1962):61.

[g]Although the aircraft could be purchased and converted for as little as $68,000 U.S. (see George C. Eads, *The Local Service Airline Experiment,* Studies in the Regulation of Economic Activity [Washington, D.C.: Brookings, 1972] p. 94), Air Canada spent $200,000 Cdn. per aircraft. See Trans-Canada Air Lines, "Initial Submission to the Air Transport Board in the Matter of Transcontinental Commercial Air Service," 1958, mimeographed, Exhibit No. 416.

[h]Almarin Phillips, *Technology and Market Structure: A Study of The Aircraft Industry,* Heath Lexington Books (Lexington, Mass.: D.C. Heath, 1971), p. 103. Prior to 1950 only Northwest bought the M202 and promptly divested itself of this aircraft.

Table 7–1. Air Canada Aircraft Fleet, 1937–1971

Year	*L-10A*	*L-14H*	*L-14-08*	*L-18*	*DC-3*	*North Star (DC-4M1)*	*Super Constellation*	*Viscount*	*Vanguard 952*	*DC-8*	*DC-8 61*	*DC-9 14*	*DC-9 32*	*B747*
1937	5	...	...	...	...	...	...	...	...	...	...	...	...	...
1938	5	11	...	...	...	...	...	...	...	...	...	...	...	...
1939	...	15	...	...	...	...	...	...	...	...	...	...	...	...
1940	...	15	...	6	...	...	...	...	...	...	...	...	...	...
1941	...	12	...	6	...	...	...	...	...	...	...	...	...	...
1942	...	1	11	12	...	...	...	...	...	...	...	...	...	...
1943	...	...	12	11	...	...	...	...	...	...	...	...	...	...
1944	...	...	12	14	...	...	...	...	...	...	...	...	...	...
1945	...	...	12	14	3	...	...	...	...	...	...	...	...	...
1946	...	...	9	14	27	...	...	...	...	...	...	...	...	...
1947	...	...	...	11	30	...	...	...	...	...	...	...	...	...
1948	...	...	...	...	27	20	...	...	...	...	...	...	...	...
1949	...	...	...	...	27	20	...	...	...	...	...	...	...	...
1950	...	...	...	...	27	20	...	...	...	...	...	...	...	...
1951	...	...	...	...	27	20	...	...	...	...	...	...	...	...
1952	...	...	...	...	27	23	...	...	...	...	...	...	...	...
1953	...	...	...	...	27	23	...	...	...	...	...	...	...	...
1954	...	...	...	...	26	22	7	...	...	...	...	...	...	...
1955	...	...	...	...	26	22	7	14	...	...	...	...	...	...
1956	...	...	...	...	24	21	9	18	...	...	...	...	...	...
1957	...	...	...	...	23	21	11	32	...	...	...	...	...	...
1958	...	...	...	...	11	21	12	46	...	...	...	...	...	...
1959	...	...	...	...	9	21	13	49	...	...	...	...	...	...
1960	...	...	...	...	7	21	12	49	3	7	...	...	...	...
1961	...	...	...	...	2	...	11	49	20	11	...	...	...	...
1962	...	...	...	...	2	...	2	48	22	11	...	...	...	...
1963	...	...	...	...	...	...	...	46	22	14	...	...		...
1964	...	...	...	...	...	...	...	39	23	16	...	...	...	...
1965	...	...	...	...	...	...	...	39	23	16	...	...	...	...
1966	...	...	...	...	...	...	...	39	23	18	...	6	...	...
1967	...	...	...	...	...	...	...	39	23	17	4	8	12	...
1968	...	...	...	...	...	...	...	39	23	20	7	...	30	...
1969	...	...	...	...	...	...	...	35	12	20	12	...	33	...
1970	...	...	...	...	...	...	...	31	12	20	18	...	36	...
1971	...	...	...	...	...	...	...	20	1	20	18	...	36	3

Sources: Air Canada, *Annual Reports,* 1937–59; International Civil Aviation Organization, *Digest of Statistics, Fleet–Personnel,* 1960–71.

Table 7–2. Characteristics of Air Canada's Pre-1950 Piston Aircraft

Aircraft	*Passenger Capacity*	*Cruising Speed*		*Full Load Cruise Range*[d] *(miles)*
		In Use[b] *(m.p.h.)*	*Listed*[c] *(m.p.h.)*	
L-10	10	175	205	500
L-14H	11	200	224	850
L-14-08[e]	11	N.A.	N.A.	N.A.
L-18	14	192	229	1000
DC-3	21[a]	180	190	850
DC-4M1	40[a]	250	280	2900[f]

[a]Introduced in service in this configuration. Some DC-3's were expanded to 28 seats in 1949. By 1957, the North Star seated 62 in tourist configuration.

[b]From Air Canada (TCA), *Annual Reports,* various years.

[c]Almarin Phillips, *Technology and Market Structure: A Study of the Aircraft Industry,* Heath Lexington Books (Lexington, Mass.: D.C. Heath, 1971), pp. 142–3.

[d]Ibid.

[e]See footnote e of this chapter.

[f]*Jane's All the World's Aircraft, 1948* (London: Sampson, Low, and Marston, 1948), p. 116C.

landing gear,[i] but also had an extremely short range anyway.[j] American Airlines, for whom the plane was designed, was the only carrier to purchase a significant number of the aircraft.[k]

The Convair 340 and the Martin 404 were relatively more successful models. For instance, the Convair 340's range was 750 miles compared to the 240's 500.[12] Eastern, National, Delta, Braniff, United, and Trans-World all purchased these aircraft. With a seating capacity of between 40 and 45, [13] both were designed for the density of the American trunk carriers' short-haul routes. However, for routes with light traffic, the DC-3 was still cheaper to operate on a passenger-mile basis.[14]

The Canadian route system at this time had very few stations generating a large volume of traffic. Table 7–3 presents the number of originating passengers per day for Air Canada's North American stations in June of 1949, one of the peak summer months. Even then, 23 of the 34 stations generated less than 40 passengers per day. These points were all served exclusively with DC-3's.[l] At

[i]Eads, *The Local Service Airline Experiment,* p. 132, reports the Convair had to fly one hour and 30 minutes when fully loaded before it consumed enough fuel to permit it to land.

[j]Aaron Jacob Gellman in "The Effect of Regulation on Aircraft Choice" (unpublished Ph.D. dissertation, Massachusetts Institute of Technology, 1968), p. 35, recounts that it could barely make 300 miles under adverse weather conditions, although its limit was supposedly 500 miles.

[k] Of the 103 Convair 240's in the U.S. domestic service in 1950, American Airlines owned 79.

[l]Only two other centers were served solely by DC-3's in 1949. These were Halifax (57.7 originations per day) and Victoria (238.4). The latter had airport facilities incapable of handling aircraft larger than the DC-3.

Table 7–3. Originating Passengers per Day for the North American Stations of Air Canada, June 1949

City	*Pass./day*	*City*	*Pass./day*
St. John's	26.2[a]	Porquis Jctn.	3.0[a]
Gander	15.9[a]	Kapuskasing	3.9[a]
Sydney	19.9[a]	Sault Ste. Marie	15.3[a]
Halifax	57.7[a]	Fort William	22.1[a]
Moncton	27.8[a]	Winnipeg	96.4
Pennfield Ridge	20.1[a]	Regina	30.4[a]
Yarmouth	6.6[a]	Saskatoon	23.2
Boston	37.1[a]	Swift Current	2.3[a]
Montreal	215.6	Medicine Hat	3.1[a]
Ottawa	77.7	Lethbridge	16.7[a]
Toronto	409.0	Calgary	107.3
New York	111.2	Edmonton	81.3
Cleveland	37.1[a]	Vancouver	290.6
Chicago	56.9	Victoria	238.4[a]
London	22.9[a]	Seattle	27.7[a]
Windsor	32.4[a]	Brandon	2.4[a]
North Bay	6.4[a]	Yorkton	3.6[a]

[a]Denotes exclusive DC-3 service in 1949.

Sources: Canada, Parliament, House of Commons, Sessional Committee on Railways and Shipping, owned, operated and controlled by the Government, *Minutes of Proceedings and Evidence,* No. 6 (April 4, 1950), p. 457; and Air Canada, Time Tables.

least 40 passengers per day would be required if the more than 40 passenger Convairs and Martins were to make two trips a day[m] at a 50 percent load factor. However, originations are not identical with traffic per route segment because of through passengers, and thus, these figures may underestimate the possibility that a larger aircraft could have been substituted for the DC-3.

That traffic was extremely light on those segments served exclusively by DC-3's is confirmed[n] by passenger flow data for June 1949.[15] The first segment of the Northern Ontario route—Toronto-North Bay—carried only 14 passengers per day on its daily flight. The two Newfoundland segments—from the mainland to Gander and from Gander to St. John's—averaged between 33 and 37 passengers per day, respectively. Two flights served this traffic. The most heavily travelled segment of the Great Lakes route—from Sault Ste. Marie to Toronto—carried only 29 passengers per day[o] and was served twice daily. The sector of the Prairie "milk run" into Regina from the east handled 23 passengers per day via two flights.[p] The larger short-haul aircraft appear impractical on

[m]Since most of the stations were connected to points both east and west, this would permit one flight per day in each direction.

[n]Even this data suffers from some inaccuracies, because of the necessity in some cases of arbitrarily assigning through traffic to one of several alternative routes.

[o]This ignores any through traffic from the west that may have used this more time-consuming route.

[p]The eastern traffic to Lethbridge is assigned to this route.

these routes for two reasons. In each of the latter three instances, larger aircraft would have meant a reduction in frequency to one flight per day. While the optimum trade-off between cost and frequency for the travelling public is difficult to determine, the benefits from a 100 percent increase in frequency from one to two by retaining the DC-3 were likely to have outweighed any minor reduction in costs that might have accrued from adopting the larger aircraft.[q] Even these savings were probably non-existent, for June was one of the summer peak months.[r] If this month could barely support one flight from the larger aircraft, no cost reductions were likely to result from year-round operations of the larger aircraft.

There were two routes—Victoria-Vancouver and Eastern Canada to the Maritimes—that offered sufficient volume to sustain a larger aircraft. The Victoria airport could not handle aircraft larger than the DC-3. However, even if the Victoria airport had been suitable, little would have been gained from substitution for the DC-3 on the Vancouver-Victoria route—the second most dense Canadian segment (after Toronto-Montreal) with 208 passengers per day in one direction. Over this short distance (only 47 miles), the larger, faster Convair could have reduced the duration of trip time by no more than two minutes,[16] and actually had higher seat-mile costs than the DC-3.[17]

The density of Maritime traffic is more difficult to calculate because the route structure even as of 1949 did not exhibit a simple linear pattern. Traffic arriving in Montreal via both Moncton and St. John totalled some 80 passengers per day. This route was served by 5 daily flights. These numbers suggest that this route would be the first to be able to sustain larger aircraft. In fact, in 1952 the 40-seat Canadair "North Star" was introduced to the Maritimes.

Thus, the second generation of short-range aircraft, because of their size, were not adopted by Air Canada. Although some traffic segments might have been able to support the larger short-range aircraft, their introduction would have required either minimal frequency of one per day or substantial reductions (percentagewise) in frequencies that were already few in number. Faced with no appropriately sized substitute for the DC-3,[s] Air Canada chose to increase the seating capacity of some of these aircraft from 21 to 28 (1949)[t] and to improve the quality of the service they provided by pressurizing them (1950).

The long-range aircraft adopted by Air Canada in the postwar period was a Canadian made hybrid of the Douglas DC-4 and the DC-6. The choice of this

[q]Adoption of only a few aircraft of one type, it is often argued, leads to higher than average maintenance costs. Thus, it is possible that this cost saving might not have existed.

[r]For instance, January system traffic was only 55 percent of June's, in 1949.

[s]Eads in *The Local Service Airline Experiment,* p. 126, concludes that with the exception of the Nord 262 no replacement for the DC-3 in terms of size was ever built.

[t]Stephen Wheatcroft, *The Economics of European Air Transport* (Manchester: Manchester U. Pr., 1956), pp. 26–39. Wheatcroft decried the lack of an adequate short-haul aircraft for European operations in the early 1950s—but for the opposite reason that their capacity was not large enough.

aircraft was dictated by a government faced with a newly developed wartime aircraft industry and the problem of its postwar conversion. In late 1943, the Canadian government decided that Air Canada was to fly a Canadian produced model of the DC-6.[u] Initially, the basic difference was that the Canadian version—eventually to be called the "North Star"[v]—was to be powered by Rolls Royce Merlin engines. The American DC-6 and the "North Star" were to enter service almost simultaneously. Air Canada's complete fleet was delivered in 1948. While the DC-6 initially entered service in the United States during 1947, it was grounded until the end of that year because of a series of fires and crashes.[18]

However, by the time the American version of the DC-6 was actually produced, it had been stretched, pressurized, and given additional speed in order to meet the challenge of Lockheed's L-049 "Constellation." The Canadian version was also pressurized and given the new DC-6 undercarriage. The result was that the North Star lay somewhere between the DC-4 and the DC-6 in terms of its characteristics. It was 80 inches shorter than the DC-6. Whereas the gross take-off weight of the DC-4 was 73,000 pounds and of the DC-6, 97,200 pounds, it was 78,000 for the North Star. While the DC-4 had listed a cruising speed of 230 m.p.h., the North Star could do 280 m.p.h. and the DC-6 was capable of 310 m.p.h.[w] Interestingly, the average capacity of the North Star and the DC-6 was virtually identical at 7 tons.[19]

The North Star was initially placed on the transcontinental run from Montreal to Vancouver (via Toronto, Winnipeg, Saskatoon, Calgary, and Edmonton), as well as the transborder routes from Toronto and Montreal to New York and Chicago. They were placed in service with a forty seat configuration[x]—four less than Phillips lists as the common seating density of the DC-4.[20] Again this was indicative of the low density of Canadian routes at this time. In 1949, an average of 118 passengers a day [21] departed from Eastern Canada for the West and were served by four North Star flights daily.[y]

The North Star appears to have been at least as expensive to operate on a plane-mile basis as the DC-6. Its capital costs were the same.[z] The price charged Air Canada for the North Star was $695,000,[22] while the DC-6 averaged

[u] A. Phillips in *Technology and Market Structure,* p. 91, reports that work was not commenced on the DC-6 in the United States until 1944.

[v] Air Canada, in line with their original announcement that the DC-6 was being produced under licence, continued to call it such until Douglas requested them to cease doing so.

[w] Normal cruise ranges for the DC-4, the North Star, and the DC-6 were 1500, 2900, and 3800 miles, respectively.

[x] In 1953, seating capacity was increased to 48; by 1955, tourist class held 62.

[y] Two DC-3's went indirectly via Sault Ste. Marie and Thunder Bay.

[z] This should not be interpreted to imply Air Canada could have purchased the DC-6 for that amount. For instance, it was reported that if they had chosen to buy the Lockheed L-049 Constellation, between duty, the exchange rate difference in 1945, and sales tax, the price of the aircraft would have been increased from $775,000 U.S. to $1,260,000 Cdn. See Canada, Parliament, House of Commons, Standing Committee on Railways and Shipping, *Minutes of Proceedings and Evidence,* no. 4 (October 30, 1945).

$680,000 [23] in 1948—the year the aircraft was delivered.[aa] In addition, because military engines generally were not built to operate for long hours between overhauls,[24] the decision to use the Merlin engine led to high maintenance costs. For instance, in 1957, whereas costs per available ton-mile for Air Canada were on the average 55 percent higher than for National Airlines,[bb] in the maintenance category they were 181 percent highter.[cc]

Actual comparison of the relative costs of the DC-6 and the North Star is difficult because of the wide variance in factor prices between the two countries.[dd] However, an intra-country comparison between the two aircraft and common models operated in both countries suggest the North Star was at least as expensive to operate as the DC-6 would have been. A 1950 study suggests that, in the United States, the DC-6 was twice as expensive to operate as the DC-3 on a plane-mile basis—68.62¢ versus 34.13¢.[ee] Table 7–4 presents the costs per aircraft-mile for the four types of aircraft operated by Air Canada in 1957. On those routes where both planes were operated, the North Star was also twice as expensive to operate as the DC-3.[ff] Since the North Star was slower and offered less seating capacity, it was therefore slightly less efficient than the DC-6.[gg]

Thus, the most obvious case of government interference in the management of the Crown airline[hh] resulted in the adoption of an aircraft whose economic

[aa]The Canadian and U.S. dollars were at par in 1948.

[bb]National operated DC-6's, DC-7's, L-18's, and Convair 340's. See Canada, Department of Transport, *Airline Competition in Canada: A Study of the Desirability and Economic Consequences of Competition in Canadian Transcontinental Air Services,* prepared by Stephen Wheatcroft (Ottawa, May 1958), p. 18.

[cc]Some of this is explained by the Super Constellation, which was introduced in 1954 to the Air Canada fleet.

[dd]For instance, fuel prices were 33 percent higher in Canada. See Canada, Parliament, House Of Commons, Sessional Committee on Railways and Shipping, *Minutes of Proceedings and Evidence,* no. 5 (April 3, 1950), p. 332.

[ee]U.S., Congress, Committee on the Judiciary, *Monopoly Problems in Regulated Industries—Airlines, Hearings* before the Antitrust Subcommittee of the Committee on the Jucidiary, House of Representatives, 84th Cong., 2nd sess., 1957, Vol. I, pp. 468–9. These figures exclude depreciation. The Air Transport Association submitted 84.27¢ and 48.06¢ per mile for 1955 operation of the DC-6 and DC-3, respectively, which is a ratio of 1.75:1 (ibid., Vol. III, p. 2067).

[ff]It is interesting to note that the ratio of L1049 to DC-3 costs was approximately the same in the two countries. In Table 7–4, for the one route on which Super Constellations and DC-3's were operated, the ratio of the plane-mile operating costs (excluding depreciation) was 2.73:1. The ratio given in the U.S., Antitrust Subcommittee, *Monopoly Problems,* Vol. III, p. 2067 for the same two aircraft was also 2.73:1.

[gg]The one caveat to this conclusion results from the fact that excise duties and tariffs on the purchase of the DC-6 may have increased the capital costs for the DC-6 relative to the North Star sufficiently to offset any operating cost advantage the former might have had. When the decision was made to go ahead with Canadian production in 1943–44, tariffs and foreign exchange control increased the cost of foreign made aircraft considerably (see footnote z in this chapter).

[hh]The other major episode occurred when the government refused to permit the airline to consolidate its Winnipeg maintenance facilities in Montreal. It was estimated that this

Table 7–4. Air Canada's Cost per Aircraft-Mile for the Super Constellation, Viscount, North Star, and DC-3, by Route, 1957 ($)

Route	*Super Constellation*		*Viscount*		*North Star*		*DC-3*
	(1)	*(2)*	*(1)*	*(2)*	*(1)*	*(2)*	*(1)*
Vancouver-Toronto	1.18	1.49	...	...	....	....	...
Vancouver-Winnipeg	1.32	1.71	...	...	....	....	...
Van-Calgary-Regina-Winnipeg	1.33	1.69	.60	.74	.99	1.01	...
Van-Edmonton-Saskatoon-Winn.	....	....	.60	.74	.95	.97	...
Calgary-Toronto	1.23	1.57	...	...	....	....	...
Winnipeg-Toronto	1.27	1.64	.57	.70	.93	.95	...
Winnipeg-Windsor-Ottawa	....	....	.55	.64	....	....	...
Toronto-Ottawa-Montreal	1.42	1.80	.65	.80	.99	1.01	.52
Pacific Coast	....	....	...	...	....	....	.57
Prairies and Foothills	....	....	.67	.83	....	....	...
Great Lakes	....	....	.61	.76	....	....	.51
Northern Ontario and Quebec	....	....	...	...	....	....	.55
Montreal-Quebec-Sept Isles	....	....	.71	.87	1.10	1.12	.55
Maritimes	....	....	.67	.81	1.02	1.04	.52
Newfoundland	....	....	...	...	1.04	1.06	...
Toronto-London-Windsor	....	....	.70	.86	1.21	1.23	.54
Toronto-Chicago	....	....	.63	.77	....	....	...

Note: (1) excludes depreciation; (2) includes depreciation.

Source: Trans-Canada Air Lines, "Initial Submission to the Air Transport Board in the Matter of Transcontinental Commercial Air Service," 1958, mimeographed, Exhibits 64A to Q.

efficiency was questionable. The DC-6 with superior speed would probably have been less expensive to operate. But then, this is the result we should expect. The public firm, it was hypothesized, is likely to find the benefits from patronizing Canadian industry far less than the benefits of being able to expand services when the most efficient equipment is adopted. Unless the benefits of choosing less efficient aircraft are suddenly increased (via direct government order), efficient equipment will be chosen. Therefore, the fact that such an order was made is perhaps indicative of the efficiency of the North Star.

THE AIRCRAFT FLEET IN THE 1950s

In 1951, the airline ordered the Lockheed Constellation L-1049C for acquisition in 1954. The L-1049C was one of a series of stretched versions of long-range aircraft first placed in service in the late 1940s (the DC-6's and L-049's), which, although faster than their predecessors because of turbo-compound engines,

would have saved the airline almost $20 million between 1966 and 1973. For a description of this episode see C.A. Ashley and R.G.H. Smails, *Canadian Crown Corporations: Some Aspects of Their Administration and Control* (Toronto: Macmillan, 1965), pp. 320–3.

were generally more expensive[ii] to operate.[25] While their adoption in the United States can be traced to the oligopolistic structure of the industry, where profits were concentrated on long-distance routes, [26] Air Canada's adoption of this aircraft can be traced to its participation in the North Atlantic cartel. With fixed prices and no opportunity to compensate for quality differences via price competition, Air Canada was forced to adopt equipment competitive with the other firms. In the late 1940s and early 1950s, it found it impossible to compete with its North Stars against DC-6's and Lockheed Constellations. For instance, as of 1952, Air Canada cancelled first class service on the North Atlantic and did not reimplement it until introduction of the Constellations. Initiation of service with this aircraft immediately increased Air Canada's share of the Canadian transAtlantic market–from 40 percent in 1953 [27] to 45 percent in 1954.[28] On its southern routes–Florida and the Caribbean–the Crown airline faced similar difficulties.

The Super Constellation was also introduced on the domestic sector–though only on the longest of the transcontinental routes–and even then it was only used sparingly. Originally begun as one flight a day in 1955 from Vancouver to Toronto stopping at Winnipeg, this service was increased to two flights a day in 1956, 1957, and to three during 1958, 1959, and 1960. By 1958, these three flights involved one non-stop of some 2100 miles and one each via Calgary and Edmonton–about 1700 miles each. With twelve Super Constellations in the fleet by the late 1950s, no more than one-quarter of these aircraft was engaged in domestic service. In 1957, the Super Constellations accounted for only 12 percent of the available seat-miles performed on the domestic system [29] and only 18 percent of the passenger-miles flown on the transcontinental route.[30]

The backbone of the fleet, starting in 1955, was the Viscount–a four engine turbo-prop, accomodating 44 passengers,[jj] with a 1000 mile range and listed cruising speed of 310 m.p.h. Although its speed was somewhat less than the later L-1049's and DC-7's,[31] it could match these two aircraft on shorter distances because of its rapid climb and descent characteristics.[kk] Its operating costs per seat-mile were 1¢ below those of the Super Constellation for those routes where they were jointly operated. Similarly, they were below the variable cost (direct operating cost less depreciation) of the North Star (see Table 7–5).

Not only was Air Canada the first North American airline to adopt the turbo-prop, but it was also, until 1960, one of the relatively few operating such service. Only Capital, Continental, and Northeast purchased the Viscount in the United States. Not until the 1960s did the American carriers adopt a somewhat

[ii] Actually Phillip's data indicates the DC-7 was more of a culprit in this respect than the L-1049. See A. Phillips, *Technology and Market Structure*, pp. 84–85, 38–39.

[jj] Seating density in the Viscount was increased to 51 in 1962.

[kk] Air Canada operated both the L-1049C and the Viscount on three routes in 1957. The average cruising speeds of these aircraft were 271 and 271; 294 and 285; 256 and 251 m.p.h., respectively.

Table 7–5. Cost per Available Seat-Mile for the Super Constellation, Viscount, North Star, and DC-3, by Route, 1957 (¢)

Route	Super Constellation (1)	Super Constellation (2)	Viscount (1)	Viscount (2)	North Star (1)	DC-3 (1)
Vancouver-Toronto	2.0008	2.5205	......	......	......	......
Vancouver-Winnipeg	2.0850	2.6957	......	......	......	......
Vancouver-Calgary-Regina-Winnipeg	2.1421	2.7187	1.3772	1.6927	1.6079	......
Vancouver-Edmonton-Saskatoon-Winnipeg	......	......	1.3796	1.6844	2.5957	......
Calgary-Toronto	1.9668	2.5010	......	......	......	......
Winnipeg-Toronto	2.0364	2.6317	1.3450	1.6446	2.0668	......
Winnipeg-Windsor-Ottawa	......	......	1.2702	1.4819	......	......
Toronto-Ottawa-Montreal	2.2401	2.8545	1.4866	1.8195	2.0451	2.5712
Pacific Coast	......	......	......	......	......	2.0812
Prairies and Foothills	......	......	1.5330	1.8821	......	2.5632
Great Lakes	......	......	1.4141	1.7581	......	2.6015
Northern Ontario and Quebec	......	......	......	......	......	2.6338
Montreal-Quebec-Saguenay-Sept Isles	......	......	1.5971	1.9492	2.1214	2.6370
Maritimes	......	......	1.5186	1.8305	1.9242	2.6666
Newfoundland	......	......	......	......	2.1593	......
Toronto-London-Windsor-Cleveland	......	......	1.5947	1.9525	......	2.5690
Toronto-Chicago	......	......	1.4331	1.7618	......	......

Note: (1) excludes depreciation; (2) includes depreciation.

Source: Trans-Canada Air Lines, "Initial Submission to the Air Transport Board in the Matter of Transcontinental Commercial Air Service," 1958, mimeographed, Exhibits 64A through Q.

larger (85 passenger) turbo-prop, the Lockheed L-188.[ll] Evidence suggests that the Viscount was less expensive to operate than the alternative short-range aircraft available—the Convair 440 and Martin 202. Phillips reports the Convair cost 1.88¢ per available seat-mile in 1957, whereas Air Canada's average was 1.68¢ (U.S.) for the Viscount.[32] Moreover, the Viscount offered superior service in terms of both speed and noise. Yet it was these latter two aircraft that were relied upon by the American carriers. It may be that imperfect capital markets along with a higher initial price ($1 million Cdn. for the Viscount [33] compared to $500 to $650 thousand U.S. [34] for the alternatives) forced the smaller U.S. airlines to buy American. Both Capital and Northeast were reported to be unable to finance[mm] additional Viscount purchases.[35] But this does not explain the behavior of the larger trunk airlines. More plausible is the contention that the United States regulatory structure in creating and perpetuating monopoly profits on the longer-distance routes concentrated most of the efforts made to improve product quality in this market.[36]

Initially applied to the transcontinental route (multi-stop service)[nn] and the denser central routes, the Viscount was being operated on virtually the whole route system by 1958. In that year, it performed two-thirds of the North American seat-miles flown.[37] Thus, the Crown airline opted for a short to intermediate range aircraft that offered comparable service but lower operating costs than longer-haul aircraft such as the Constellation. Compared to the shorter-haul pistons, the Viscounts were no more expensive to operate and offered service of higher quality.

THE AIRCRAFT FLEET IN THE 1960s

In late 1956, the airline ordered, as replacements for the North Star and Super Constellation, the Douglas DC-8 and the Vickers Vanguard. The DC-8 entered service in early 1960; the Vanguard in 1961 (Table 7–1). With cruising speed of 550–575 m.p.h.,[oo] a seating capacity of 127,[pp] and a range of 3800 miles, the DC-8 was meant to handle long-distance traffic. It was placed on non-stop Toronto-Vancouver and one-stop (initially Winnipeg, later Calgary or Edmon-

[ll] Although available in 1959, it was grounded shortly thereafter because of several disastrous crashes caused by sympathetic vibrations engendered by the engines.

[mm] Eads, in *The Local Service Airline Experiment,* pp. 136–42, partly attributes the delay in the introduction of turbo-props in local airline service to financing difficulties.

[nn] Long-distance direct traffic was still extremely light. In September 1957, Toronto-Montreal to Vancouver traffic amounted to only 77 passengers per day. See Canada, Air Transport Board, *Report to the Minister of Transport on Transcontinental Air Services,* (Ottawa, December 1958), p. 34.

[oo] Air Canada powered its first versions with Rolls-Royce rather than the standard Pratt and Whitney engines.

[pp] The stretched version seating upwards of 196 passengers was purchased in 1967.

Table 7–6. Cost per Plane-Mile and per Available Seat-Mile for the Viscount, Vanguard, and DC-8, 1963

Type	*Cost per Plane-Mile ($)*	*Average Number of Seats*	*Cost per Available Seat-Mile (¢)*	*Stage-Length Approx. Miles*
Viscount	1.28	51	2.501	250
Vanguard	2.10	108	1.954	375
DC-8	2.08	131	1.590	1100

Source: Canada, Sessional Committee on Railways, Airlines and Shipping, *Minutes of Proceedings and Evidence*, No. 1 (December 2, 3, 4, 1963), p. 53.

ton) transcontinental service. The Vanguard, a four engine turbo-prop[qq] with listed cruising speed of 420 m.p.h., a seating capacity of 96 to 108, and a range of 2200 miles, was used to replace the North Star and supplement the Viscount on intermediate range routes. It was introduced extensively on the Maritimes, the central Canadian routes (including Chicago and New York), and the transcontinental routes.

That the long-range jet aircraft had costs far below those of the generation of piston aircraft that they had replaced has been well documented elsewhere.[38] Canadian costs were about the same as American for this aircraft. In 1966, Canadian operators (both Air Canada and CP Air) operated DC-8's at 1.171¢ U.S. over an average stage-length of 2400 miles on the North Atlantic, while the American carriers' DC-8 costs on international operations were 1.214¢ U.S. per seat-mile with an average stage-length of 2,000 miles.[39]

Of greater interest was the appropriateness of the choice of the Vanguard.[rr] Table 7–6 compares the average costs per seat-mile of the Viscount, the Vanguard, and the DC-8 in 1963, while Figure 7–1 presents the estimated relationship between the direct operating costs of Air Canada's fleet in the middle 1960s. It is evident that the Vanguard was cheaper to operate per seat-mile than the Viscount over all stage-lengths. For distances up to 1,000 miles, it had lower seat-mile costs than the DC-8. Optimal aircraft choice, of course, entails more than mere minimization of costs. But at least the Vanguard with its somewhat slower speed and noisier ride was not more costly than the jet alternative.[ss] The Boeing 727, the first jet that would have obviously bettered

[qq]The Vanguard, like the Electra, had vibration problems, though unlike its American counterpart it did not suffer crashes as a result of these problems.

[rr]The only other airline to purchase this aircraft was British European Airways.

[ss]Nor was it more expensive than the alternative Lockheed L-188. The Vanguard's cost of 1.8¢ U.S. per available seat-mile compares favorably with the 2.2¢ U.S. given for the L-188 at a stage-length of some 200 miles in the early 1960s. See Straszheim, *The International Airline Industry*, p. 259.

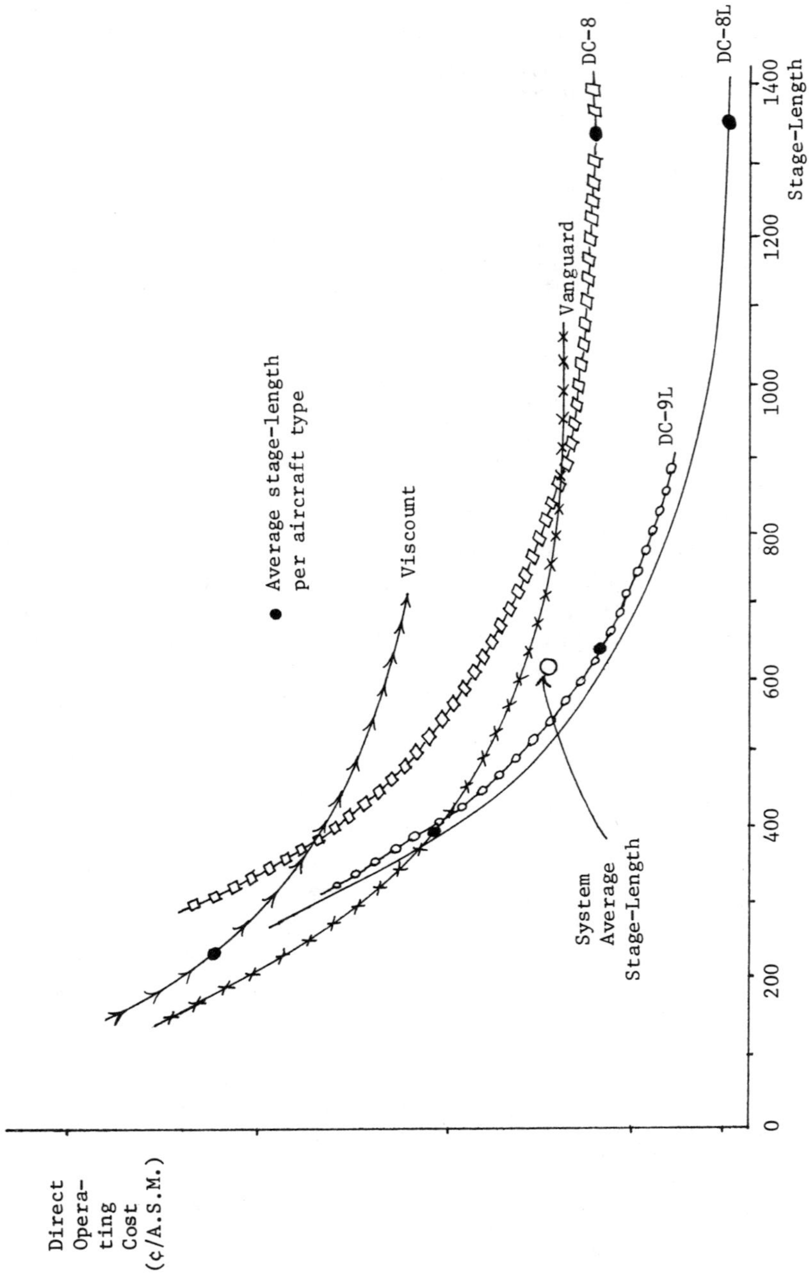

Figure 7-1. Direct Operating Costs (Cents per Available Seat-Mile) for the Viscount, Vanguard, DC-9, and DC-8.

the Vanguard's costs over shorter distances[tt] became available in 1964. The airline passed this up to purchase the DC-9 in 1966—an aircraft with even lower costs than the 727, especially over the shorter routes.[40] In 1967, Air Canada reported that the DC-9 cost 1.45¢ per available seat-mile at an average stage-length of 600 miles.[41] This aircraft—94 passengers, 560 m.p.h., 1600 mile range—that had a cost curve intersecting that of the Vanguard between 300 and 400 miles (see Figure 7–1) and that was of comparable size eliminated much of the cost advantage of the Vanguard over intermediate stage-lengths. One year following the advent of the long-bodied DC-9 in 1967,[uu] the Vanguard fleet was reduced by 50 percent (Table 7–1) and phased out by the end of 1970.[vv]

The airline was not particularly slow in adopting the technologies that with each new generation of jet aircraft offered a superior product at less cost. Acquisition of the DC-8, the DC-9,[ww] and the Boeing 747 during this period was relatively prompt. In all cases, the Crown airline was operating these aircraft within one year of their first going into service in the United States.

CONCLUSION

Apart from the North Star, little government pressure appears to have been exerted on the Crown airline to influence its equipment purchases. Although the decision to purchase the DC-9 resulted in great public debate [42] —the objection came mainly from a group of Quebec Members of Parliament who argued in favor of the French-made Caravelle—the government itself refused to intervene.[xx]

While the North Star was the only choice directly influenced by the government, it was also the only aircraft whose purchase was at all questionable. For the density characteristics of Canadian routes, the Lockheed series L-10 through L-18 offered a service superior in speed and at less cost per passenger than the DC-3—the one most commonly in use on American routes. The DC-3, when adopted, provided service at lower cost per passenger and higher frequencies than the larger short-haul aircraft then being adopted in the United States. The Viscount not only offered cost savings, but also service improve-

[tt]Ibid., p. 86. The Boeing 720B, a precursor of the 727, had extended the jet economics to shorter routes, but it was the 727 that sharply reduced them on the medium stage-lengths.

[uu]The short DC-9's cost per available seat-mile corresponded to the DC-8 curve. It was the long bodied version of this aircraft that produced the cost reduction.

[vv]The airline had planned to depreciate the aircraft in ten years, whereas it became obsolete in eight.

[ww]The introduction of the DC-9 was delayed because of a shortage of aircraft engines caused by the American participation in the Vietnamese War.

[xx]The French company never made any firm offers for manufacture of the Caravelle in Canada, while Douglas Aircraft had already committed itself to building in Toronto the tail section of every DC-9 manufactured.

ments in terms of speed relative to the short-haul aircraft used in the United States during the late 1950s.

The earlier hypothesis is borne out. The Crown airline, except when directly ordered to purchase the North Star in order to support the Canadian aircraft industry, or when forced by the service rivalry engendered by the rigid price structure and monopoly profits created by the North Atlantic cartel to order one of the expensive long-range turbo-compound aircraft spawned by this competition, chose to operate aircraft that compared favorably either in cost or service characteristics with those operated elsewhere.

This, of course, is no proof that inefficiencies did not exist. But, at least as far as operating costs are concerned, there are two sources of evidence to confirm the relative efficiency of this Crown corporation. With the advent of the Viscount, the direct operating costs quoted above compare favorably with those of the American carriers. Secondly, the one comprehensive attempt to evaluate the relative efficiencies of the airlines of different countries places Air Canada amongst the most efficient operators.[43] This corroborates the contention that support maximization in the Canadian context required minimum costs—that is, support maximization found consumer support rather than factor support a more efficacious method of ensuring survival.[yy]

[yy]It is difficult to argue that the entry of other carriers forced the adoption of efficient equipment. The decision to adopt the Viscount (1952), the DC-8 and the Vanguard (1956), and the DC-9 (1963) respectively preceded the introduction of transcontinental competition (1959) and the expansion of regional carriers (1966).

Chapter Eight

Manifestations of Support-Maximizing Behavior—Price and Product Policy during the 1950s

An examination of Air Canada's fare and product policy in effect during the 1950s provides further corroboration for the proposed model of a Crown airline. Between 1950 and 1959, Air Canada faced little or no competition on its domestic route system. In choosing that level of fares and product quality that best fulfilled its objectives, it was unhampered by direct competition.[a] It has been hypothesized that the airline will develop support by establishing substantial equality in the fare per mile and/or the service provided to different routes across its system. This period provides an opportunity to examine the extent to which the Crown airline did so. In addition, it provides an example of the manner in which both the fare structure and the quality of the product offered to different regions responded to decreases in costs brought about by the introduction of new aircraft.

FRAMEWORK FOR THE ANALYSIS OF THE FARE STRUCTURE

It has been argued that any change in profits available to the Crown airline from operations in one market should affect prices and service quality across the route system. In particular, a "public" airline should react to a decrease in costs specific to one market by changing the prices and/or the service frequency in all sectors of its route system. It has also been postulated that for any one route the direction and magnitude of these changes will depend upon whether the city-pair belongs to a profit or a loss sector. Therefore, it is important to differentiate routes on the basis of profitability. But it is also important to classify routes

[a]The airline may have been constrained on some routes by indirect competition. The Vancouver-Toronto passenger could always travel Vancouver-Seattle-Chicago-Toronto. However, the number of routes offering similar alternatives was small.

according to the region in which they are located, for it is possible that the degree of support generated from a route varies from region to region and that the airline will not favor all regions equally.

For the purpose of analyzing the effect different events have had on Air Canada's fare structure, its route system is divided into five segments. These will be referred to as (1) transcontinental, (2) corridor, (3) northern Ontario and Quebec, (4) Maritimes, and (5) east-west sectors. Transcontinental flights are defined as those connecting points between Victoria and Winnipeg and those from western Canada into Ontario and Quebec. As Chapter Six demonstrated, during the 1950s, it was in this sector that profits were generated to support the other four. The corridor sector is assigned all routes that connect city-pairs between Windsor, Ontario, and Sept Isles, Quebec. This sector includes the densest Canadian routes—the Toronto, Ottawa, Montreal triangle. The northern Ontario and Quebec sector encompasses the routes extending northward from Toronto and Montreal into northern Ontario and Quebec. Although this sector is composed of loss routes and is situated in the same general region as the corridor routes, it is separated in this analysis from the latter because of its lower traffic density and the relative isolation of the points served theron. The Maritimes sector is designated to include all flights within the Atlantic provinces as well as external flights to points located within Ontario and Quebec. Routes connecting points west of Ontario with Atlantic destinations are assigned to the east-west category. They are separated from the transcontinental routes for two reasons. First, they involve connecting flights and, therefore, are inherently more costly than a route of corresponding length on the transcontinental sector. Secondly, each of these routes is comprised partially of a transcontinental sector, partially of a Maritimes segment. A priori, it is therefore not apparent how a combination of the two would be treated by the airline.

To provide a concise description of the fare structure for a particular year, linear regressions of price on distance are estimated.[b] In addition, covariance analysis will be used to test whether or not, in any one year, the fare equation varied across different sectors.[c] So as to reduce the number of observations to manageable proportions, only city-pairs with an annual passenger volume in 1968 of more than 1000 are utilized.[1] Table 8–1 presents the characteristics of the resulting sample. The longest mean stage-length occurs on east-west routes; the shortest on the corridor. The transcontinental route provides the widest range of stage-lengths, which vary from 42 to almost 2500 miles. Both the corridor and northern Ontario sectors contain routes all of which have stage-lengths of less than 900 miles.

[b]Volume was also included, but its influence was found to be insignificant.

[c]In order to test whether the differences might really be the result of the linearity assumption adopted, several non-linear relationships were also estimated. Their fit was so poor that they were discarded in favor of the alternate hypothesis that the fare equation was linear, but differed for the routes chosen.

Table 8–1. Characteristics of the Sample of Routes Used to Analyze the Fare Structure

Sector	*Number of City-Pairs*	*Mean Stage-Length (miles)*	*Range of Stage-Lengths (miles)*
Transcontinental	76	1,180	42 - 2486
Corridor	23	360	69 - 839
Northern Ontario	18	370	68 - 717
Maritimes	56	600	102 - 1389
East-West	13	2,450	1521 - 3361

Fares for the regressions are taken from Air Canada time tables. The fare adopted is the lowest non-promotional price available—generally tourist class in the 1950s and economy class in the 1960s. Ticket prices are reduced by the amount of the round trip discount when it existed. If the fare was not published, it is calculated from connecting segments. All distances are taken from those filed by Air Canada with the Air Transport Committee in 1970.

A study of the fare structure should involve an examination of the comparability of the rates per mile not only within each sector but also amongst the various sectors. The Crown airline may choose to adopt the same fare equation for each sector in order to guarantee that all city-pairs of identical stage-length, but irrespective of sector, have the same fare per mile.[d] Or, it may choose fare equations that differ between sectors, but still argue that different sectors receive roughly the same treatment. To do so, the airline could argue that some measure of the average fare per mile in each sector was the same across sectors. One such candidate is the rate per mile calculated at the mean stage-length. For this reason, it shall be reported along with the regression equations.

Since we are interested in whether the fare regressions differ across sectors, the nature of the difference is important. Specific comparison between routes across sectors may be sufficiently infrequent that the Crown airline can afford different fare sturctures for different sectors.[e] But routes within a sector may be more readily compared—especially if the sector is geographically homogeneous—and thus the Crown airline may attempt to minimize the difference in the fare per mile charged within such a sector. If fares are derived from a linear equation of the type estimated here, then the size of the intercept affects the spread of the fare per mile amongst city-pairs within each sector.[f] The larger the intercept, the greater this difference will be between routes of different stage-lengths in

[d]Should there also be no distance-related taper in the uniform fare structure, then all routes irrespective of distance will be treated alike.

[e]As pointed out above, it may still attempt to minimize the difference across sectors in some measure of average fare paid even if it adopts a different fare structure in each region.

[f]$P_1/D_1 - P_2/D_2 = a_1\ (1/D_1 - 1/D_2)$ where $P_i = a_i + b_i D$, $i = 1{,}2$.

any one sector. If a sector also has a range of routes confined to the shorter stage-lengths, the Crown airline has an additional reason to minimize the intercept of the fare equation, for the larger the intercept of the fare equation in a sector whose routes are short, the larger will be the spread in the fare per mile between the longest and the shortest routes therein. The same size of intercept for a sector whose routes have the same range of distances but all of which are generally longer will lead to a smaller difference in the fare per mile between the shortest and the longest routes therein. To the extent that public pressure is a function of the perceived differentials in each sector, the same intercept will lead to greater outcry from the sector with the shorter routes. Thus, whenever a sector is characterized by short stage-lengths or geographic homogeneity, we shall be interested in examining whether the airline maintained greater intra-sectoral comparability than elsewhere and whether it effected fare changes by a shift in the slope or a shift in the intercept of the fare equation.

Three sectors—the corridor, northern Ontario and Quebec, and the Maritimes —not only consist mainly of short routes, but are also geographically homogeneous. On the other hand, the transcontinental sector includes routes from different regions and many of its routes are therefore less likely to be compared one with another. However, there is a subset of the transcontinental route system that may be subject to some intra-sectoral comparison because of a common characteristic of the routes contained therein. This subset contains those routes connecting one region to another—that is, the set of routes that tend to be regarded as a homogeneous group for purposes of government competition policy (see Chapter Nine). However, these routes are generally longer than those found in sectors mentioned above. Therefore, in light of the previous discussion, these characteristics lead us to predict that, *ceteris paribus* (fare per mile at mean stage-length held constant), the fare structure on the three loss sectors should be characterized by lower intercepts and higher slopes than the fare structure on the transcontinental sector.

Table 8-2 presents the fare equations estimated from all the city-pairs for the years chosen for study. The equations reported therein assume there is no difference between sectors—that one equation adequately represents the fare structure for all sectors. This assumption is dropped in the subsequent section. The insignificant intercept exhibitied for the 1951 equation indicates that at the beginning of the period, the average fare per mile was approximately the same across all routes. However, between 1951 and 1958, the aggregate equation rotated in a clockwise direction as a distance-related taper in the average fare per mile was introduced. The reason for this rotation and the manner in which individual sectors were adjusted to give this result are examined in the next section. It will serve not only to corroborate the predictions of the public airline's reactions to shifting cost curves, but also to illustrate the varying impact its actions have had upon different regions.

Table 8–2. Regressions of Fare on Distance, Aggregate Results for 1951, 1955, 1958, 1962, 1968, and 1971

Year	*Intercept*	*Distance Slope Coefficient*	F^a	R^2
1951	1.15 (1.21)[c]	.068 (88.6)[c]	85.42 (1,139)[b]	.983
1955	2.02 (2.35)	.060 (82.5)	23.90 (1,182)	.974
1958	4.73 (8.41)	.052 (108.8)	252.11 (1,183)	.984
1962	9.72 (14.94)	.049 (88.5)	155.16 (1,183)	.977
1968	10.41 (17.94)	.055 (109.4)	416.94 (1,180)	.985
1971	11.29 (27.15)	.057 (160.3)	875.41 (1,178)	.993

[a]$F(1,150)_{.01} = 6.81$.

[b]Figures in parentheses in this column indicate degrees of freedom for the F statistic.

[c]Figures in parentheses in these columns are t statistics for the estimated regression coefficients.

The data required for this investigation is provided in Tables 8–3, 8–4, and Figure 8–1. Table 8–3 contains the results of the fare regressions for 1951, 1955, and 1958, which are now allowed to differ across sectors. Empty cells indicate the coefficient of the equation for that sector is identical to that presented for the east-west sector.[g] The *t* statistics in columns three through ten indicate the extent to which the slope or the intercept of the fare equation for that particular sector deviates from that estimated for the east-west route. This table permits evaluation of the existence of differing fare structures amongst regions. In addition, it can be used to infer the importance attributed by the airline to equality in the rate per mile within each sector.

Table 8–4 presents the fare per mile calculated from the estimated regressions using the mean distance for each sector. It has been hypothesized that minimizing their inter-sectoral differences may be an important objective for the Crown airline.

Figure 8–1 graphs the relationship between the average fare per mile and distance as given by the estimated regressions. This figure permits a comparison of the fare per mile across sectors for all stage-lengths as well as the course of the fare structure from 1950 through 1958.

[g]If covariance analysis suggested that the estimate of a separate intercept or slope coefficient was insignificant, then it was not estimated separately, and the relevant coefficient may be read from the intercept or slope estimates provided in the first two columns of Table 8–3.

Table 8–3. Fare Regressions, Disaggregated by Sector, 1951, 1955, 1958

Year	Standard		Deviations from the Standard Intercept (Col. 1) and Slope (Col. 2)							
	East-West		Transcontinental		Maritimes		Corridor		N. Ontario	
	(1) Intercept	(2) Slope	(3) Intercept	(4) Slope	(5) Intercept	(6) Slope	(7) Intercept	(8) Slope	(9) Intercept	(10) Slope
1951	.546 (.45)[a]	.068 (80.5)[b]	....	....	−1.89 (0.81)	.006 (2.04)[b]	....	....	....	....
1955	2.82 (3.14)[b]	.060 (82.1)[b]	....	....	....	....	....	....	5.49 (1.36)	−.021 (2.87)[b]
1958	3.74 (4.68)[b]	.052 (83.8)[b]	3.04 (2.24)[b]	−.001 (0.58)	....	.002 (2.01)[b]	....	....	....	−.004 (1.26)

[a]Figures in parentheses are t statistics. Those for the standard equation indicate whether the estimates differ from zero. Those beneath the other estimates indicate whether they are significantly different from the standard estimates contained in columns (1) and (2).
[b]Indicates significant t statistic (at 5 percent level).

Table 8–4. Fare per Mile at Mean Stage-Length, by Sector, 1951, 1955, 1958 (¢)

Year / Period	East-West		Transcontinental		Maritimes		Corridor		N. Ontario	
	Fare	*Change*	*Fare*	*Change*	*Fare*	*Change*	*Fare*	*Change*	*Fare*	*Change*
1951	6.82 (0.05)[a]		6.85 (0.06)		7.19 (0.15)		6.98 (0.33)		....	
1951–1955		–.70 (.08)[b]		–.61 (.08)		–.72 (.17)		–.22 (.38)[c]		....
1955	6.12 (0.06)		6.24 (0.05)		6.47 (0.09)		6.76 (0.19)		6.16 (0.44)	
1955–1958		–.77 (.08)		–.56 (.06)		–.44 (.13)		–.55 (.26)		–.34 (.50)[c]
1958	5.35 (0.05)		5.68 (0.04)		6.03 (0.10)		6.21 (0.18)		5.82 (0.24)	

[a]Figures in parentheses indicate the standard error of the estimate.

[b]The standard error of the difference in the mean fare per mile was calculated assuming the errors in each time period were independent of one another.

[c]Indicates the change in mean fare per mile was not significant for $t_{.025,180}$.

Source: Table 8–3.

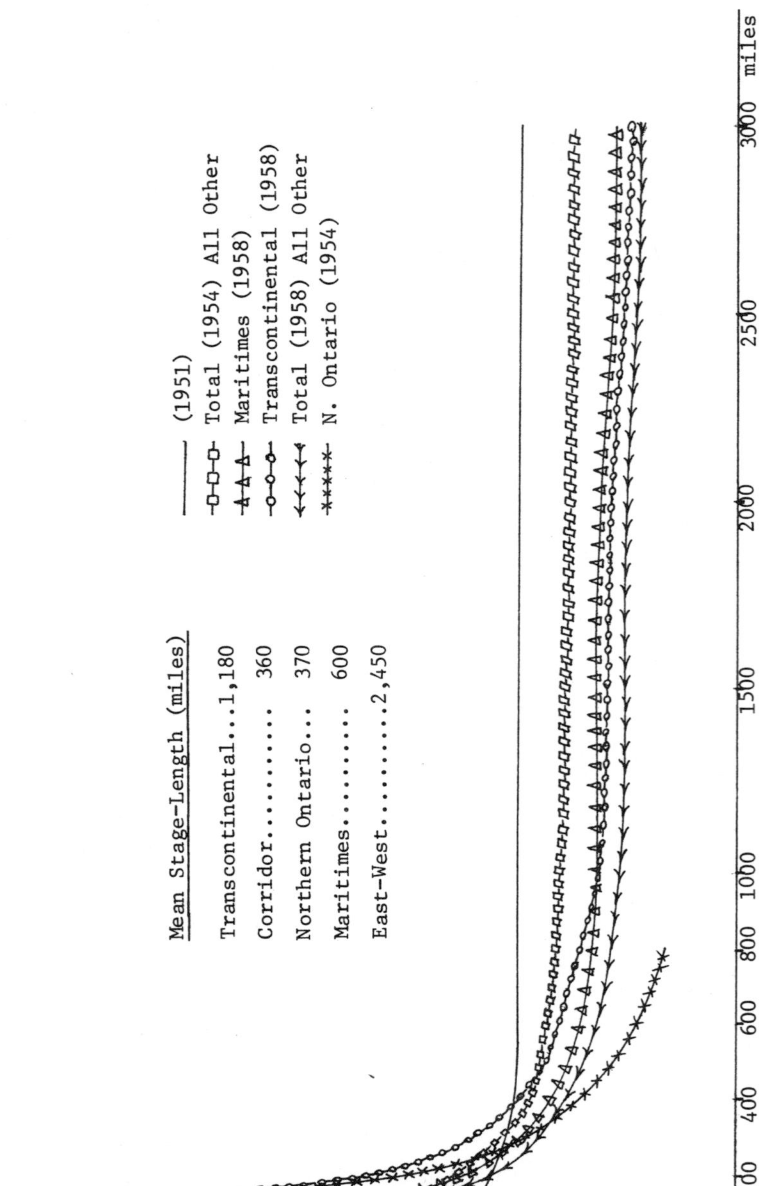

Figure 8-1. Estimated Fare Structure—Cents per Mile Plotted against Distance, 1951, 1954, 1958.

THE FARE STRUCTURE IN 1951

Upon emergence from the period of subsidies in the late 1940s, Air Canada should have had a fare structure that minimized fare differentials. For it is precisely when direct government subsidies are being paid to a Crown airline that specific groups of the public may feel most justified in demanding "parity" of treatment. Tables 8–3 and 8–4 confirm this hypothesis. Table 8–4 shows that in 1951, the first postwar year in which a subsidy was not required, the mean fare per mile was virtually identical in all sectors but the Maritimes.[h] The reason for this is evident from Table 8–3. The estimated fare equations do not differ across sectors (again with the exception of the Maritimes). Of equal importance, the intercept of the common fare equation is not significantly different from zero. Thus, both inter- and intra-sectoral differences in the fare per mile charged were virtually non-existent.

This pattern cannot be attributed to the pattern of costs incurred on the different routes. Prior to the introduction of the North Star, the use of the DC-3 meant that there was little or no cost advantage for longer flights.[i] However, with the replacement of the DC-3 by the North Star in 1948, the cost on the transcontinental routes, compared to that on the shorter routes, fell.[j] By 1951, the North Star accounted for the majority of seat-miles produced on the transcontinental run. The DC-3's continued to serve the Maritimes, many parts of the corridor, including the Montreal-Toronto run, and some of the shorter routes in the west such as Victoria-Vancouver, Calgary-Edmonton, and the "milk" run from Winnipeg across the southern Prairies to Lethbridge. Thus, the lack of distance-related taper in the fare structure must, if we can assume fixed costs were minimal, have resulted in the rate of return earned on the longer routes being substantially greater than that earned on the shorter routes. Both the route results reported in Chapter Six and the fare structure of the early fifties suggest the Crown airline was cross-subsidizing one part of its route system with another.

The lack of fare taper was not unique to Canada. The institutional framework in the United States—private airlines receiving public subsidies, subject to a regulatory authority—produced a fare structure that until 1952 provided no variation in the fare per mile with respect to distance.[2] This may have been the result of a pricing strategy that attempted to maximize sales and the rate base on which subsidy was calculated.[3] Or, in line with the discussion in

[h]The reason for this was the high per mile rate charged for the routes into Newfoundland—higher even than the rate applicable to the shorter routes elsewhere in the Maritimes. Newfoundland had only joined Confederation in 1949, and Air Canada had apparently not adjusted for the changed political circumstances by 1951.

[i]This ignores the somewhat greater utilization that can be obtained for equipment on longer flights because of night flying.

[j]See Chapter Seven, Table 7–5.

Chapter One on regulation, it may have been no more than a reflection of the objectives of the regulatory agency. But what is of greater interest is that, when no longer benefiting from subsidies, airlines in the United States altered the fare structure to approximate costs more closely. Notwithstanding the difficulty of concerted action to raise fares on the short hauls relative to the longer routes,[4] the American industry managed to increase the taper with $1.00 across-the-board fare increases in 1952, 1958, and 1961.

Air Canada, as long as it was the sole domestic trunk operator, failed to change the fare structure in so drastic a fashion. As described below, it introduced some distance-related taper by selectively introducing lower-priced "tourist" service—primarily on long-haul routes. However, Table 8–5 indicates that until 1961 the majority of the airline's passengers continued to avail themselves of first class service. The fares thereon remained unchanged between 1951 and 1961—except for a reduction in the round trip discount from 10 to 5 percent in 1958. Thus, the actual yield received by the airline could have shown very little variance with respect to distance during the 1950s.

The introduction in the United States of lower priced "coach" service, concentrated on longer-haul routes, [5] tended to reinforce the taper created by the flat, across-the-board fare increases.[k] To the extent that a greater percentage of total traffic availed themselves of these fares and the ratio of the coach to the regular fare was lower in the United States than in Canada, then the difference in the fare taper between the two countries was further accentuated. Table 8–5 shows that until 1961 penetration of the market by lower-priced service was greater in the United States.[l] In 1953, the ratio of the coach fare to the standard fare, weighted by volume, was 64.3 percent [6] in the United States. In Canada, coach fares were set at 80 percent of first-class fares when first introduced in 1954.[m] Thus, an inter-country comparison indicates that the nationalized corporation not the regulatory agency was the more "efficient" institution for maintaining equality in the fare per mile charged for different routes.[n] In turn, this implies the Crown airline provided a higher degree of cross-subsidization than the regulated industry. But then, this was the hypothesized rationale for a government's preferring the former institution to the latter.

[k]This would not be so if the service when offered in the dense short-haul markets had a lower ratio of coach price to regular price. This does not appear to have been the case. See U.S., Antitrust Subcommittee, *Monopoly Problems*, Vol. I, p. 286.

[l]The difference is actually greater than Table 8–5 indicates. The percentage of North American services accounted for by the tourist class was 23.0, 25.1, 21.9, and 18.8 for the years 1954, 1955, 1956, and 1957, respectively. See Trans-Canada Air Lines, "Initial Submission," 1958, mimeographed, Exhibit No. b-431.

[m]Following the decrease in tourist fares in 1958, the Canadian ratio was still only about 70 percent.

[n]This assumes similar taper in the cost curves of the industry in each country—a not unreasonable assumption in light of the discussion in Chapter Seven—and similar elasticities of demand for both short- and long-haul routes in the two countries.

Table 8–5. Comparison of the Percentage of Total Traffic Carried in Coach Class for American Carriers versus Tourist Class for Air Canada, 1949–1964 (%)

Year	*United States Domestic Trunk*	*Air Canada System*
1949	3.7	. . .
1950	13.6	. . .
1951	12.5	. . .
1952	19.4	. . .
1953	26.0	. . .
1954	32.8	. . .
1955	35.0	32
1956	37.3	33
1957	38.7	30
1958	41.1	37
1959	43.6	39
1960	49.2	44
1961	57.8	79
1962	65.6	88
1963	67.6	87
1964	71.9	88

Source: Air Canada, *Annual Report,* 1964, p. 16; U.S., Civil Aeronautics Board, *Handbook of Airline Statistics,* Washington, D.C., 1965, p. 58. These percentages include both coach and economy traffic.

THE FARE REVISION OF 1954

In 1954, the Super Constellation was introduced on the transcontinental and international routes. The Super Constellation was used sparingly on the domestic North American routes—that is, it accounted for only 12 percent of the available seat-miles performed in 1957. As Table 7–5 indicated, the cost per available seat-mile was greater for the Super Constellation than for the North Star on those routes where both these aircraft were used. Cost reductions were not the reason for the Super Constellation's introduction. The benefits that accrued from the adoption of this aircraft were derived from increased traffic generation—especially on the North Atlantic. Because of the rigidity in the cartel prices that the International Air Transport Association set for this market, Air Canada, operating the North Star, had found it extremely difficult to compete with the DC-6B's and Super Constellations operated by other carriers. In the first year of operating the Super Constellation, Air Canada more than offset any increased costs with increased traffic; its share of the Canadian North Atlantic market jumped from 40 to 45 percent.[o] As a result, the Crown airline's profits and rate

[o]Similarly, it is possible that, if previously there had been any diversion of transcontinental Canadian traffic to the United States, the introduction of the Super Constellation on the domestic transcontinental run generated new traffic thereon.

of return both increased in 1954.[p] The model of the Crown airline predicts that this increase in profits available for cross-subsidization should have resulted in at least an improvement in services or a reduction in prices to the mainline sector and possibly to the loss sector as well. Air Canada's behavior in this instance supports this contention.

The previous discussion of support-maximizing behavior centered upon the Crown airline's choice of an optimal combination of price-frequency characteristics for its existing route system. But the airline might also be expected to consider broadening its base of support by extending its route system when the profit contraint of Figure 5–2 shifts inward. In the early 1950s, Air Canada suffered from a serious gap in its domestic route system in that it had no service to points in Quebec outside of Montreal. It was a "serious" gap for a support-conscious government corporation since as of 1973 Liberal party governments have been in power federally for all but five years since the inception of the airline, and Quebec has provided the Liberals with a substantial proportion of their strength throughout this period. Following the introduction of the Super Constellation, the airline, in 1955, traded Canadian Pacific Airlines its international routes from Eastern Canada to Mexico in return for several points in northern Ontario and Quebec,[q] and the Montreal-Quebec City-Sept Isles run. These two routes together incurred losses that in 1957 amounted to $2.1 million on a fully allocated cost basis.[r] The extent of this expansion in the airline's loss services is emphasized by the fact that these routes accounted for over 25 percent of the total loss incurred on all the unprofitable sectors in that year.[s]

The airline reacted to its increased profitability not only by extending its loss services but also by revising its fare structure. This was accomplished via the introduction of "tourist" rates for a select group of city-pairs from Vancouver to St. John's, Newfoundland.[t] These rates were available only on North Star aircraft which were converted to a 48 seat configuration from the previous 40 for the new service. The Super Constellation was to provide only first-class service.[u] During the next four years, tourist class accounted for 23.0, 25.1, 21.9, and 18.8 percent of North American revenue passenger-miles.

That this reduction was limited to a specific class of travellers might be

[p] See Tables 6–2 and 6–4.

[q] Val d'Or, Rouyn-Noranda, and Timmins.

[r] See Table 6–5.

[s] It is difficult to argue that these route acquisitions were merely market development investments, since some fifteen years later they were still unprofitable on a fully allocated cost basis.

[t] The points connected were Vancouver, Calgary, Edmonton, Regina, Saskatoon, Winnipeg, Windsor, London, Toronto, Ottawa, Montreal, Moncton, Halifax, Sydney, Stephenville, Gander, and St. John's. Not all combinations of these points received the lower fares.

[u] Not until 1957 was a joint tourist–first-class configuration provided on the Constellation.

explained, in retrospect, by the fact that the increase in profits generated by the introduction of the Super Constellation was relatively small and that the demand for services was not highly elastic. Using the fact that the new fare was 20 percent lower, that tourist traffic averaged 24 percent of the North American total in 1954–55, that traffic on those routes where tourist service was introduced comprised about 80 percent of the system total, and assuming all tourist traffic was newly generated yields a rough estimate of the price elasticity of -1.5.[v] This implies a general fare reduction was likely to be relatively expensive. The price reduction afforded by the relatively small improvement in profitability was likely to be so small as perhaps to be unappreciated. Instead, the airline appears to have tailored a much larger and therefore more visible decrease in fares to a specific group.

The new lower fares were, at first glance, an attempt to compensate for the differential in product quality brought about by fleet reequipment. Nevertheless, the level and pattern of the new fares implemented in different sectors is consistent with the support-maximization hypothesis. The tourist fares were set at 80 percent of the value of a one-way first-class ticket. Since the previous fare structure was characterized by neither inter- nor intra-sectoral differences in the price per mile, the new fares by themselves also had no distance-related taper. All sectors that received the new service were treated in like fashion—insofar as the fare per mile was the same. However, when the fare structure of those routes that both did and did not receive the new service is analyzed, several interesting patterns arise.

As Table 8–4 indicates, the improved profitability of both the international and possibly the transcontinental sectors lowered the mean fare per mile for all sectors. This result bears out the model developed in Chapter Five.[w] The actual pattern of fare adjustments on the different loss routes provides the first evidence as to the relative importance of each sector to the airline. Of the two loss sectors, the decrease in the mean fare per mile for the Maritimes was the greatest. The airline used the occasion of this new service to bring the fare structure of the Maritimes, which had been above the average in 1951, into line with the rest of the system (Table 8–3). Although the mean stage-length on the Maritime routes was considerably less than on the transcontinental (approximately 600 versus 1200 miles), the decrease in the mean fare per mile is greater for this loss route (Table 8–4).

[v] $\eta_p = -24/80 \big/ 20/100$.

[w] An alternate explanation of the fare reduction was that it applied only to those routes that were profitable—even though some of these routes have been classified as falling in loss sectors. Footnote t of this chapter lists those points that were offered tourist service. If this were the case, the Crown airline responded to increased profits from its mainline sectors by decreasing prices thereon but by leaving prices on its loss routes unchanged. This interpretation is equally compatible with the model developed in Chapter Five, but it would rule out the alternative model that contained the absolute value of the price variables in the Crown airline's objection function (see the discussion in Chapter Five).

The corridor routes received less of a decrease in the mean fare per mile than the Maritimes. But then, losses thereon had already been substantially increased as the result of the extension of service into Quebec. Still, two of the three densest routes were provided with tourist service at fares below the average tourist fare of 6.24¢ per mile on the transcontinental run. Toronto-Montreal with a stage-length of 340 miles received a tourist fare per mile of 5.6¢; Montreal-Quebec City at 160 miles, 5.9¢ per mile. Only two of the transcontinental city-pairs had lower rates per mile. Compared to the Maritimes, the benefits extended to the corridor were concentrated on service expansion and select price reductions.

The model of the public airline also predicts that the price spread between the profitable and unprofitable sectors should have increased as the result of the introduction of the Super Constellation. As Table 8–4 indicates, the transcontinental routes did receive a greater decrease than the corridor routes. That this did not also hold for a comparison between the transcontinental and Maritime sectors must be attributed to the fact that the Crown airline cannot be described as being in equilibrium vis-à-vis these latter routes before the price change.[x]

Finally, as of 1955, the only sector to have a significantly different fare structure from the rest was the newly acquired northern Ontario and Quebec route (Table 8–3). As Figure 8–1 shows, the average fare per mile on distances above the mean stage-length of some 300 miles had significantly lower fares per mile than the rest of the system. This was the result of the low level of the fares from Montreal to the northern points in this sector. Again we are presented with corroborating evidence as to the importance of the new service to Quebec points.

Therefore, the technological change that increased North Atlantic profits served to decrease the inequality between Maritime and transcontinental rates, to expand services on the corridor, and to open up a new loss sector serving northern Ontario and Quebec, at the same time as providing low fares from Montreal to northern points in this sector.

PRODUCT POLICY–CROSS-SUBSIDIZATION AND THE EXTENSION OF NEW EQUIPMENT TO THE LOSS ROUTES

The mid-1955 introduction of the Viscount caused a sharp downward shift in the airline's cost curve.[y] System costs per available ton-mile fell from 42.84¢ in 1954 to 37.97¢ in 1955. While fare reductions had resulted from the introduction of the Constellation, the airline in this instance chose initially to

[x]See footnote h of this chapter.
[y]See Table 7–5.

react to this reduction by improving the quality of the service offered across its route system.

Equity of treatment has been hypothesized to be an important target for the Crown airline; the visibility of a specific instrument a measure of its relative importance. Questions posed in the House of Commons and to its Sessional Committee responsible for Air Canada's operations indicate that equality of service standards as measured by the type of aircraft providing service garnered as much attention as the fare structure. In the late 1950s, Members of Parliament from both the Prairies [7] and Newfoundland [8] requested an extension to their constituencies of the Viscount service then being accorded to other areas. Similarly, in 1964, before the airline had even introduced the DC-9, Members from the Maritimes let it be known that they wished such service to be implemented at the earliest possible date.[9]

Introduction of Viscount service improved the quality of service both by reducing load factors,[z] and thereby improving accessibility to desired flights, as well as by equalizing the quality of equipment provided the different regions. Between 1954 and 1959, the latter being the year by which the entire fleet of Viscounts was acquired, domestic load factors fell from 76.5 to 68.7 percent.[aa] While cost per available ton-mile decreased from 42.8¢ to 37.1¢, a decrease of 13.5 percent, cost per revenue ton-mile decreased only by 4 percent. However, not all of this reduction in load factors was caused by a general expansion in capacity. Some can be attributed to the extension of Viscount service to the less dense, unprofitable sectors.

Viscount service was initially introduced on the transcontinental system and the Ontario sector of the corridor stretching from Windsor to Montreal in 1955. In 1956, the number of transcontinental Viscount services was expanded from 2 to 6. It was not until 1957 that the Maritimes received this aircraft, and then only as far east as Halifax. In the same year, Viscount service was also inaugurated on the Montreal-Quebec segment of the corridor. The final expansion occurred in 1958 to the routes in northern Ontario, east of Halifax to St. John's, and east of Quebec City to Sept Isles.

By 1958, the Viscount performed 64 percent of seat-miles flown on North American services; the North Star, 22 percent; the Super Constellation, 12 percent; and the DC-3, 2 percent.[10] Only Victoria and several airports on the Prairie "milk" run did not receive Viscount service.[bb] As a result, the reduction

[z]The load factor is defined as the number of passenger-miles sold divided by the number of seat-miles flown. The higher this number the fewer empty seats are available and the less likely a passenger will be in obtaining a seat without substantial advance planning.

[aa]Actual domestic load factors were 74.0, 76.5, 73.1, 75.9, 72.8, 72.7, and 68.7 for the years 1953 through 1959. See Canada, Dominion Bureau of Statistics, Aviation Statistics Centre, *Civil Aviation–Annual,* Cat. No. 51–202, various years.

[bb]Service to London, Ontario, was delayed until 1957 because of inadequate airport facilities there. See Canada, Sessional Committee on Railways and Shipping, *Minutes of Proceedings and Evidence,* no. 2 (March 21, 25, 26, 1957), p. 291. Viscount service to Victoria and Prairie towns was constrained for the same reason.

Table 8–6. Comparison of Viscount and DC-3 Direct Operating Costs per Available Seat-Mile, 1957

Route	*Average[a] Stage-Length (miles)*	*Viscount (¢)*	*DC-3 (¢)*	*Ratio of Operating Costs (%)*
Toronto-Ottawa-Montreal	250	1.8195	2.5712	70.8
Prairies and Foothills	128	1.8821	2.5974	72.5
Great Lakes	303	1.7581	2.6445	66.5
Eastern Quebec[b]	190	1.9492	2.6815	72.7
Southern Ontario[c]	136	1.9525	2.6106	74.8
Maritimes	236	1.8305	2.6666	68.6

[a]Approximate–estimated from 1963 data. The actual stage-lengths flown by each aircraft varied slightly from these averages.

[b]Montreal-Quebec-Saguenay-Sept Isles. The Viscount was used only on the 160 mile Montreal-Quebec segment.

[c]Toronto-London-Windsor-Cleveland.

Source: Trans-Canada Air Lines, "Initial Submission to the Air Transport Board in the Matter of Transcontinental Commercial Air Service," 1958, mimeographed, Exhibit 64.

in the variance of the quality of service across the route system was considerable. Previously, many points in the Maritimes, northern Ontario, and the corridor (southern Ontario and the area east of Montreal) had received service from DC-3's, while the transcontinental received North Star and Super Constellation service. The Maritimes had not received North Stars until 1952–4 years after their introduction elsewhere, and were not to receive the Super Constellation.[cc] Thus, the introduction of the Viscount permitted a substantial equalization of service standards across the country. This behavior stands in sharp contrast to that of American carriers. In the United States, the major trunk carriers continued to serve isolated points with propeller-driven Martins and Convairs during this period.

Whereas substitution of the Viscount for the North Star on transcontinental routes involved a reduction in costs which averaged about 15 percent [11] per available seat-mile, cost savings as a result of its substitution for the DC-3 were less immediate. Table 8–6 indicates the relative costs of the Viscount and the DC-3 during 1957 when both were being operated on the same routes. The seat-mile costs of the Viscount averaged 30 percent below those of the DC-3. But the Viscount seated 44; the DC-3, only 28. If traffic on those routes previously served by the DC-3, or the number of flights remained the same after

[cc]Actually the Super Constellation was used in the Maritimes for a few months in 1961 before finally being phased out of service.

Table 8–7. Operating Results for Air Canada, by Route, 1956–1957

Route	*Operating Profit 1956*	*1957*	*Load Factor 1957*
	($000)		*(%)*
Vancouver-Toronto	.....	302	68.8
Vancouver-Winnipeg	– 176	– 149	52.3
Vancouver-Calgary-Regina-Winnipeg	1347	1023	71.2
Vancouver-Edmonton-Saskatoon-Winnipeg	1026	614	68.0
Calgary-Toronto	300	470	69.0
Winnipeg-Toronto	3726	4016	75.3
Winnipeg-Windsor-Ottawa	.....	109	69.7
Toronto-Ottawa-Montreal	– 537	– 951	72.5
Pacific Coast	– 964	–1334	67.8
Prairies and Foothills	–1107	–1403	63.9
Great Lakes	– 14	– 118	68.3
Northern Ontario	–1027	–1193	63.4
Toronto-London-Windsor	– 964	–1071	69.2
Montreal-Quebec-Sept Isles	– 644	– 861	66.4
Maritimes	–1203	–1801	65.5
Newfoundland	– 109	– 342	64.8

Source: Canada, Air Transport Board, *Transcontinental Route Hearings, Exhibit Book,* TCA Exhibits 64 and 420.

introduction of the Viscount, load factors would have fallen by 37 percent, thus making the Viscount actually more expensive per unit of traffic carried.[dd]

Therefore, increased profits from the transcontinental sector were probably used to expand Viscount service to the "social" routes at a somewhat faster pace than would otherwise have occurred. Proof of this contention would ultimately require route data showing that the loss per passenger-mile increased during the period of introduction of these services. Unfortunately, this is lacking. However, other evidence may be used to infer the same conclusion. Net profits peaked in 1956, the year the Viscounts had been placed in large numbers on the transcontinental run, and fell in the two subsequent years of their extension to the loss routes.[ee] Table 8–7 indicates that between 1956 and 1957—the year Viscount service was launched on the Montreal-Quebec segment and in the Maritimes—the losses on these routes[ff] grew twice as fast as losses elsewhere.

[dd]The same problem did not arise on the transcontinental route since the North Star in first-class configuration (the flights replaced by the Viscount) seated 48.

[ee]See Table 6–2. It is difficult to attribute this to a downturn in the business cycle since the growth in operating revenues averaged 14.9 percent in 1957 and 1958 compared to 15.2 percent in the previous two years.

[ff]The Newfoundland route is included in these calculations because, in lieu of the introduction of Viscount service, the airline deliberately increased North Star service. See Canada, Sessional Committee on Railways and Shipping, *Minutes of Proceedings and Evidence,* no. 2 (March 21, 25, 26, 1957), pp. 289–96.

Equally suggestive of cross-subsidization during the transitional phase is the difference between the load factors that existed on the transcontinental and the social routes. As Table 8–7 indicates, load factors averaged 71 percent on the transcontinental, but only 66 percent on the social routes.[gg] The difference is even more pronounced when load factors on Viscounts alone are compared. On the transcontinental sector, Viscount load factors averaged over 75 percent; on Montreal-Quebec, 68 percent; and on the Maritimes, only 64 percent. Of course, a profit-maximizing airline will not necessarily equalize load factors across routes. Higher prices and lower load factors might be chosen where the demand is for high frequency rather than inexpensive service. A once-a-day service on a so-called social route might be an example of this type of operation. But we have already seen that the fare per mile was unrelated to distance on first-class service—and the Viscount during this period was only offered in this configuration. Therefore, on the social routes—all of which had short stage-lengths—the lower load factors were not offset with higher fares. At worst, this implies the airline required additional profit on the transcontinental segment to temporarily support introduction of the Viscounts elsewhere. At best, it suggests they were constrained from reducing these load factors by the necessity of equalizing service across the system as soon as possible.[hh]

THE FARE REVISION OF 1958

Once Viscount service had been extended to social routes, the airline implemented its second major fare revision. In 1958, tourist fares[ii] were reduced by an average of 13 percent [12] while the round-trip discount on first-class service was reduced from 10 to 5 percent.

Since this fare reduction was not an immediate response to a route-specific cost reduction, the Crown airline might be expected to minimize the inter-sectoral differences in the fare reductions. For it is in this situation that it becomes particularly vulnerable to criticism, since it cannot argue that a specific cost reduction merits special consideration be given to one route over another. In fact, the changes actually implemented in tourist fares were almost identical—that is, average decreases in the fare per mile of 0.87¢ for the transcontinental route; 0.87¢ for the Montreal-Toronto route;[jj] and 0.80¢ for the Maritimes sector.

[gg] Montreal-Toronto is excluded from both sectors because its extremely high density differentiates it from the routes included in the other two categories.

[hh] This hypothesis might be confirmed if, following the extension of the Viscount across the system, load factors had declined on the transcontinental sector. They did; but unfortunately, competition had been introduced in 1959 on this sector, thereby destroying the *ceteris paribus* conditions required for this test.

[ii] Tourist service was still not provided on Viscounts, but as of 1957 had been made available on Super Constellations.

[jj] This was the only corridor city-pair to receive direct point-to-point tourist service.

While the changes in the tourist fare were almost identical, this does not mean the resulting fare structure left the price spread between the profitable and the loss sectors unchanged. For the model of the public airline predicted that the spread should have increased. Indeed, as Table 8–4 shows, because the tourist service was not offered on every route and because the discount on first-class round-trip fares was reduced, the price spread—as measured as the fare per mile at mean stage-length—between the transcontinental and the loss sectors did widen.

These changes also served to decrease the inter-sectoral disparity amongst the loss sectors (Table 8–4). The northern Ontario and Quebec routes, which had enjoyed an advantage over the other two loss sectors in 1955, received the smallest fare reduction.[kk] The mean fare per mile for all Maritime city-pairs—not just those receiving tourist service—that had in 1954 received a greater decrease than the mean for the corridor, now benefited from a slightly lower reduction. The result was that the spread amongst these loss sectors decreased.

It is also noteworthy that following the fare revisions, the three loss sectors had a significantly lower intercept than the transcontinental sector (Table 8–3). The fare reductions on the transcontinental sector were effected mainly on the longer routes,[ll] thereby rotating the fare equation clockwise and increasing the difference in the fare per mile between short- and long-distance city-pairs within the transcontinental system. The significantly lower intercept for the three loss routes indicates the importance to the airline of maintaining comparability of fares per mile within these sectors when reducing the mean price. Thus, the airline appears to have attempted to minimize not only inter- but also intra-sectoral differences on the loss routes.

CONCLUSION

During the period when Air Canada faced virtually no competition either on its domestic mainline or regional routes, its product and fare policy closely matched the predictions arising from the model of the publicly owned firm. It was hypothesized that one effect of the establishment of a Crown airline would be a reduction in the variation of prices and service quality across the route system—at least in comparison to that which a more competitive market would offer. Comparison of the performance of the Canadian and American airline industries tends to corroborate this hypothesis. Throughout the 1950s the distance-related taper in the fare per mile Air Canada charged was less than for American carriers. By the mid 1950s, Air Canada also had equalized the quality

[kk] As Table 8–4 indicates, the reduction in the fare per mile at the mean stage-length was not significantly different from zero for the northern Ontario and Quebec sector.

[ll] The average stage-length for these routes was 1300 miles compared to 730 for those city-pairs that did not receive direct tourist service.

of service across its route system—as measured by type of aircraft used—to a greater degree than had American carriers.

The predictions of the model as to the effect of exogenous events upon the Crown airline's behavior were also borne out. An increase in profits originating in the international or domestic mainline system was felt in fare and service changes across the route system. After the introduction of the Super Constellation, new loss services were initiated into an area of the country that, it was argued, was of critical importance to a support-maximizing Canadian public corporation. Profits generated by the introduction of the Viscount on mainline routes were also used to improve the quality of service to regional points—this time by extending this very aircraft to regional centers. Fares responded to both these events by moving downward. In addition, there is evidence to indicate that the spread between the loss and profitable sectors widened, which again is a finding in accordance with the model. Finally, by the end of the two fare revisions, the estimated fare regressions indicate that the Crown airline was maintaining more intra-sectoral fare equality in the geographically homogeneous loss sectors than on the transcontinental mainline routes.

The model of the Crown airline was used to derive predictions of the Crown airline's response to two events: an increase in profits on the mainline routes due to the introduction of a new aircraft thereon and a sudden decrease in profits earned on those same routes due to the entry of a second carrier. This chapter has examined the response of Air Canada to the first event. The next chapter examines its response to the second.

Chapter Nine

Competition and Government Policy: The Transition from Monopoly to Duopoly on the Transcontinental Route

INTRODUCTION

Postwar aviation policy in Canada has continuously wrestled with the issue of the degree of "competition" to be allowed on the mainline transcontinental run. Air Canada's monopoly position of the early 1950s has been eroded until by 1972 most of its transcontinental system from St. John's, Newfoundland, to Victoria, British Columbia, was shared with at least one and often two carriers.[a]

The impetus given to events by a change in the market structure on the transcontinental route provides the setting for a somewhat imperfectly controlled experiment to test the theory of a Crown airline. For instance, in providing a clear manifestation of public support for the airline when threatened by new entrants, it indirectly serves to validate the treatment of cross-subsidization as survival-oriented. It also provides a test as to whether the effects of this change in market structure correspond to those which the model of a public airline would have predicted.

While these events test the relevance of the behavioral model of the public airline, they also serve to emphasize the importance of adopting this framework both in formulating and evaluating government policy. In particular, the "monopoly" appellation as applied to a public firm contains emotive behavioral implications based on the profit-maximizing behavioral assumptions applicable to a privately owned firm. If these assumptions are not relevant for the behavior of a public firm, policy prescriptions implicitly founded on an inappropriate model are likely to lead to incorrect predictions of the effect of "competition" on the actions of the public firm.

[a]Canadian Pacific Airlines and/or one of the regional carriers–Pacific Western, Transair, Quebecair, Nordair, and Eastern Provincial.

THE INAUGURATION OF "COMPETITION"

An easing of the rigid government-imposed entry barriers on the transcontinental sector occurred in 1959. In 1957, the Liberal government, responsible for the founding of the government airline, was defeated for the first time in the postwar era. Throughout this period, Air Canada had retained its position as the sole transcontinental carrier. With the profits earned on the transcontinental and international sectors,[b] it had aggressively expanded its domestic system.[c]

Its chief rival was Canadian Pacific Airlines (CP Air)–a subsidiary of the Canadian Pacific Railway Company. The railroad, after its refusal in 1937 to participate on a minority basis in Trans-Canada Air Lines, entered the airline industry by purchasing a number of bush carriers during the Second World War.[d] As early as 1944, it was pushing for entry to the transcontinental and international routes.[1] The government, at this time, reiterated its original position that Air Canada was to be sole carrier on the transcontinental and international routes.[2] The first reversal in this policy occurred in 1949 when CP Air was granted the North and South Pacific international routes.[e] Subsequently, expansion in CP Air's route system occurred when it added routes from Vancouver to Mexico and Lima (1954); from Vancouver to Amsterdam (1955); from Toronto to Mexico (1955), Buenos Aires (1956), and Lisbon and Madrid (1957). However, prior to the Liberal defeat, CP Air was still denied entry to the transcontinental system.

Members of the Conservative government elected in 1957 had previously been highly critical of Air Canada's protected domestic position. The Conservative Member of Parliament who was to become Minister of Transport had in 1956 called for "all-out competition" between the government airline and private airlines on the transcontinental run.[3] Members of the Conservative party espoused the sale of the government airline to private interests.[4] The result was that as soon as it took office, the Conservative government received an application from CP Air for transcontinental rights.[f] A government with an avowed preference for more competition in the airline market,[g] and an airline

[b]The North Atlantic did not show a profit until after 1952.

[c]The airline's description of its policy in this period is somewhat lower key. "As long as our profitable routes were left to us, we would make enough money to carry the unprofitable ones." See Canada, Sessional Committee on Railways, Airlines and Shipping, *Minutes of Proceedings and Evidence,* No. 4 (November 27, 28, 1962), p. 330.

[d]See Chapter Three.

[e]The extent of the reversal is emphasized by the fact that Air Canada had already set up an operating base in Vancouver preparatory to launching this service. See Corbett, *Politics and the Airlines,* p. 168.

[f]CP Air had just been turned down by the former Liberal government in its bid for a transcontinental air freight service.

[g]Ironically, the leader of the Conservative party in 1937 had been an active supporter of the airline originally being set up as a government enterprise. See Corbett, *Politics and the Airlines,* pp. 111–2.

eagerly seeking to expand into the transcontinental market thus presented Air Canada with the most serious challenge it had yet encountered.

Subsequent events were to demonstrate the effectiveness of the Crown airline's cross-subsidization policy in generating support for Air Canada's position. Air Canada publicly stated that transcontinental competition would mean that the "extension of unprofitable services would be curtailed."[5] In response, groups from those areas of the country served by loss routes came forth to profess varying degrees of opposition to the proposed change in policy. The Regina Municipal Air Board requested a guarantee that the result of competition would not be an abandonment of the existing Prairie routes.[h] The Maritime Provinces Board of Trade made clear it did not oppose the notion of competition per se, but it demanded assurance that all Canadians would continue to get the services they were then receiving.[6] The Quebec City Board of Trade was the most forceful in that they asked for outright dismissal of the application. Having experienced service from both carriers,[i] they extolled the advantages of Air Canada compared to CP Air.[j]

The support so exhibited was effective. The newly elected Conservative Minister of Transport specified that competition would be considered only if it did not cause "major detrimental effects to existing operations."[7] With these terms of reference, two inquiries were made at his request into the desirability of competition on the transcontinental route.[8] Both concluded that competition on the scale proposed by CP Air would cause Air Canada to incur large deficits. The premise governing both reports, therefore, had to be the inconceivability that Air Canada's loss routes would be phased out[k] or that prices or service standards would alter so as to reduce the amount of cross-subsidization required.

Once the government decided to retain the support of those groups that benefited from the Crown airline, it was confronted with a decision as to whether to substitute direct subsidies for the existing indirect subsidies internal to the industry. Cross-subsidization, it has already been argued, will generally be preferred to direct subsidies by support-minded governments. Air Canada's own estimates placed the costs of competition for the first three years at over $30 million in lost revenue.[9] Faced with the choice of implementing competition

[h]*Globe and Mail* (Toronto), October 10, 1958, p. 20. The Saskatchewan government, controlled by a socialist party, opposed the extension of transcontinental rights to private enterprise.

[i]Air Canada had acquired this route in 1955 from CP Air in exchange for Eastern Canada to Mexico City.

[j]*Globe and Mail,* October 21, 1958, p. 2. Air Canada had replaced CP Air's DC-3 service with Viscount service.

[k]To be fair, both reports do mention that transfer of loss routes from Air Canada to regional carriers might be considered. However, their off-hand treatment of this critical issue is indicative of the unpalatable nature of this alternative.

that would entail contributing from government revenues a sum of uncertain but probably large magnitude for direct subsidies or continuing to provide service to outlying points via cross-subsidization at no cost to the treasury, the government predictably gravitated in the latter direction. If there had been no costs to ignoring its original promise to introduce competition, there might have been no change in the number of carriers on the transcontinental system.

But there were other complications the government could not ignore. Extensions of CP Air's route system to Mexico from eastern Canada (1955), to Buenos Aires (1956), and to Lisbon and Madrid (1957) had led this airline to report losses of $113,000 in 1957, $1.9 million in 1958, and $3.9 million in 1959.[l] The airline let it be known that continuation of its unprofitable services—both foreign and domestic[m]—depended upon the introduction of cross-subsidization. CP Air, in the words of its president, required "some 'cream' routes to balance its economics." [10]

The Air Transport Board, therefore, recommended that in order "to strengthen the position of C.P.A. in the international field . . ." [11] one flight per day between Vancouver, Winnipeg, Toronto, and Montreal be granted the airline. The government implemented the Board's recommendation in May of 1959. Thus, what had started out as an exercise in competition became really just an extension of the policy of cross-subsidization. The transcontinental traveller was now to support CP Air's domestic and international passengers as well. That the resulting competition was so limited obviated the necessity of implementing a program of subsidies for Air Canada's social routes—which alternative was so unpalatable that it was not explicitly discussed in any of the studies that examined the desirability of a change in market structure. The decrease in profits likely to be occasioned the Crown airline by this marginal change in market structure promised to be sufficiently small that the price or service adjustments required to offset these losses would draw little public attention.

THE EFFECT OF COMPETITION ON THE FARE STRUCTURE

Although service was initially implemented with 89-seat Britannias, CP Air by 1962 was able to offer some 141 seats per flight in DC-8's.[n] This gradual expansion in capacity permitted the airline to maintain a relatively constant share of the transcontinental market from 1959 through 1965—some 12.7

[l]Canadian Pacific Railway Company, *Annual Report, 1959,* p. 15, blamed low load factors on these international routes for its poor performance.

[m]It operated routes north from Vancouver through British Columbia, the Yukon and north from Edmonton into the North West Territories. It is difficult to judge whether the government worried more about losing the domestic or the international routes.

[n]The DC-8 which was introduced in 1961, replaced the Bristol Britannia that had been bought in late 1957.

percent of the passenger-miles flown.[o] The effect of the "competition" policy was therefore to reduce the potential profit available to the Crown airline for cross-subsidization purposes.

To conform to the proposed model, Air Canada should have reacted by increasing prices or reducing services on the loss sectors. As already seen, the model is less explicit as to the direction in which prices or service frequencies on the transcontinental sector are predicted to move. The model, however, as presently developed, has ignored the ramifications of the particular manner in which profits available for cross-subsidization are changed. Entry of a second carrier may no longer permit the initial occupant unilaterally to set fares it would find optimal. Should collusion break down, we might expect fares to decrease rapidly. Fortunately for our predictions, the manner by which the second participant was introduced removes this complication. The restriction of one flight per day imposed upon CP Air made it extremely unlikely that Air Canada would feel itself constrained from adopting the fare level it desired. As evidence of this, from April 1962 through April 1965, Air Canada permitted CP Air to adopt lower fares on the four transcontinental sectors it served.[p] Thus, Air Canada may be treated as having been capable of varying service or fare levels unhindered by strategic considerations.[q]

But competition policy was not the only force at work that should have affected prices. A significant downward shift in cost curves resulted from the introduction of the DC-8 in April 1960 and the Vickers Vanguard in 1961. System operating costs per available ton-mile fell from 37.1¢ in 1959 to 31.3¢ in 1961. Since both the DC-8 and the Vanguard were initially applied to the transcontinental sector,[r] the effect of this change was, *ceteris paribus,* to increase the potential profits available from the transcontinental run.

Thus, the effect of changing technology on fares should have been the opposite to that resulting from the government's relaxing of the entry barriers on the transcontinental run. The relative magnitude of the effect that these two offsetting events had on profit potential must be determined if a testable hypothesis as to the direction of price changes is to be developed.

Between 1959, the year before the new equipment was introduced, and 1962,

[o]Canada, Department of Transport, "Further Airline Competition in Canada: A Study of the Consequences of any Further Development of Domestic Mainline Competition in Canada" (unpublished paper prepared by Stephen Wheatcroft, Ottawa, February 1966, mimeographed), p. 11. The annual shares were in 1959, 11.4%; 1960, 13.0%; 1961, 9.8%; 1962, 14.2%; 1963, 14.7%; 1964, 14.4%; and 1965, 11.6%.

[p]The fares for Air Canada and CP Air were: Vancouver-Toronto, \$109 and \$99; Vancouver-Montreal, \$120 and \$110; Vancouver-Winnipeg, \$63 and \$58; Winnipeg-Toronto, \$52 and \$47; Toronto-Montreal, \$23 and \$20.

[q]This assumption has additional support since the president of Air Canada testified that up until the day of filing the new 1962 rates he was under the "impression . . . mistaken or otherwise" that CP Air would duplicate the fares. See Canada, Sessional Committee on Railways, Airlines and Shipping, *Minutes of Proceedings and Evidence,* No. 1 (December 2, 3, 4, 1963), p. 28.

[r]The Maritimes also were to receive Vanguard service almost immediately.

the year the fare structure was revised, operating costs on the transcontinental route fell from 27.07¢ per available ton-mile to 21.40¢.[12] During the same time period, interest costs for the entire system increased from 1.05¢ to 1.94¢ per available ton-mile.[13] If this figure is added to operating costs on the transcontinental route, total costs thereon decreased from 28.12¢ to 23.34¢ per available ton-mile. However, this was accompanied by a decrease in load factors resulting from the replacement of 82-seat Super Constellations and 62-seat North Stars with 133-seat DC-8's and 108-seat Vanguards. By using the transcontinental weight load factor, the 1959 and 1962 cost per revenue ton-mile becomes 53.15¢ and 45.15¢, respectively.[14] But, introduction of the new aircraft not only reduced costs, it also resulted in a shift of traffic from first class to economy (see Table 8–5). As we shall see, 1962 transcontinental fares generally were either unchanged or were above their 1959 levels; yet, passenger revenue per revenue ton-mile thereon fell from 57.70¢ in 1959 to 50.60¢ in 1962. The net effect of the revenue and cost reductions arising from the introduction of new aircraft was to increase the margin between passenger revenue and costs per revenue ton-mile from 4.55¢ to 5.45¢—or by 20.8 percent.[s]

On the other hand, the introduction of CP Air to the transcontinental market reduced Air Canada's profits on this route by at least the share of the market captured by the new entrant and perhaps by more if there were economies of scale in this market. Between 1959 and 1965, CP Air captured an average of 12 percent of the market. But much of the transcontinental market consists of local traffic—from which very little profit was generated. If this traffic is excluded and Toronto-Montreal traffic is also ignored, CP Air's share in the early 1960s amounted to over 30 percent. Therefore the net effect of the introduction of new aircraft and competition on the transcontinental sector was to shift the Crown airline's potential profit frontier downward.[t]

Substantiation of this conclusion is provided by the fact that deficits of $2.6, $6.5, and $3.5 million were subsequently incurred in 1960, 1961, and 1962, respectively. A brief but ill-fated experiment in lower fares was attempted but quickly rescinded in 1961.[u] By 1962, a new fare structure was adopted that, because it lasted for six years, shall be assumed to have reflected the airline's objectives. Since the net effect on profits of the change in market structure and

[s]This estimate is biased upwards because the increase in interest charges used to generate total costs for the transcontinental route was derived from system averages whereas most of this increase was directly attributable to only a portion of the routes—primarily the international and transcontinental sectors.

[t]The strength of this deduction is reinforced if the profit frontier is regarded not as a one period constraint but as the present value of future profits. Then the Crown airline faced with limited but successful entry might now consider its long-run profit frontier to have fallen.

[u]The 1961 fare revision is ignored here since its brief duration indicates that it was no more than part of a search procedure on the part of the airline's management for an optimal fare structure.

technology was negative, to conform with the predictions of our model, the resulting fares should have shown an increase at least on the loss sectors. In fact, as Table 9–1 indicates, the mean fare per mile was increased significantly on all three loss routes. The Maritimes, however, received a much smaller increment than either of the other two loss routes. This accords with the support-maximizing behavioral hypothesis, for during the Air Transport Board's hearings into the desirability of transcontinental competition, the majority of groups supporting the maintenance of Air Canada's transcontinental monopoly came from the Maritimes.[v] As Chapter Eight recounted, the airline had previously been reducing the disparity in the mean fare per mile amongst its loss sectors. Provided now with more accurate information on the support it would receive when threatened, Air Canada chose to readjust the relative benefits that each loss sector received.[w]

The model of the public airline also predicted that the price spread between sectors should have widened in response to the decrease in profit potential occasioned by entry. The results in Table 9–1 indicate that the difference in the statistic being used here to approximate the average fare per mile charged the mainline and loss sectors widened between 1960 and 1962.[x]

Finally, the effects of the change in technology and in government policy served to offset one another on the transcontinental and east-west routes, and to leave their mean fare per mile virtually unchanged (Table 9–1). However, as Table 9–2 indicates, the fare equations for these two routes were twisted in a clockwise direction. This resulted in increasing the average fare per mile for routes with stage-lengths of less than 1000 miles (see Figure 9–1). It might be surmised that the lack of support the airline had received from many of the communities along the transcontinental route reduced the importance of maintaining comparability of fares per mile amongst city-pairs in this sector.

An equally plausible explanation of the twisting of the fare structure is that many of the shorter routes on this sector incur losses and therefore should have received price increases according to the model proposed herein. Figure 9–1 lends support to this interpretation. It indicates that the fare structures of the corridor and northern Ontario and Quebec routes shifted upwards to result in a mean fare per mile approximately equal to the fare per mile for transcontinental

[v]Air Transport Board, *Transcontinental Air Services,* p. 8. This region was singled out as being the most strongly opposed to CP Air's bid. There is therefore a strong presumption that this was not only the area most sensitive to changing services, but that it was also the best area in which to buy support in terms of per dollar of loss incurred.

[w]Earlier it was reported that Quebec City had been a strong supporter of the Crown airline. Quebec routes are included in the corridor sector and thus whether the Crown airline remembered this support or chose to value it is obscured in Table 9–1. Closer examination of this sector produces the observation that the mean fare per mile for the Quebec routes increased less than for the other routes in the corridor.

[x]That it did so rules out the competing model–I(A)–discussed in Chapter Five, for this model predicted that fare differentials should have narrowed as a result of entry to the mainline sector.

Table 9–1. Fare per Mile, at Mean Stage-Length, by Sector, 1958, 1962 (¢)

Year / Period	*East-West*		*Transcontinental*		*Maritimes*		*Corridor*		*N. Ontario*	
	Fare	*Change*	*Fare*	*Change*	*Fare*	*Change*	*Fare*	*Change*	*Fare*	*Change*
1958	5.35 (0.05)[a]		5.68 (0.04)		6.03 (0.10)		6.21 (0.18)		5.82 (0.24)	
1958–1962		–.09[c] (.06)[b]		+.07[c] (.06)		+.46 (.16)		+1.41 (0.35)		+1.86 (0.42)
1962	5.26 (0.04)		5.75 (0.05)		6.49 (0.12)		7.61 (0.30)		7.68 (0.34)	

[a]Figures in parentheses indicate the standard error of the estimate.

[b]The standard error of the difference in the mean fare per mile was calculated assuming the errors in each time period were independent of one another.

[c]Indicates the change in mean fare per mile was not significant for $t_{.025,180}$.

Source: Table 9–2.

Table 9–2. Fare Regressions, Disaggregated by Sector, 1958, 1962

Year	*Standard*		*Deviations from the Standard Intercept (Col. 1) and Slope (Col. 2)*							
	East-West		*Transcontinental*		*Maritimes*		*Corridor*		*N. Ontario*	
	(1) Intercept	*(2) Slope*	*(3) Intercept*	*(4) Slope*	*(5) Intercept*	*(6) Slope*	*(7) Intercept*	*(8) Slope*	*(9) Intercept*	*(10) Slope*
1958	3.74 (4.68)[a]	.052 (83.8)[b]	3.04 (2.24)[b]	–.001 (0.58)	....	.002 (2.01)[b]	....	....	....	–.004 (1.26)
1962	11.14 (9.89)[b]	.048 (67.2)[b]	....	....	–5.27 (2.90)[b]	.007 (3.19)[b]	–7.38 (2.77)[b]	.018 (3.05)[b]	–5.72 (1.79)	.014 (1.92)[b]

[a]Figures in parentheses are t statistics. Those for the standard equation indicate whether the estimates differ from zero. Those beneath the other estimates indicate whether they are significantly different from the standard estimates contained in columns (1) and (2).

[b]Indicates significant value for two-tailed t test with 5 percent level of significance.

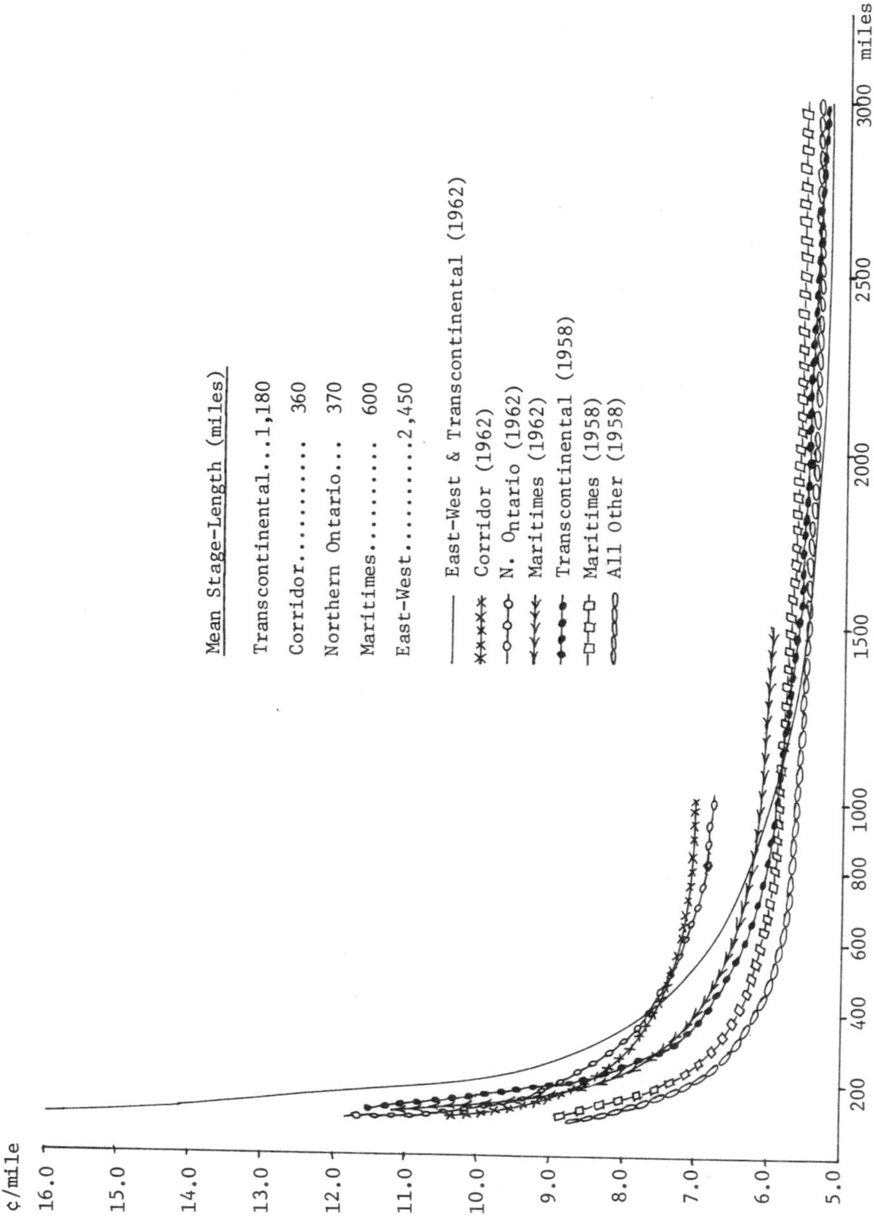

Figure 9-1. Estimated Fare Structure—Cents per Mile Plotted against Distance, 1958, 1962.

routes having a stage-length equal to the loss routes' mean. It is interesting to note that Table 9–2 indicates this latter shift was accomplished primarily by an increase in the slope of the fare equation of the loss sectors. Although the mean price increased on these loss sectors, their greater regional homogeneity resulted in more importance being laid upon minimizing the intra-sectoral differences thereon than on the transcontinental route.

Thus, the change in fare structure resulting from the introduction of competition on the transcontinental sector conforms closely with the interpretation of the behavior of a government-owned airline proposed herein.

THE PRAIRIE BRANCH LINE ABANDONMENT

The reaction of the Crown airline to an increased potential for cross-subsidization in the 1950s was an extension of its domestic route system. It is, therefore, not surprising to find that, conversely, the loss in profits due to the introduction of a second carrier on the transcontinental sector led to the abandonment of some routes.[y] In 1961, Air Canada applied to the government for the right to abandon the so-called "Prairie Milk Run"—the local route from Winnipeg to Brandon, Yorkton, Regina, Swift Current, Medicine Hat, and Lethbridge.

Ostensibly, the reason for discontinuation was that only DC-3's could operate into the airports along this route and that maintaining only two aircraft of this type in an otherwise all turbine fleet had become impractical. However, since other airlines have operated fleets with very few aircraft of a single type,[15] a more important consideration was at stake. Practicality for a government airline must be measured in terms of support per dollar of subsidy. Air Canada was losing $300,000 per year on this route, [16] while average boardings were less than 2.5 passengers per flight.[17] This particular route was the most costly deficit sector operated by Air Canada. As Table 9–3 shows, the loss per passenger on the Prairies and Foothills route was greater than anywhere else. Equally important, the deficit offered a very low return to the airline. Outside of CP Air's home province of British Columbia, the Prairies had evinced the least support for the government airline during the transcontinental hearings.

Even so, the route was abandoned in such a way as to cause the government the least discomfiture. No other airline would take the route over without promise of subsidy payments.[z] Because this was apparently not acceptable to

[y]It is true that service to Trois Rivières was initiated in 1963 but this action involved special circumstances. The reason for inauguration of this service was explained by the airline. "The Minister of Transport had a certain affiliation with Three Rivers and he asked that we make a study [of landing there]." See Canada, Standing Committee on Railways, Canals, and Telegraph Lines, *Minutes of Proceedings and Evidence* no. 3 (June 22, 23, 1964), p. 359. The Minister of Transport was the Member of Parliament from Trois Rivières.

[z]See the section on regional airlines for a description of the evolution of regional aviation policy.

Table 9–3. The Relative Cost per Passenger of Generating Support on the Loss Sectors, 1957

Route	*Loss* ($000)	*Revenue Passenger-Miles* (000)	*Loss per RPM* (¢)	*Average Stage-Length*[a] (miles)	*Loss per Passenger* ($)
Toronto-Ottawa-Montreal	951	161,489	0.6	248	1.49
Pacific Coast	1,334	17,482	7.6	60[b]	4.56
Prairies and Foothills	1,403	23,818	5.9	154[b]	8.09
Great Lakes	118	32,606	0.4	303	1.21
Northern Ontario and Quebec	1,193	21,848	5.4	147	7.94
Toronto-London-Windsor-Cleveland	1,071	33,292	3.2	136	4.35
Montreal-Quebec-Saguenay-Sept Isles	861	24,619	3.5	190	6.65
Maritimes	1,801	123,267	1.5	236	3.54
Newfoundland	342	36,678	0.9	235	2.12

[a]Taken from Air Canada route system, 1963.

[b]Since no category existed in 1963 corresponding to these two classifications, the average was worked out from the Air Canada time tables for 1957.

Source: Air Transport Board, *Transcontinental Route Hearings, Exhibit Book,* TCA Exhibits No. 64 and 420.

the government, Air Canada provided an indirect subsidy. A Viscount and two DC-3's, along with spare parts, that together were worth $220,000[aa] were given Transair in return for a guarantee that it would provide service on this route for three years.[18]

CONCLUSION

Although the introduction of a second carrier to the transcontinental sector was billed as a major shift in competition policy, the restriction of CP Air to one flight per day meant this change was hardly a radical alteration in market structure. Yet, it is precisely in the case of such marginal changes that the model of the Crown airline is most likely to be applicable.

Air Canada, faced with a loss of potential profits from its transcontinental sector—profits which would have been used to subsidize support-generating loss services—made adjustments on both margins. The unprofitable or "social" routes suffered an increase in prices and a decrease in services. The transcontinental route was denied a rate decrease—a reduction which in the light of the Crown airline's behavior in the 1950s should have resulted from the introduction of the

[aa]One suspects the actual value was higher since Air Canada managed to dispose of a Viscount for $400,000 that year, and also because the penalty clause in the Transair contract amounted to $500,000 if service was discontinued.

long-range jet aircraft. Although prices did not increase everywhere on this sector, profit margins must have done so since the introduction of long-range jet aircraft substantially reduced costs. Thus, the fact that prices on the transcontinental sector did not increase was the result of a "fortunate" juxtaposition of the change in competition policy with the introduction of new cost-reducing technology. The lack of this coincidence when the second change in market structure was implemented (Chapter Eleven) meant that similar behavior on the part of the Crown airline led to a very different result—that is, marked increases in the prices of all sectors.

Thus, even though the introduction of a second carrier (CP Air) into the transcontinental market offered a choice of carriers for the first time to the public travelling thereon,[bb] it involved a cost. Prices were either increased to or maintained at levels higher than they would have otherwise been. Merely treating Air Canada as a normal profit-maximizing monopolist would have led to this conclusion only with special assumptions—a joint production process, and increasing returns to scale.[cc] The power of the model of the public airline lies in the fact that its prediction about the effect of entry is not dependent upon prior determination of the industry's production function, which is an advantage not easily ignored given the conflicting econometric evidence as to the existence of economies of scale in the airline industry.[19] Thus, the reactions of Air Canada to CP Air's initial occupancy of the transcontinental market accord with the actual degeneration in the performance of all markets—a degeneration the possiblity of which was ignored by those who relied upon standard models of the firm.

[bb] Corbett (*Politics and the Airlines*) stresses the importance of this choice theme in his inter-country comparison of the air transport industry without ever coming to grips with any other aspect of the performance of the industry.

[cc] The concluding chapter examines whether this particular alternative serves to explain more than this episode.

Chapter Ten

The Demand Function for the Crown Airline's Services

Estimates of the demand curves faced by Air Canada along with the theory of the public corporation will be used in a subsequent chapter to explain the Crown airline's pricing and product policy in the late 1960s. The airline's behavior in response to CP Air's 1958 entry to the transcontinental run has already been adduced as corroboration for the model. In this particular case, the price on the mainline sectors remained relatively constant—though the mark-up of price over cost increased—while the loss sectors suffered increases in both prices and mark-ups. But the model suggests the Crown airline's response to entry could very well have been to increase the price charged in the profitable sector. Indeed, as Chapter Eleven will show, this was the result of a second round of entry that occurred in the late 1960s. In order that this accord with the model, the Crown airline's fare would have to have been below the profit-maximizing price on these sectors. This chapter provides estimates of the price elasticities for a select sample of Air Canada's routes. In combination with cost data, these estimates will be used in the following chapter to justify treating the Crown airline's pricing policy on the transcontinental and international routes as corroborating the support-maximizing model. These estimates also serve another purpose. Although the theory suggests that cross-subsidization will occur within the route system of a Crown airline, it does not stipulate how close to the profit-maximizing level prices in some sectors will move. Combination of the estimates of the price elasticity along with evidence on costs helps to answer this question.

THE MODEL

Time series regressions of the demand for air travel have been beset by the fact that a complex set of factors has governed the growth of air travel in the last 25 years. The rise in real income and the fall in air fares, the reduction in travel time, increased schedule frequency, and better safety records have all led to greater air travel. The simultaneous occurrence of these factors is not so much a problem as is the lack of data containing independent variation in these variables.[1] Time series data are often so highly correlated that long-run trends dominate the movement of all other variables.[2]

While multicollinearity and paucity of degrees of freedom affect the statistical reliability of many of the time series analyses, the highly aggregative nature of the equations makes interpretation of the resulting parameter estimates difficult. Most studies have aggregated across both routes and classes of service.[3] The estimated elasticities—associated with such dependent variables as speed, yield, or income—are really weighted averages of the elasticities of the underlying micro-relationships.[4] This average may be composed of non-corresponding micro-elasticities. For example, the estimate of the aggregate fare elasticity may be affected by the micro-income elasticities. Furthermore, the weights used to construct the macro-variable will critically influence the value of the estimated macro-elasticity. For instance, if the average uses fixed weights summing to one to construct the macro-variable (as Bartlett does), the weights applied to the micro-elasticities will not sum to one.[a]

Further problems with these aggregative studies arise from their failure to consider the effects of the supply side of the market process. The availability of lower-priced coach service has not been universal. It was first offered on long-haul routes and only later on the shorter, more dense routes. Failure to recognize this tends to result in elasticities higher than would have resulted had prices moved downwards uniformly on all routes.[5]

In order to minimize these difficulties, regressions of the demand for the Crown airline's services were performed at the route level. This automatically reduces the problem of interpretation arising in aggregative studies. The results will confirm the existence of differences between routes and thus the appropriateness of this separation. Five Canadian routes were chosen for estimation purposes. Three are long-distance—Toronto-Vancouver, Canada-United Kingdom, and Toronto-Montreal-Florida. The first represents a trans-continental route that contains a mix of business and tourist traffic. The second is a trans-Atlantic route, on which tourist travel predominates, that others have claimed is price elastic.[b] The Florida route is also dominated by tourist traffic, but of a kind one might or might not expect to be price-conscious.[c] It is on

[a]A detailed discussion of the problems of aggregation in estimating the demand for air travel is contained in Phillip K. Verleger, Jr., "A Point-to-Point Model of the Demand for Air Transportation" (unpublished Ph.D. dissertation, Massachusetts Institute of Technology, 1971), pp. 50–63.

[b]Stephen Wheatcroft in "Elasticity of Demand for North Atlantic Travel" (unpublished paper prepared for the International Air Transport Association, Montreal, 1964, mimeographed), p. 5, calculates the summer elasticity as −2.0 and the winter elasticity as −1.8 for Canadian North Atlantic travel.

[c]Paul W. Cherington in *Airline Price Policy: A Study of Domestic Airline Passenger Fares* (Boston: Division of Research, Graduate School of Business Administration, Harvard

these three routes that Air Canada earns the profits that are used for cross-subsidization purposes. The other two routes—Toronto-Montreal and Toronto-New York—are short-distance flights. Compared to the long-distance routes, business and government personnel account for a greater percentage of traffic on these two routes. However, while rail service offers competition for air service on the Toronto-Montreal route, there is virtually no acceptable alternative to air travel on the Toronto-New York route. Therefore we might expect the former to be more price elastic than the latter.

The problems of interpretation that have beset other attempts to estimate the price elasticity of air travel are further reduced in this study by disaggregating the demand equation, not only by route, but also by class of service. Since survey evidence indicates the two classes often differ substantially as to the percentage of traffic accounted for by business or by pleasure travellers,[6] and since for some of the routes under consideration here first-class traffic often composed up to 20 percent of the total, it seemed unrealistic to treat the two classes as if they exhibited the same price and income elasticity.[d] The approach adopted here disaggregates by the most prominent division—first class versus economy. However, to the extent that more than one price still existed in each class, aggregation problems have not completely disappeared. Fortunately "special fares" were not as widespread in Canada as in the United States. During the period in question, neither youth, military, "Golden Age," standby, night coach, or "Discover Canada" fares were applicable to the markets chosen.

The problem of specifying the demand equation was reduced by choosing a relatively homogeneous time period—the years 1961 through 1966.[e] Many of the influences that affect air travel but are difficult to quantify, such as safety, growing public acceptance, and the introduction of new equipment, were relatively constant over this period. Air Canada made no major equipment changes[f] while frequency and schedules were not violently altered. Although alternate modes of travel existed, either they were no longer viable alternatives, such as rail from Toronto to New York, or their price and service characteristics remained relatively constant. Monthly data, 70 observations,[g] were used so that the advantage of homogeneity in removing non-quantifiable variables from consideration is not offset by a paucity of data.

The choice of variable to represent the effect of the general level of economic activity upon air travel presented a problem. To a degree, this choice should hinge upon the relative proportion of business and pleasure travellers. It might

---

University, 1958), p. 168, relates the completely different reaction to price reductions of the New York to Florida and Chicago to Florida markets.

[d]Straszheim, *The International Airline Industry*, p. 271, also has voiced some doubts as to the suitability of treating price elasticities as the same across different classes of service.

[e]As the next section explains, this was modified for the first-class demand equations to include only the period 1962 through 1966.

[f]This obviates taking the change in travel time into account.

[g]The November 1966 strike and subsequent month were omitted.

be reasonable to assume that business travellers are more likely to be affected by a change in overall business activity (G.N.P.); pleasure travellers more by their real personal disposable income. However, because of the high degree of collinearity behind most of the national accounts series, the choice is less crucial than it would seem. Taylor, in the context of a general macro-model, using a principal-components analysis, found no more than three or four independent series [7] and that one, "general prosperity," accounted for over 97 percent of total variation. Bartlett, in estimating the demand for air travel, experimented with a large number of variables that might be used to represent business activity and found that his estimates of price elasticity were not affected by the choice of income variable.[8]

However, the advantage of the short-run case-study approach to demand estimation adopted here is somewhat reduced by the difficulty of obtaining other than annual data series on income levels, and in particular, on local income levels.[9] Since good monthly figures exist for Canadian labor income, this is the series used—for both first- and economy-class traffic. This raises two questions. First, it may not be the relevant variable for either class. Secondly, it may not be the correct figure for individual routes. In answer to the first, it seems that it is likely to be relevant for coach class, and collinear to whatever variable is "relevant" to first class. Secondly, experiments with other variables—industrial production, and new orders which were virtually collinear with labor income—had little effect on estimated price elasticities.

The use of monthly data presents several further complications. First, the travel market differs across seasons—because of the changing mix of business and vacation travel. The use of monthly data is meant to use the additional variation across months to estimate price elasticities. Therefore, the data was not deseasonalized using a smoothing process. To do so would have confused the relationship between changing prices and changing fluctuations in air travel—especially over a season. In fact, it is difficult to determine just how much information would be left in the time series. Instead seasonal dummies were used for intercept terms.[h]

Secondly, it might be argued that it is unlikely that there is a unique price elasticity for the whole year. The reaction to price changes will differ both because of differing socio-economic characteristics of each market and because of special fare packages in existence in different seasons. Although the regressions employed a simple linear functional form, binary variables are used to test the existence of a significant variance in the estimated elasticities for different seasons.

As already indicated, previous demand studies for air travel have ignored the

[h]The number of seasonals required for each route varied depending upon the route's traffic profile. If, for instance, traffic appeared to have three distinct peaks, three seasonals were chosen.

influence of supply factors. It has been argued that the period chosen for this study is relatively homogeneous and that it was so chosen because most quality differences are hard to quantify. But there is one factor that was changing during this period that undoubtedly affected demand. This is the probability that a given flight could be caught, or a given fare obtained. This probability is a function of the load factor on a given route—the ratio of passenger-miles to available seat-miles. Although the exact level of the load factor at which traffic suppression begins to occur is difficult to specify, the routes chosen for this study often experienced load factors as high as 80 percent. The experiments that attempt to account for the effect of this capacity or supply constraint will be discussed in the next section.

THE RESULTS

Economy Traffic

The demand for economy travel (Q_E) is essentially postulated to be a function of the economy price (*PE*), the first-class price (*PF*), and the income variable (*Y*). Other time series studies of air travel demand have experienced some difficulty with multicollinearity.[10] Fortunately, the independent variables on most of the routes exhibit very little collinearity. Holding the influence of other variables constant, only the partial correlation coefficients between the economy- and the first-class price for the United Kingdom route and between the economy price and income for the Toronto-New York route are significantly different from zero.[i]

Table 10–1 presents the regression results for each of the five routes.[j] Own-price elasticities are all negative and significant[k] except for Toronto-New York, which exhibits a positive elasticity not significantly different from zero. Of those routes with a price elasticity significantly different from zero, the transcontinental route exhibits the highest price-elasticity (–2.1); Toronto-Montreal, the least (–0.32). The long-haul routes, Florida, the United Kingdom, and Toronto-Vancouver, are price elastic; the short-haul routes are price inelastic.[l] The cross-elasticities with respect to the first-class price are all positive; however, only on the transcontinental and Toronto-Montreal routes are they significantly different from zero. The highest estimated cross-elasticities (0.88 and 0.84) are found on the United Kingdom and transcontinental routes. All income elasticities are significantly positive—the highest values are found on the

[i] A two-tailed test at five percent level of significance was used.

[j] All elasticities are calculated at the mean value of the variables concerned.

[k] The Durbin-Watson statistic indicates that autocorrelation exists for the transcontinental and United Kingdom regressions and may therefore have biased our test in favor of rejecting the null hypothesis of zero-price effect.

[l] Only the short-haul routes are significantly different from –1.

Table 10–1. Price and Income Elasticities of the Demand for Economy Class, by Route

Route	*Economy Price Elasticity* $\eta(PE)$	*First-Class Price Cross-Elasticity* $\eta(PF)$	*Income Elasticity* $\eta(Y)$	R^2	*F*	*Durbin-Watson Statistic*
Transcontinental	−2.06 (2.09)[c]	0.84 (2.30)	3.96 (10.93)	.83	87.6 (1,66)[d]	.96[a]
Florida	−1.26 (2.20)	0.31 (0.51)*	1.80 (5.05)	.86	56.7 (1,61)	1.65[b]
United Kingdom	−1.58 (2.48)	0.88 (1.42)*	2.50 (5.74)	.84	75.4 (1,65)	1.32[a]
Toronto-Montreal	−0.32 (2.22)	.33 (2.07)	1.61 (21.64)	.95	200.1 (1,52)	1.74
Toronto-New York	0.45 (0.72)*	0.19 (0.61)*	1.12 (4.72)	.73	27.3 (1,51)	1.76

[a]Reject hypothesis that there is no autocorrelation.

[b]Indeterminate range of the Durbin-Watson; no serial correlation using Theil-Nagar test.

[c]The t statistic; an asterisk indicates $t < t_{.025}$ for the degrees of freedom relevant to that equation.

[d]Indicates degrees of freedom of the F statistic; all are significant to the 1 percent level.

long-haul routes (3.96 for the transcontinental); the lowest on the short-haul routes (1.12 for Toronto-New York).[m]

Although these results are less aggregative than most, they still neglect the possibility that price elasticities differed across seasons. In order to test whether or not seasonal differences are significant, the demand equations were re-estimated using binary variables to allow the price elasticity to vary in different seasons. Table 10–2 reports the results of the estimates for the price elasticity for specific periods within the year. The second column reports the elasticity for what is in effect the excluded category—the months not specifically considered in column three.

For all routes this disaggregation shows the peak period traffic to be more price elastic than travel during the rest of the year. The economy price elasticity on the transcontinental route during the summer months increases to –3.40 as compared to –2.1 reported in Table 10–1; Toronto-Montreal increases to –0.82 from –0.32, but still remains price inelastic; while Toronto-New York shows an increase to –1.47 from +0.45.[n] On the United Kingdom route, the summer price elasticity remains at –1.5, close to the previous result. Florida also exhibits a higher price elasticity during the peak period January-February (–1.93) as compared to the previously estimated yearly average of –1.3.

If the first-class price is treated in the same manner, the cross-elasticity in the off-peak season is found to increase. Equation (10–1) reports the results of this approach for the transcontinental route. In these results, $\eta(PE)_1$ and $\eta(PF)_1$, are the estimated economy price elasticity and first-class price cross-elasticity respectively for the summer months of May through September. $\eta(PE)_0$ and $\eta(PF)_0$ are the same elasticities but applicable to the rest of the year. The t statistics indicate whether the reported elasticity is significantly different from zero. The cross-elasticity outside the summer months has increased from .84 to 1.3, while it is not significantly different from zero during the summer months. Similar results were obtained for the other routes.

[m]It is possible that heteroscedasticity of the error terms may have existed in this formulation and that the t values were therefore biased. To test whether this problem existed, Bartlett's test was run for each of the equations reported in Table 10–1. Each sample was divided at its mid-point. The χ^2 statistics for the transcontinental, Florida, United Kingdom, Toronto-Montreal and Toronto-New York routes were calculated as 4.25; 1.30; 2.06; 1.12; and 1.49, respectively ($\chi^2_{.05}$ = 3.84; $\chi^2_{.01}$ = 6.635). Although this test is only approximate, it indicates that apart from the transcontinental route, the assumption of homoscedasticity is not violated. To further substantiate this, additional regressions were run after dividing through each variable by number of employed and including it as an additional variable. The results were not much different from those initially obtained. For instance, the own-price elasticity for Vancouver was estimated to be –3.02 (t = 2.79), for Florida as –1.13 (t = 2.00), and for the United Kingdom as –1.46 (t = 2.01).

[n]This is the only peak period elasticity which is not significantly different from zero at the significance level of 5 percent adopted here.

Table 10–2. Regressions for Economy Class with Price Elasticities Allowed to Vary Across Seasons, by Route

Route	*General Economy Price Elasticity*[a]	*Specific Period Economy Price Elasticity*[b]					*First-Class Price Cross-Elasticity*	*Income Elasticity*	*F*	R^2	*Durbin-Watson*
Transcontinental	0.56 t=(0.50)*[c]			−3.40 (2.20) [3.43][d]			0.89 (2.60)	3.82 (11.40)	83.9 (1,66)[f]	.86	1.08
Florida	−1.93 (3.02)	−1.18 (1.22)* [0.73]*	−1.76 (0.38)* [1.77]*	0.31 (0.06)* [1.91]*	2.58 (0.49)* [2.51]	0.64 (0.20)* [1.68]*	0.40 (0.67)*	1.72 (4.80)	37.7 (1,57)	.87	1.85
United Kingdom	0.26 (0.26)*		−1.15 (1.94)* [3.47]	−1.46 (2.33) [1.28]*[e]			0.34 (0.63)*	2.32 (5.11)	74.5 (1,63)	.88	1.67
Toronto-Montreal	−0.28 (1.63)*		−0.37 (0.95)* [0.36]*	−0.82 (2.18) [1.71]*			0.39 (2.42)	1.56 (18.66)	146.4 (1,50)	.95	1.90
Toronto-New York	1.76 (2.16)	1.21 (0.90)* [0.44]*	−1.47 (1.44)* [3.50]	1.12 (0.72)* [0.58]*			−0.42 (1.38)*	1.06 (4.78)	24.8 (1,48)	.79	1.84

[a]Indicates price elasticity for periods not specifically covered in column 3.

[b]The periods covered vary route by route. That for the transcontinental route refers to the months May through September; for Florida the individual periods are March-April, May-June, July-August, September-October, and November-December, respectively; for the United Kingdom they refer to May-June-September-October, and July-August, respectively; for Toronto-Montreal, May-June-October, and July-August-September, respectively; for Toronto-New York, April-May-June, July-August-September, October-November-December, respectively.

[c]The t statistics in parentheses indicate whether the elasticity is significantly different from zero. An asterisk indicates $t < t_{.025}$ for the number of degrees of freedom relevant to that equation.

[d]The t statistics in brackets indicate whether the elasticity for specific periods differs from the general economy elasticity reported in column 2.

[e]This t statistic indicates whether the July-August elasticity differs from the May-June-September-October elasticity.

[f]Indicates degrees of freedom for the F statistic. All are significant to the 1 percent level.

	$\eta(PE)_0$	$\eta(PE)_1$	$\eta(PF)_0$	$\eta(PF)_1$	$\eta(Y)$	R^2	$F(1,63)$	D.W.[o]	
	0.85	−3.21	1.31	0.48	4.18	.86	70.3	1.08	(10–1)
t =	(0.69)	(2.65)	(3.52)	(0.80)	(12.99) .				

Both of the above formulations, with the income variable included in simple unlagged form, ignore the influence of past income levels on demand. When as many as 20 percent of the travellers on the transcontinental system decide upon their trip 8 to 12 months in advance, this may lead to biased results. Of course, whereas past income levels may affect trip planning, it may equally well be argued that it was present income levels that ultimately determined the final trip decision. Equation (10–2) reports a test of the importance of including past income levels in the estimation of demand for the transcontinental route. Economy traffic (Q_E) is assumed to be a function of present economy price (PE) and present and past levels of income (Y). The coefficients on the income term are assumed to decrease at a constant rate. This yields the estimating equation:

$$Q_E = \alpha + \beta PE - \beta\theta PE_{-1} + \delta\theta Y + \theta Q_{E_{-1}} \quad 0 \leqslant \theta \leqslant 1 ,$$

where θ is the multiplicative factor that reduces the initial impact of a change in income by $\delta\theta$ over time. The estimated elasticities from this formulation are reported in equation (10–2).

$\eta(PE)$	$\eta(Y)^p$	θ	R^2	$F(1.63)$	D.W.[q]	$h[11]$	
−1.81	3.50	0.58	.90	122.8	1.31	3.96	(10–2)
(1.89)	(2.31)	(6.86) .					

The estimated price elasticity has fallen slightly (although still elastic) while the long-run income elasticity, $\eta(Y)$, is close to that derived from the original formulation. Although no restriction was placed on the relationship between the coefficients during the estimating procedure, the results did meet the required restrictions. However, multicollinearity between PE and PE_{-1} (r^2 = .73) and $Q_{E_{-1}}$ and Y (r^2 = .84) did lead to substantially larger standard errors for the elasticities and reduced their precision. Since the relative ranking of the elasticities is not affected by this formulation, it will not be reported for the other routes.

The estimates presented in Table 10–1 and 10–2 may be biased because of another problem. While other demand studies have recognized the simultaneous

[o] The Durbin-Watson statistic.
[p] This is the long-run income elasticity of the demand for economy-class travel.
[q] The Durbin-Watson statistic.

nature of most markets, the area of transportation studies has not followed suit. Air transportation is a service industry where the production unit (available seat-miles) is larger than the demand unit (revenue passenger-miles) when averaged over time units such as years, quarters, or months. As a result, there has been a tendency to ignore the supply aspects of the travel market. Shifts in the supply curve have been regarded as tracing out the demand curve. However, a load factor of less than 100 percent does not guarantee the non-existence of a capacity constraint. The existence of these constraints preclude the observed price-quantity observations from lying on the demand curve.

Although the exact load factor at which diversion occurs depends on the nature of the peak in demand, the size of aircraft used, and airline schedules, the figure of 60 percent has been suggested as the critical value.[r] In the years 1961–66, the average load factor varied on the Canadian routes under consideration from 60 percent on the Toronto-Montreal route to 51 percent on the transcontinental. However, even on this latter route, capacity constraints were occasionally operative since load factors averaged over 75 percent during the peak summer months.

The discussion of capacity constraints usually centers around load factors. However, the relevant variable to be included in a regression should be seats not utilized rather than load factor. A sixty percent load factor on a route served by a 100 seat aircraft implies a greater number of excess seats than if a 44 seat aircraft had been used. Therefore, the difference between available seats (A_S) and passengers (Q_E)—i.e., (A_S–Q_E)—will be used as a proxy to indicate the probability that capacity constraints were operative. The smaller this variable, the more likely some flights were full and passengers were turned away.

Assume that the desired level of demand, $Q_E{}^*$, is a linear function of the economy price (PE), the first-class price (PF), and income (Y).

$$Q_E{}^* = f(PE, PF, Y) = \alpha + \beta PE + \gamma PF + \delta Y. \qquad (10\text{–}3)$$

However, due to capacity constraints, the demand is not entirely met in peak periods. The difference between desired demand, $Q_E{}^*$, and actual demand, Q_E, is postulated to be a function of the excess capacity, (A_S–Q_E)—that is,

$$Q_E{}^* - Q_E = f(A_S - Q_E) = \text{v} + e\,(A_S - Q_E);\quad e < 0. \qquad (10\text{–}4)$$

Two implicit assumptions underly this relationship. The first is that the greater the difference between the sum of all seats made available and passengers carried over a given time period, the greater the percentage of total flights during that

[r]Informal discussion with regulatory personnel. Stephen Wheatcroft in the report he made for the Department of Transport, entitled *Airline Competition in Canada,* uses a similar number.

period that are not capacity constrained. The second is that the larger the percentage of flights that are not capacity constrained, the closer is actual demand to potential demand.

Rearranging (10-4) and substituting (10-3) for $Q_E{}^*$ gives:

$$Q_E = \frac{\alpha - \nu}{1-e} + \frac{\beta}{1-e} PE + \frac{\gamma}{1-e} PF + \frac{\delta}{1-e} Y - \frac{e}{1-e} A_S . \qquad (10\text{–}5)$$

It is possible that the capacity constraint enters equation (10–4) only when load factors exceed a certain level. When excess capacity is high, the desired level of demand and actual demand are likely to be identical. If many such observations exist, they may bias the estimates of the price and income elasticity of the demand for air travel. The same problem has been recognized in cross-sectional studies of consumption functions when large numbers of a cross-sectional sample do not purchase the good whose demand curve is being estimated. In order to correct for this problem, equation (10–5) was also estimated with the supply constraint considered operative only for load factors greater than 60 percent—the figure believed relevant by industry sources.

The results for each of the five routes are reported in Table 10–3. The first row of estimates for each route assumes the supply constraint to be operative for all observations. The estimates of economy price elasticities that result from this assumption are all more elastic than the results reported in Table 10–1. The most dramatic change occurs on the transcontinental route where the economy price elasticity has increased in absolute value from 2.1 to 7.4. But the latter estimate is not significantly different from zero. In addition, this formulation yields unrealistic estimates of the income elasticity for all three long-distance routes—estimates that are either negative or that do not significantly differ from zero. This suggests that, in the case of the longer routes, assuming that the supply constraint was operative at all load factors may be inappropriate.

The second row of estimates for each route in Table 10–3 assumes the capacity constraint becomes operative only when load factors exceed 60 percent. In the case of the transcontinental route this assumption yields an estimate of the economy price elasticity of -2.6. The estimate previously obtained using an unconstrained procedure was only -2.1. The estimate of the economy price elasticity on the United Kingdom route has increased only slightly in absolute value to 1.66 from the estimate of 1.58 reported in Table 10–1. In both cases, the income elasticity of the demand for air travel falls slightly compared to the unconstrained estimates.

The formulation assuming that the capacity constraint is operative for all load factors is more satisfactory for the short-haul routes. The economy price elasticity for the Toronto-Montreal route, which was -0.32 in Table 10–1, becomes -0.33, while the income elasticity decreases from 1.6 to 1.3. The estimate of the economy price elasticity of Toronto-New York becomes negative

Table 10–3. Economy-Class Price and Income Elasticities by Route, with Supply Constraints Hypothesized to be Effective at Varying Load Factors

Route	Load Factor Above Which Supply Contraint is Considered Operative	Economy Price Elasticity $\eta(PE)$	First-Class Price Cross-Elasticity $\eta(PF)$	Income Elasticity $\eta(Y)$	R^2	F^b	Durbin-Watson
Transcontinental $\eta(PE) = -2.1$[a] $\eta(Y) = 4.0$[a]	All	–7.4 (1.8)*[c]	–2.3 (2.1)	–0.8 (0.5)*	.97	433.1	1.85
	60%	–2.6 (2.1)	0.7 (1.4)*	2.5 (2.7)	.91	122.1	1.12
United Kingdom $\eta(PE) = -1.6$[a] $\eta(Y) = 2.5$[a]	50%	–1.96 3.13	0.13 (0.16)*	0.40 (0.48)*	.96	314.9	1.71
	60%	–1.66 (2.17)	1.44 (2.04)	2.40 (3.72)	.92	138.9	1.70
Florida $\eta(PE) = -1.3$[a] $\eta(Y) = 1.8$[a]	50%	–1.77 (2.03)	1.31 (2.35)	0.60 (0.91)*	.95	134.7	2.26
	60%	–0.71 (0.94)*	0.73 (0.98)*	1.62 (3.76)	.90	68.57	2.10
Toronto-Montreal $\eta(PE) = -0.3$[a] $\eta(Y) = 1.6$[a]	50%	–0.33 (1.58)*	0.25 (1.14)*	1.28 (2.99)	.97	244.9	1.50
	60%	–0.27 (1.77)*	0.24 (1.46)*	1.52 (9.37)	.96	210.6	1.67
Toronto-New York $\eta(PE) = 0.5$[a] $\eta(Y) = 1.1$[a]	50%	–1.79 (1.12)*	1.41 (1.70)*	1.02 (0.91)*	.90	75.6	1.61
	60%	0.16 (0.24)*	–0.31 (0.95)*	1.28 (5.19)*	.80	34.6	1.71

[a]These results were taken from Table 10–1 for comparison.

[b]All F statistics are significant to the 1 percent level.

[c]An asterisk indicates $t < t_{.025}$ for the number of degrees of freedom relevant to that equation.

for the first time, but is not significantly different from zero.[s] Its income elasticity remains virtually unchanged.

That long- and short-haul routes apparently require different formulations of the capacity constraint has a plausible explanation. Marketing surveys indicate that a larger percentage of travellers on long-haul routes both decide upon their trip and make reservations earlier than on short-haul routes. This means the airline has a greater chance of meeting peaks in demand on the long-haul routes. A priori, this implies that for the same average load factor, more people are either inconvenienced or turned away on the shorter routes than on the longer ones. In turn, this implies that the supply effect should become operative at a lower average load factor for the shorter routes. Indeed this is what the results in Table 10–3 imply.

In summary, the introduction of the notion that demand may be supply constrained would appear on average to make each route only slightly more price elastic and to reduce the income elasticity relative to the original formulation.[t] In addition, whether one adopts the first or second formulation of the effect of the supply constraint does not affect the original conclusion that both short routes are extremely price inelastic. In neither case is either of their economy price elasticities significantly different from zero.

First Class Traffic

First class traffic was assumed to be a function of its own price, the economy price and the income variable. Observations for 1962 through 1966 were chosen[u] because this market was still adjusting in 1961 not only to the introduction of economy fares, but more importantly to an increased fare differential that had occurred in January 1961. For example, in 1961 the transcontinental first-class to economy fare ratio increased to 1.5:1 from 1.4:1 in 1960. In 1962, this ratio stabilized in the 1.38:1 range. Since the 1960 figures

[s] That introducing the capacity variable on the Toronto-New York route should have a greater effect on the estimate of the price elasticity than on the Toronto-Montreal route might be explained by the fact that Air Canada was not the sole carrier on the former route but faced virtually no competition on the latter route—only one flight a day from CP Air.

[t] An alternative specification of capacity constraints which was discarded because of multicollinearity between the variables was $Q_E = Q_E^*(1-c\ 1/A_S)$ where $Q_E^* = f(PE, PF, Y)$ is desired demand.

This yielded the estimating equation: $D = \alpha + \beta PE + \delta PF + \mu Y - \alpha c - \beta c\ PE/A_S - \delta c\ PF/A_S - \mu c\ Y/A_S$.

The results for Florida were:

	$\eta(PE)$	$\eta(PF)$	$\eta(Y)$	R^2	D.W.
	−1.45	0.73	2.70	.90	2.02
t =	(1.43)	(0.86)	(4.06) .		

This approach was hampered by severe multicollinearity (the determinant was zero to six decimals) and the t value for the partial correlation coefficients between PE and PE/A_S, PF and PF/A_S, and Y and Y/A_S were 2.87, 2.61, and 3.57, respectively.

[u] The observations were from July 1962 for Toronto-Montreal and Toronto-New York; from January for the other routes.

Table 10–4. Price and Income Elasticities of the Demand for First-Class Travel, by Route

Route	*First-Class Price Elasticity* $\eta(PF)$	*Economy Price Cross-Elasticity* $\eta(PE)$	*Income Elasticity* $\eta(Y)$	R^2	*F*	*Durbin-Watson*
Transcontinental	–0.61 t = (2.30)[b]	1.00 (1.20)*	2.20 (6.70)	.83	71.9 (1,52)[a]	1.11
Florida	–1.58 t = (2.61)	0.10 (0.17)*	0.52 (1.45)*	.89	75.2 (1,62)	2.21
United Kingdom	1.11 t = (1.13)*	–3.56 (1.67)*	2.32 (2.68)	.64	18.7 (1,52)	.85
Toronto-Montreal	–0.13 t = (0.29)*	0.50 (1.14)*	.002 (.006)*	.32	4.34 (1,52)	1.26
Toronto-New York	–1.90 t = (4.07)	0.24 (0.27)*	–0.71 (2.03)	.49	8.75 (1,46)	1.00

[a]Indicates degrees of freedom for the F statistic. All are significant to the 1 percent level.

[b]An asterisk beside a t statistic indicates $t < t_{.025}$ for the number of degrees of freedom relevant to that equation.

were unavailable, both 1960 and 1961 have been omitted and only observations from 1962 through 1966 are utilized.

Table 10–4 presents the results. The elasticity with respect to first-class fare is greatest for Toronto-New York and Florida. Toronto-Montreal is the most inelastic. Although for the United Kingdom the price elasticity is positive and insignificant, this result can be explained by the multicollinearity previously reported to exist between the independent variables used for the estimates obtained for this route. Removing the economy price yields an estimated elasticity of -.10, which is statistically insignificant from zero. While for all but the United Kingdom route, the cross-elasticity with respect to the economy price is of the right sign, it is never significant at the 5 percent level.[v] The income elasticity is highest for the transcontinental and United Kingdom routes while smallest on the short-haul Toronto-Montreal and Toronto-New York routes.

Since it was felt that the capacity constraints in economy might affect first-class travel, the economy load factor was included and the results are reported in Table 10–5. The economy load factor has the right sign for all routes, but is only significantly different from zero for the two short-haul routes. Intuitively this would appear to make sense. Only on the short routes where a business trip may not be planned very far in advance are travellers willing to pay the extra fare to switch classes when a seat is not available in economy.

[v]If all observations 1961 through 1966 are used, the cross-elasticity becomes significant while the income elasticity is usually reduced substantially and is commonly negative.

Table 10–5. Price and Income Elasticities for First Class, by Route, with the Influence of Capacity Constraints in Economy Class Taken into Account

Route	*First-Class Price Elasticity* $\eta(PF)$	*Income Elasticity* $\eta(Y)$	*Economy Load Factor Elasticity*	R^2	*F*	*Durbin-Watson*
Transcontinental	– .48	2.53	0.01	.83	57.2	1.04
	t = (1.83)*[b]	(9.44)	(0.20)*		(1,52)[a]	
Florida	–1.51	0.48	0.02	.89	75.3	2.23
	t = (2.52)	(1.43)*	(0.32)*		(1,62)	
United Kingdom	0.26	2.82	.03	.60	18.4	.77
	t = (0.36)*	(3.33)	(1.54)*		(1,52)	
Toronto-Montreal	–0.22	–0.23	0.25	.27	5.04	1.06
	t = (0.49)*	(1.04)*	(1.93)*		(1,52)	
Toronto-New York	–2.50	–0.15	.22	.61	14.96	1.15
	t = (5.92)	(0.76)	(3.12)		(1,46)	

[a]Indicates degrees of freeom for the F statistic. All are significant to the 1 percent level.

[b]An asterisk beside the t statistic indicates $t < t_{.025}$ for the number of degrees of degrees of freedom relevant to that equation.

Chapter Eleven

Pricing Policy on the Two Profitable Sectors—the North Atlantic and the Transcontinental—during the 1960s

INTRODUCTION

This chapter examines the pricing behavior of Air Canada on its two profit-generating sectors—the trans-Atlantic and the transcontinental—during the late 1960s. Neither market was highly competitive—the former was a tightly controlled cartel; the latter, a duopoly. Both sectors underwent changes in market structure and the result was that Air Canada actively pressed for fare revisions. But, while it sought to lower prices on the trans-Atlantic, Air Canada increased prices on the transcontinental sector. The previous chapter provides estimates of the demand curves facing the airline on both routes during this period. Combined with the costs of operation on each sector, these estimates may be used to explain the contrasting behavior of the Crown airline. It will be argued that, in the case of the trans-Atlantic market, the air fare was above that which would have maximized profits for the airline, but for the transcontinental route, the price was below that level. A change in the market structure of each market combined with the airline's cross-subsidization policy served to elicit opposite price responses in the two sectors.

THE DOMESTIC FARE STRUCTURE

By 1962, Air Canada had adjusted its fare structure to compensate for the introduction of a second carrier on the transcontinental route. Between 1962 and 1967 no further changes in the domestic market structure occurred, and the domestic fare structure remained relatively constant. Yet, during this period, the airline was able to increase its rate of return from 3.1 percent in 1962 to an average of 6.5 percent in the years 1965 through 1967 (see Table 6–4). This was accomplished both via a reduction in costs—from 29.7¢ in 1962 to 27.4¢ per available ton-mile in 1965—and via an increase in the percentage of output

Table 11–1. Air Canada Passenger Load Factors, by Sector, 1960–1965

Sector	*1960*	*1961*	*1962*	*1963*	*1964*	*1965*
International	63.9	55.7	53.1	53.0	62.4	62.7
Transcontinental	65.9	67.4	62.1	59.8	62.7	68.2
Montreal-Toronto	68.3	68.9	67.4	66.1	68.2	66.8
Transborder	68.6	67.5	65.5	64.0	66.2	66.6
Other Domestic	64.5	62.4	57.1	57.3	58.2	59.1
System	66.0	64.1	60.2	59.6	63.4	65.2

Source: Canada, Department of Transport, "Further Airline Competition in Canada: A Study of the Consequences of any Further Development of Domestic Mainline Competition in Canada" (unpublished paper prepared by Stephen Wheatcroft, Ottawa, February, 1966, mimeographed), Appendix 3.

sold—passenger load factors increased system-wide from 60 percent in 1962 to 65 percent in 1965. However, the adjustment in capacity provided, relative to traffic growth, was not spread equally across the system. Table 11–1 indicates that while load factors on the high density Toronto-Montreal and transborder routes remained relatively constant, and those on other domestic routes actually fell, the load factor on the transcontinental route increased to a level above that prevailing in 1960.

Prior to CP Air's entry into the transcontinental sector and Air Canada's introduction of new and larger equipment thereon in 1961 and 1962, the load factors on the transcontinental routes had been higher than on the rest of the domestic system (see Table 8-7). Both of these changes lowered the transcontinental load factor relative to the other routes, a situation apparently unacceptable to the Crown airline. The early sixties saw the airline gradually re-establishing the former relationship—that is, by the end of this period load factors on the profitable sector were once more equal to or higher than load factors on both the dense Montreal-Toronto route and other less heavily travelled domestic routes.

On March 27, 1967, the government announced the second major change in its domestic competition policy. CP Air, which since 1958 had been limited to one flight daily from Vancouver to Montreal, was to be allowed to expand its service thereon.[1] Initially, the airline was to be permitted to double its capacity in the 1967 calendar year. In addition, CP Air was granted approval to increase its capacity in stages until it accounted for 25 percent of the total transcontinental capacity.[a] This was to be accomplished by 1970.

It has been argued that a government-owned airline, even when in a poisition to do so, is not likely to set prices so as to maximize profits. The Crown airline will, however, generate some profits for the purpose of cross-subsidization. It follows from the model developed to predict the behavior of the Crown airline

[a]Transcontinental capacity was defined as available seat-miles provided between Vancouver-Edmonton-Calgary-Saskatoon-Regina-Winnipeg-Toronto-Ottawa-Montreal.

that a change in market structure, ostensibly meant to break down the monopoly position of the Crown airline in these profitable sectors, could very well lead to price increases thereon and should cause prices on the loss sector to go up.

Prior to 1967, Air Canada had only one flight per day from CP Air to contend with on the profitable transcontinental route. Thus, the demand curve facing Air Canada was that of the total market less that taken by CP Air's one flight per day. The only constraint on setting a monopoly price would have been a threat by CP Air not to follow suit and the lever this would have provided its competitor in arguing for relaxation of the capacity controls placed upon it. However, evidence indicates that the fare that was established was jointly agreed upon by both airlines.[b] Thus we may regard the price established as being unconstrained by the existence of the private carrier.

The estimated demand equation for economy traffic on the transcontinental route yielded a price elasticity of -2.06 during the middle sixties (Table 10-1).[c] Since throughout this period the economy price between Vancouver and Toronto was $109, this implies that marginal revenue was $56 (with an upper confidence limit [5%] of $82).[d] The cost per seat-mile of Canadian carriers on this route in 1966 was 2.89¢ or $61 per seat.[2] With an average load factor of 73 percent, [3] the average cost per passenger was $84.[e] If the average cost per passenger is regarded as equal to the long-run marginal cost, the fact that estimated marginal revenue was below marginal cost indicates that the Crown airline was not fully exploiting its monopoly power. There still was scope for a price increase should a further deterioration in the Crown airline's market share on the profitable mainline routes reduce the potential profits it could earn thereon.

The 1967 expansion in CP Air's share of the transcontinental market served to reduce the profits available to the Crown airline for cross-subsidization purposes. While the effects of the first expansion of the private carrier into the transcontinental market in the late 1950s had to be disentangled from those resulting from a simultaneous reduction in costs, no similar problem arises in this instance. Although the DC-9 had begun to replace the Viscount, the Crown airline's average cost per available ton-mile remained relatively constant prior to the fare revision in 1968—27.35¢ in 1965, 27.34¢ in 1966, 26.87¢ in 1967.

Tables 11–2 and 11–3 and Figure 11–1 permit analysis of the resulting

[b]CP Air did not actually follow Air Canada's 1962 fare increase until 1965, but initially it had indicated it would do so. See Canada, Sessional Committee on Railways, Airlines and Shipping, *Minutes of Proceedings and Evidence,* no. 1 (December 2, 3, 4, 1963), p. 28.

[c]This should be compared to the rough estimate of −1.5 obtained in Chapter Eight from data relating to the introduction of tourist service in 1954.

[d]If the elasticity calculated using the supply constraint were used, the estimate of marginal revenue is $67 with an upper confidence limit of $90.

[e]Using the average transcontinental load factor from 1962 through 1965 yields an average cost per passenger of $96.

Table 11–2. Fare Regressions, Disaggregated by Sector, 1962, 1968, 1971

Year	*Standard*		*Deviations from the Standard (Col. 1) and Slope (Col. 2)*							
	East-West		*Transcontinental*		*Maritimes*		*Corridor*		*N. Ontario*	
	(1) Intercept	*(2) Slope*	*(3) Intercept*	*(4) Slope*	*(5) Intercept*	*(6) Slope*	*(7) Intercept*	*(8) Slope*	*(9) Intercept*	*(10) Slope*
1962	11.14	.048	....	....	–5.27	.007	–7.38	.018	–5.72	.014
	(9.89)[a]	(67.2)[b]			(2.90)[b]	(3.19)[b]	(2.77)[b]	(3.05)[b]	(1.79)	(1.92)
1968	6.15	.057	6.64	–.005	....	.005	....	.012		.011
	(6.74)[b]	(95.6)[b]	(4.73)[b]	(5.34)[b]		(3.73)[b]		(4.17)[b]		(3.49)[b]
1971	11.10	.056	1.01	.001	....	....	....	....	....	....
	(23.95)[b]	(125.3)[b]	(1.06)	(1.04)						

[a]Figures in parentheses are t statistics. Those for the standard equation indicate whether the estimates differ from zero. Those beneath the other estimates indicate whether they are significantly different from the standard estimates contained in columns (1) and (2).

[b]Indicates significant value using two-tailed t test with 5 percent level of significance.

Table 11–3. Fare per Mile at Mean Stage-Length, by Sector, 1962, 1968, 1971

Year	*East-West*		*Transcontinental*		*Maritimes*		*Corridor*		*N. Ontario*	
Period	*Fare*	*Change*	*Fare*	*Change*	*Fare*	*Change*	*Fare*	*Change*	*Fare*	*Change*
1962	5.26 (0.04)[a]		5.75 (0.05)		6.49 (0.12)		7.61 (0.30)		7.68 (0.34)	
1962–1968		+.59 (.06)[b]		+.53 (.06)		+.74 (.15)		+.99 (.38)		+.80 (.43)
1968	5.85 (0.05)		6.28 (0.04)		7.23 (0.09)		8.62 (0.23)		8.48 (0.26)	
1968–1971		+.20 (.06)		+.44 (.05)		+.23 (.11)		+.05 (.25)[c]		+.14 (.28)[c]
1971	6.05 (0.03)		6.72 (0.03)		7.46 (0.06)		8.67 (0.10)		8.62 (0.09)	

[a]Figures in parentheses indicate the standard error of the estimate.

[b]The standard error of the difference in the mean fare per mile was calculated by assuming the errors in each time period were independent of one another.

[c]Indicates the change in mean fare per mile was not significant for $t_{.025,180}$.

Source: Table 11–2.

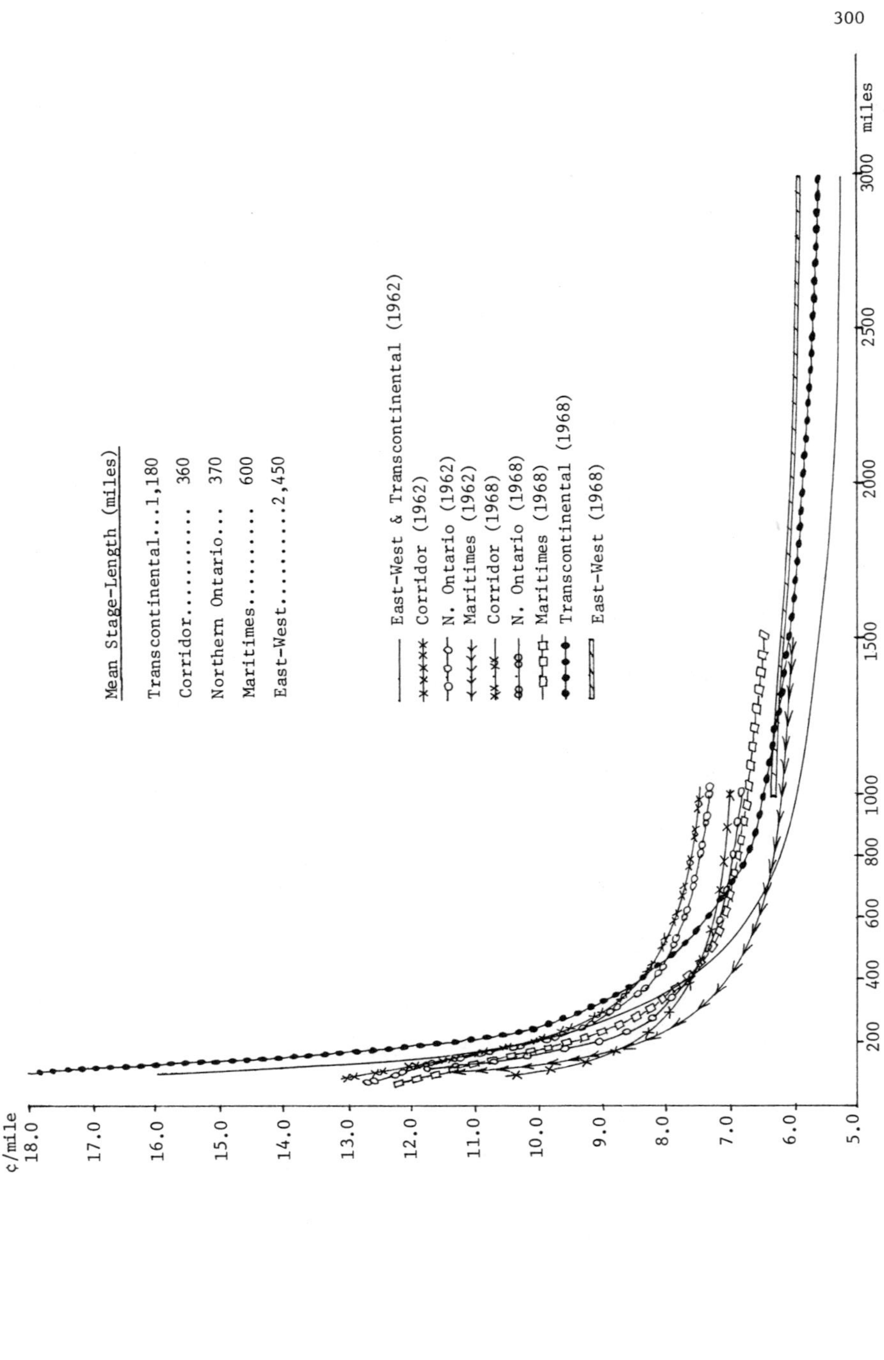

Figure 11–1. Estimated Fare Structure—Cents per Mile Plotted against Distance, 1962, 1968.

change in the fare structure. As the model developed in Chapter Five predicted, entry to the profitable mainline routes caused the mean price on all the loss sectors to increase (Table 11–3).[f] The model is ambiguous as to the sign of the change expected on the mainline routes. But the airline's response to a combination of entry and the introduction of cost-reducing technology in the late 1950s was to increase the price-cost mark-up thereon. This time with no perceivable cost reduction, a similar result was achieved with an increase in the mean price on the transcontinental route (Table 11–3). The airline took advantage of the discrepancy between marginal revenue and marginal cost on the transcontinenatl sector to reduce the degree to which higher prices on the regional sectors would be required to offset the initial loss in profits.

It should be noted that the increase imposed on the transcontinental sector was less than that on the loss routes. Again this accords with the model's prediction that the price spread between the profit and loss sectors should have increased—a prediction that was also borne out in the fare changes that resulted from entry in the late 1950s.

Of equal interest was the effect of this general fare revision on the relative level of prices within each sector. Table 11–2 indicates that the increase for both the profit and the loss sectors was accomplished via an upward shift in both the intercept and the slope of the estimated fare regression. But the intercept of the loss sectors' fare equation was still significantly below that of the mainline routes. Thus the intra-sectoral differences were less on the loss routes. The apparent importance of maintaining intra-sectoral comparability on the latter sectors has already been noted in Chapter Nine's discussion of the 1962 fare revisions. Perusal of Figure 11–1 does indicate, though, that for the first time the fare per mile for both the corridor and the northern Ontario and Quebec sectors, at their mean stage-lengths, was approximately the same for routes on the transcontinental system of equal stage-length. The Maritimes still enjoyed a slight advantage.

Between 1968 and 1970 Air Canada was faced both with a continued expansion from CP Air and with a major incursion from the regional carriers. Although the Minister of Transport had announced the Regional Aviation Policy in 1966, it was not until late 1968 and 1969 that any significant route awards were made to the regional carriers. Transair was not granted the Regina-Winnipeg-Toronto route until early 1970. Eastern Provincial Airways received Montreal-Charlottetown in late 1968 and Halifax to St. John's in early 1970. Quebecair was allowed increased leeway to compete against Air Canada between Montreal and Sept Isles in 1969. The expansion of CP Air and to a lesser extent

[f]The reader should be reminded that profitable and unprofitable are relative terms. While unprofitable and loss are used loosely as synonyms, all that "loss" implies is that the airline is earning a lower rate of return on these sectors than on the profitable ones. In some cases, as evidence in Chapter Six indicated, the rate of return on a "loss" sector may have been negative.

that of Transair both served to reduce the Crown airline's potential transcontinental profits. The expansion of Quebecair and Eastern Provincial served to increase the losses earned on the corridor and the Maritimes sectors.[g]

Simultaneously, the Crown airline was replacing its DC-9's and DC-8's with the respective long-bodied version of each aircraft, which at least in the case of the latter were used only on the transcontinental sector. This served to decrease Air Canada's system average cost per available ton-mile by 17.1 percent between 1967 and 1970—from 26.87¢ to 22.27¢. However, as was the case when turbine replaced piston aircraft in 1960 and 1961, load factors fell somewhat—this time by 13.9 percent. In the domestic market, this decrease was almost entirely accounted for by a fall in the transcontinental load factor. The net effect of entry to the mainline route and the cost reduction was probably to leave Air Canada's potential profits thereon relatively unchanged. On the other hand, with less extensive use of these two aircraft on the loss sectors—the stretched DC-8 was not used at all thereon—the net effect here would have been to increase the Crown airline's potential losses.

The resulting fare revision in early 1971 bears this interpretation out. The model of the Crown airline predicts that an increase in losses incurred in the unprofitable sectors should have led to an increase in prices on the profitable sector. Table 11–3 indicates that the 1971 fare revision significantly increased the mean fare per mile on the transcontinental sector. The model permits the sign of the resulting change in loss sector prices to be positive, zero, or negative. Two of the three sectors suffered no significant change. Only the Maritimes received a significant increase. That the Maritimes suffered relative to the other loss sectors is consistent with the fact that it was here that the Crown airline received the most extensive duplication of its services. Perusal of Figure 11–2 shows that the advantage the Maritimes had enjoyed as of 1968 over the other loss sectors finally disappeared with the 1971 fare revision. Finally, the model is compatible with the observation that an increase in losses on its unprofitable sectors was accompanied by a decrease in the per mile fare differential between the profitable and unprofitable sectors. The results in Table 11-3 indicate that this is what occurred.

Table 11–2 also indicates that the intercepts of the fare regressions for the loss sectors were significantly increased. As a result, the intra-sectoral differences in the fare per mile charged different routes in each loss sector widened. With an intercept approximately equal to that of the regression for the transcontinental sector, the loss sectors no longer had greater intra-sectoral comparability than the mainline routes. There are two explanations for this result. First, the entry of the eastern regional carriers can be regarded as primarily affecting the

[g]This does not imply that entry occurred only on unprofitable routes—though this is part of the explanation judging by the increase in subsidies paid these two airlines during this period. It is quite possible that some routes in what have been classified as loss sectors were profitable and that these were the routes on which entry occurred.

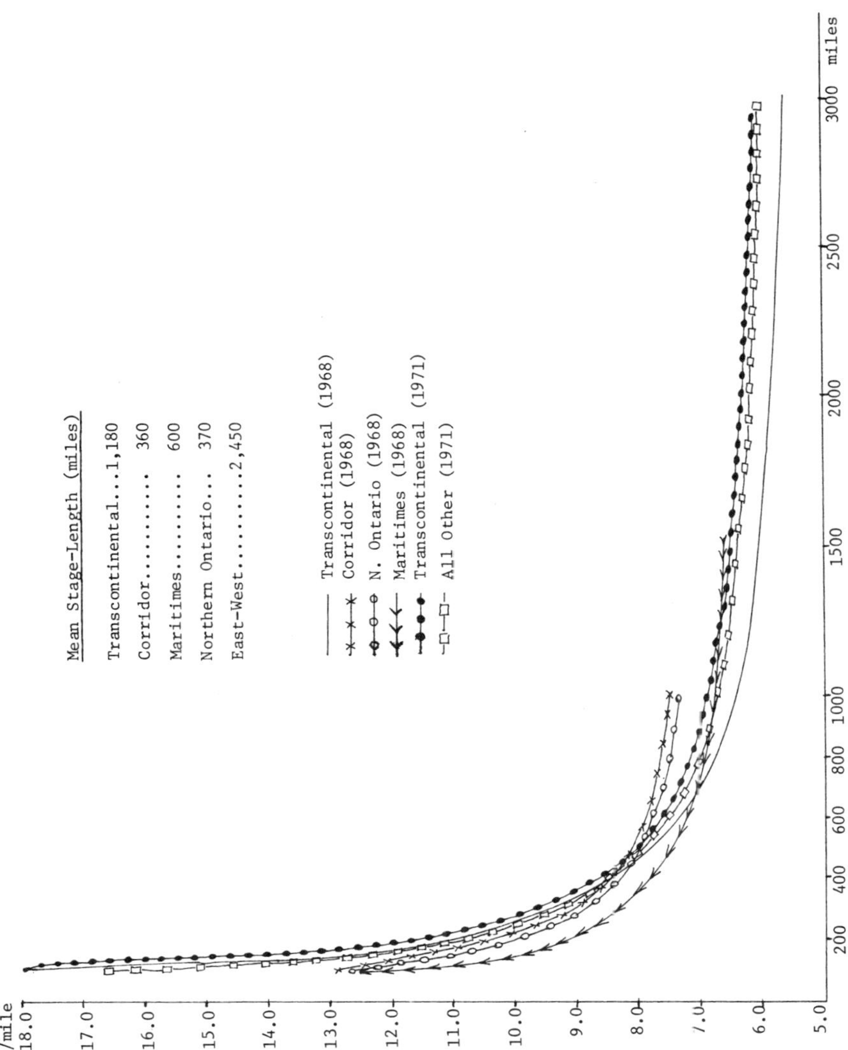

Figure 11-2. Estimated Fare Structure—Cents per Mile Plotted against Distance, 1968, 1971.

longer-distance, profitable routes of the Crown airline in this area of the country. While the Maritimes and the corridor routes have generally been described as loss routes, it is unrealistic to claim that every route contained therein was unprofitable. The concluding chapter, which develops price-cost margins for Air Canada's routes, suggests that the very routes that were most affected by the expansion of the eastern regionals—Montreal-Sept Isles, Quebec-Sept Isles, and Montreal-Moncton—were profitable (see Table 12–1). The model developed in Chapter Five predicts that entry to profitable routes should increase the price spread between the profitable and unprofitable routes. Since the data in Table 12–1 also indicates that the shorter routes in both the corridor and the Maritimes fall in the latter category, entry to the former should have increased the distance-related taper in the fare per mile in each of these sectors. The upward shift in the fare regression's intercept accomplished this. However, the fact that a similar increase in the fare per mile taper also occurred on the northern Ontario and Quebec sector—an area where the Crown airline faced no entry—lends credibility to a second explanation of this change in the fare structure of the loss routes. It can be argued that minimizing intra-sectoral fare differences no longer was as important to the Crown airline. Faced with competitors on its loss sectors which charged higher fares on their shorter distance routes than the Crown airline did,[h] Air Canada could more readily argue that differences in route costs required greater intra-sectoral fare differentials, and promptly readjusted its fare schedule accordingly.

THE TRANS-ATLANTIC MARKET

The trans-Atlantic market has, since its inception, been organized as a cartel.[4] Following conflicts as to the degree of competition that would be allowed to prevail in the postwar international aviation markets, the International Air Transport Association (IATA) was designated as the body through which fares were to be regulated. All member countries were convened about once a year to set international fares. Backed by member governments, who control entry to their respective markets and who are party to these agreements, the cartel was able to count on extremely effective sanctions against renegade carriers—that is, their exclusion from the market.

Since the motivations that led to the creation of the cartel were based on the desire of some governments anxious to nurture the success of their own carriers, [5] and evidence suggests that there was considerable variance in the efficiency of international carriers, [6] the existence of unduly high prices was to be expected. The price in the early sixties was in fact considerably above the average total cost per passenger of the Canadian carriers. The average cost per

[h]See the discussion in Chapter Six and Tables 6–7 and 6–8.

passenger between Montreal and London was $151, while the off-season fare was $210, the peak season fare was $245.[7]

Maintenance of these fare levels by the cartel was not achieved without rancorous internal debate. Air Canada, both by its actions and by the bargaining strategy it adopted, has proven to be one of the more active proponents of lower fares.[i] It has, however, been constrained both by the international institutional framework, which prevents the unilateral implementation of lower fares, as well as by its inability to physically separate the Canadian from the American North Atlantic travel market. In 1970, only 12.2 percent of the total market originated or terminated in Canada. With only short distances separating the large United States Midwest and East Coast markets from Canadian gateways, IATA could ill afford to permit the Canadian portion of the market to go its own way. However, the Crown airline has on two notable occasions adamantly negotiated for lower fares.

In 1962, some four years after the introduction of the long-range jet with its attendant cost reductions, IATA agreed to a 5 percent increase on regular North Atlantic fares. Although both Canadian and American carriers were against this increase, their support was sought in return for the implementation of a new fare—the "affinity group" fare—that was 38 percent lower than the regular economy fare.[8] The "affinity group" fare was to be restricted to travellers who belonged to approved groups and who booked a block of seats together. Characteristic of a monopoly, the cartel was attempting to perfect a pattern of discriminatory prices. All IATA agreements on fares must be approved by member governments. Both Canada and the United States initially refused to accept the higher fares. European governments, led by the United Kingdom, promptly threatened to take "action" against the aircraft of any carrier that refused to abide by the higher fares. In the face of this confrontation, the amount of the increase was somewhat ameliorated. Nevertheless, economy fares moved upwards even though costs were falling.

The aftermath of this battle was a rancorous debate that developed in 1963 over fare reductions. At the time, the round-trip economy fare on the North Atlantic was approximately $500. The leading American carrier proposed a reduction to $320; Air Canada suggested $360 during the peak summer season and $290 during the off-peak winter months.[9] The European carriers, mindful of bad public relations that would result from being labelled "high fare" carriers, publicly announced that they too favored lower fares. But their proposals were as before to increase the extent of price discrimination by further reduction of promotional fares.[10] The compromise agreed upon by the majority of carriers

[i]K.G.J. Pillai, *The Air Net: The Case Against the World Aviation Cartel* (New York: Grossman, 1969), p. 96, recounts one story attributing failure of the cartel to reach agreement on fares to Air Canada's "rigid stand for lower fares."

amounted to a 3 percent reduction in season and a 20 percent reduction off-season—economy fares of approximately $485 and $400, respectively.[11] Air Canada refused to agree to these reductions, arguing that they were inadequate.

IATA requires unanimous consent to a fare schedule before it can be submitted to member countries' governments for approval. Wheatcroft has claimed that this "gives a powerful bargaining weapon to an airline which is trying to reduce the level of fares and rates."[12] On the contrary, this episode illustrates just how ineffective this unanimity provision is when one airline insists on reducing fares. Although Air Canada vetoed the agreement, the other carriers filed the new rate schedule with their governments and promptly received acceptance. Air Canada was faced with an alternative. Either it would have to acquiesce or it would have to negotiate individually with every European country for a new bilateral treaty. If it adopted the latter approach, it would have had to negotiate mutually agreeable fares with each country. Faced with the possibility of total exclusion from the cartel, the Canadian airline chose to join the agreement.

Air Canada's actions in pressing for lower fares might be interpreted in one of two ways. Either it felt that the discrepancy between North Atlantic and transcontinental fares—7.8¢ on Montreal-London versus 5.1¢ per mile for Toronto-Vancouver in 1963—was as unacceptable as domestic differences had been, or the existing price was above that at which Air Canada's profits would have been maximized. Evidence in the previous chapter placed the price elasticity for this route at -1.6. With a peak season one-way fare of $254 in 1963 this meant that the marginal revenue would have been $95. In 1966, the average cost per passenger for the two Canadian carriers on this route was approximately $151.[13] Accepting this as the best estimate of the long-run marginal cost facing the airline, the trans-Atlantic fare would appear to have been below the profit-maximizing price for Air Canada.

However, calculation of the price elasticity based only on scheduled service traffic is erroneous, for it ignores an important feature of the market. A large proportion of total traffic on the Canada-Europe segment travelled via non-scheduled or charter services. In 1964, charter traffic carried by IATA airlines operating to and from Canada amounted to 40 percent of their scheduled traffic.[j] Should the Crown airline have felt it would lose this traffic unless it reduced its regular fare, then the elasticity of demand would have been considerably higher than that estimated from the scheduled traffic alone. Charter passengers were travelling at a round-trip fare of about $250 versus the regular fare of $500. If it is assumed that the point elasticity estimated for the scheduled service applied to such a large price decrease, and that the regular fare

[j]Straszheim, *The International Airline Industry*, p. 54. The corresponding figure for the American segment of the North Atlantic market was only 13.5 percent.

would have to have fallen to $250 to retain the charter traffic, the fare elasticity was really much more elastic—that is, about -2.4.[k] Using this figure produces an estimate of the marginal revenue of a one-way fare at 1963 prices of about $148. But marginal cost of one-way passage would not have been $150—the average cost per passenger of scheduled service quoted above. Charter flights operated at much higher load factors. If the charter flights are assumed to have been operating at 100 percent load factors, then weighting the average cost per passenger of each type of service by their share of total traffic gives an average cost of only $132 per passenger. This calculation suggests that the level of fares on the North Atlantic at this time was above that which would have maximized the Canadian Crown airline's profits.

Of course, there is no need to reduce prices generally if price discrimination can be effectively maintained. However, there was good reason for the Canadian airline to distrust its ability to do so. The licensing of new non-IATA charter carriers in this market in the early sixties [14] reduced the ability of IATA to segment its markets. To IATA, the charter market was an integral part of its price discrimination scheme. In order to ensure that it would not be used to implement general fare reductions, IATA itself enforce the regulations with an investigative agency and a schedule of fines. Nominally, the non-scheduled carriers were supposed to observe the same eligibility rules for charter flights that IATA enforced. But they had no higher priced market to protect and every incentive to violate them in order to attract as many passengers as possible. Although member governments took the responsibility for enforcing these regulations against the non-scheduled carriers, in practice they have been loath to do much.

Table 11–4 compares the growth of charter and scheduled traffic on the North Atlantic. The growth rate for charter traffic was greater than that for scheduled traffic. In addition, the non-scheduled share of the charter market grew rapidly. By 1968 the non-scheduled carriers had surpassed those of IATA in terms of the number of charter passengers carried. The Canadian scheduled carriers' share of the charter market began to decline in 1964.[15] In that year, Air Canada's charter traffic amounted to 40 percent of its scheduled traffic;[16] in 1970, it accounted for only 22 percent.[l] Whereas Air Canada maintained its relative position in the scheduled market—50 percent in 1964, 47 percent in 1970—its share of charter traffic fell from 37 percent [17] in 1964 to less than

[k]The elasticity is equal to $\eta_1 + C/Q / \Delta P/P$ where η_1 is the calculated elasticity from scheduled services, C/Q the ratio of charter to scheduled and $\Delta P/P$ the percentage price reduction. $C/Q = .40$ while $\Delta P/P = .5$.

[l]Canada, Dominion Bureau of Statistics, Aviation Statistics Centre, *International Air Charter Statistics,* Cat. No. 51–003, Vol. 1, No. 3 (July-September 1970), pp. 12–16, and *Air Transport World* VIII, no. 4 (1971):10. In order to compute this figure, it was assumed that Air Canada and CP Air split North Atlantic charter traffic in the same proportion as their division of total charter traffic.

Table 11–4. Division of North Atlantic Traffic between Scheduled and Non-Scheduled Services, 1963–1970 (000)

Services	*1963*	*1964*	*1965*	*1966*	*1967*	*1968*	*1969*	*1970*
IATA-scheduled	2422	3069	3611	4198	4987	5258	5997	7201
IATA-charter	414	482	480	503	517	495	780	817
Other-charter	35	112	197	303	510	753	1411	1758
Other-scheduled	67	95	128	146	166	165	183	262
Total	2958	3758	4418	5149	6180	6671	8371	10,038

Source: International Air Transport Association, *World Air Transport Statistics,* No. 16 (1971), p. 56.

20 percent[m] in 1970. This development tends to confirm the earlier hypothesis that the demand curve faced by Air Canada was much more price elastic than a demand curve estimated from scheduled services alone would have indicated.

In 1971, Air Canada entered the IATA fare conference determined to recapture the charter traffic it had lost. The airline, hoping to tap the charter market, proposed a reduction in the 21-day excursion fare from $400 to $250 in the peak season and from $350 to $200 in the off-season.[n] A new bargaining strategy was adopted. In 1963 Air Canada had learned that threatening to veto the IATA rate package and permitting an open rate situation to develop had been singularly unsuccessful. By early 1970, the airline had developed a contingency plan to make the threat more credible than it had been in 1963. Air Canada temporarily reached an agreement with Ireland's international carrier, so that if Air Canada was again bypassed, it would adopt the proposed low fares itself, become virtually a charter carrier, and fly only to Ireland. From Ireland, the passengers could then make their way elsewhere to Europe via regular services. These arrangements were sufficiently convenient to most price-conscious travellers that there was a good chance that a substantial portion of the Europe-bound passengers would be diverted from the more expensive IATA flights.

In the end, this strategy was moderately successful. Excursion fares (22 to 45 days) were reduced to $300 in peak-season; $210 for winter and $232 for a new intermediate category—the "shoulder" season (May, June, September, and October)—for the Toronto-London route.

Thus, the Crown airline acted vigorously on two separate occasions in an effort to force the North Atlantic fares downwards. Although it has been argued

[m]Together Air Canada and CP Air carried only 20 percent of all European-Canadian charter traffic. Canada, Dominion Bureau of Statistics, *International Air Charter Statistics,* Cat. No. 51–003 (July-September 1970), p. 12.

[n]*Globe and Mail,* June 26, 1971. The airline felt the 21 to 45-day excursion fare would compete for 80 percent of the charter market.

that the optimum price for Air Canada was below that in existence for most of this period, the timing of the airline's actions needs explanation. The increasing importance of non-scheduled carriers must have played a role in its decisions; but it is more than coincidental that its actions followed closely on changes in domestic aviation policy that reduced potential profits for cross-subsidization. First in 1959, then in 1968, the introduction of competition on the domestic system would have served to stimulate the airline to compensate for these losses by looking to its other profitable opeations—the North Atlantic. The initiation of the arrangements for the 1971 IATA session must have commenced in 1970—the year in which CP Air finally expanded to fill 25 percent of the transcontinental market. The 1963 threat was the culmination of three years of unsuccessful attempts to reduce fares that had begun in 1959—one year after CP Air received its first transcontinental flight.[o]

CONCLUSION

We are thus provided with evidence from three episodes—the initial introduction of competition on the transcontinental route in 1958, its subsequent expansion in 1967–68, and finally the extension of the regional carriers between 1968 and 1971—evidence that can be used to judge the appropriateness of the model of the Crown airline. In each case, the interdependence of the Crown airline's fare structure across sectors was illustrated. Whether the event was new entry to the transcontinental or to the regional routes, the fare structure of all sectors was altered. Moreover, the sign of the fare change was as predicted—always positive for at least the sector not experiencing entry.

The magnitude of the perverse movement in prices that resulted was not insignificant. For example, on the heavily travelled Vancouver-Toronto route, the two successive fare adjustments in 1968 and 1971 raised the fare by $24 from $109 to $133. At the same time introduction of the stretched DC-8 served to reduce the cost per passenger on this route by about $13 (see Table 12–1). On both the Calgary-Toronto and Edmonton-Toronto routes, prices were increased by $20 from $89 to $109, while the stretched DC-8 resulted in about a $10 decrease in the cost per passenger (see Table 12–1). In all three cases, the ratio of the sum of the fare increase and the cost decrease—the amount by which the markup was increased—to the fare originally in effect before implementation of the second phase of the government's "competition" policy is 34 percent.

Up to this point, this work has almost completely ignored the International operations of the Crown airline. This chapter also demonstrates that, as we should have expected, the Crown airline's performance on the domestic sector is not independent of the profitability of its international routes. Even though

[o]As we saw in Chapter Six, the airline had incurred losses between 1960 and 1962.

considerably restricted as to the price level chosen for its international routes because of the existence of the cartel thereon, loss of potential profits from its domestic system has led to its actively seeking a change in North Atlantic fares on two occasions–a change that would have helped to offset a change in domestic profits occasioned by shifts in the government's domestic "competition" policy.

Part III

Conclusion

Chapter Twelve

Conclusion

ALTERNATE THEORIES OF THE BEHAVIOR OF THE PUBLIC FIRM

Treating the public firm as a rational political entity yielded several testable hypotheses. First, it was predicted that the public airline would develop a policy of internal cross-subsidization. Secondly, it was hypothesized that a cost decrease, apparently specific to only one route, might well cause prices to fall elsewhere. Thirdly, the model forecast that the introduction of a competitor on certain of the Crown airline's routes would cause prices elsewhere to increase. Finally, the introduction of equipment that increases demand but does not affect costs was predicted to cause prices to change on those routes not benefiting from this equipment. Following development of the implications of the model of the Crown airline, evidence from the Canadian Crown airline's behavior was adduced in an attempt to substantiate this theory.

The corroborating evidence that was presented may be less than totally persuasive—especially to those who are loath to abandon more traditional models of the firm. The attractiveness of any model depends upon its relative simplicity, the acceptability of its assumptions, and the degree to which it can explain events that generally accepted alternative models cannot account for. It is to the last issue that this section addresses itself. Admittedly, the occasion is rare when a set of events is compatible with only one underlying model. Nevertheless, this issue cannot be completely ignored. To the extent that the more obvious alternatives can be ruled out, the theory of the public firm as proposed herein will be strengthened.

Instead of treating the public firm as responsive to the political process, it might well have been modeled as a profit-maximizing firm. Perhaps those who argue that regulatory agencies do no more than promote the interests of regulated firms would feel equally at ease with the argument that a public carrier, when unhindered by competition, is merely a profit-maximizing monopolist in disguise.[a] However, this approach in and by itself does not explain the interdependence that was found to exist amongst the prices charged in different markets. In order to do so, special characteristics must be ascribed to airline markets.

If the production process is characterized by joint costs or if the demand in any one market is a function of that in others, then interdependence of prices across markets will result. It is therefore necessary to ask whether either or a combination of both would yield all the other predictions that emanate from the support-maximizing model. If certain restrictions on the nature of the cost function are required to produce the same results, we must then investigate whether these are characteristic of aviation markets.

If part of the production process is joint and if the marginal cost function is declining then most of the predictions hold. First, when the difference between price and average cost is calculated for all sectors, some routes appear to be subsidizing others. Secondly, a downward shift in the marginal cost function of that portion of costs not joint will lead to a decrease in prices on other routes. Thirdly, if the demand curve on one route shifts to the right, then the price in other markets will decrease. Finally, if a change in market structure reduces the number of passengers carried on one route, prices will increase elsewhere.

But the existence of scale economies in that portion of costs that is joint is not sufficient to yield the same predictions about changes in fare differentials as are generated by the support-maximizing model. For instance, the support-maximizing model predicted that entry to the profitable mainline routes would increase the fare differential between profit and loss sectors. A profit-maximizing, price-discriminating monopolist sets the price difference between two products, $P_2 - P_1$, such that

$$P_2 - P_1 = \left[\frac{1}{(\frac{1}{\eta_2} + 1)} - \frac{1}{(\frac{1}{\eta_1} + 1)} \right] MC,$$

where η_1, and η_2 are the price elasticities of each product and MC is the marginal cost.[b] If marginal cost increases because of a loss in traffic caused by

[a]As an alternative the public firm could be treated as a regulated firm with even more incentive than a private firm to augment the managers' utility at the expense of shareholders. See Armen Alchian and Reuben Kessel, "Competition, Monopoly and the Pursuit of Money," *Aspects of Labor Economics,* a Conference of the Universities–National Bureau Committee for Economic Research, a Report of the National Bureau of Economic Research, New York, Special Conference Series, No. 14 (Princeton, N.J.: Princeton U. Pr., 1962), pp. 157–83.

[b]The analysis remains unaffected if it is recognized that there is a portion of airline costs that does not appear to be joint. Thus the marginal cost should differ for each route.

entry to one sector or the other, the price differential will widen if the elasticities remain constant. Since the essence of government policy was to guarantee and restrict the new entrant to a set share of the market, treating the elasticity as constant is not too unrealistic.[c] Only if we regard $|\eta_i|$ as increasing dramatically in response to entry will it be possible to obtain the movements in the price differential, P_2-P_1, which the support-maximizing model predicted or which were observed. Given the rigid governmental restrictions that have been imposed on each new entrant, this interpretation of events while possible appears implausible. It would garner greater credence if, in the face of entry, prices had actually fallen on the sector affected.[d] But as we have seen this did not occur.

Since the alternative explanation that depends on the existence of economies of scale cannot be completely ruled out, it behooves us to inquire whether there is solid evidence that some portion of costs are joint and subject to increasing returns to scale. The relevance of this alternative model is subject to empirical test. Airline costs are generally placed in one of two categories—direct or indirect operating costs. Direct operating expenses include air crew costs, fuel, maintenance, and depreciation. Scale effects that do exist for this category are related to stage-length and route density [1] and do not appear joint in any meaningful sense.[2] Indirect costs include passenger service and handling, aircraft and traffic servicing, promotion and sales, and general and administrative expense. Although production for contiguous routes is joint in this case, numerous statistical studies have been unable to uncover the existence of economies of scale in this category.[3] Unfortunately, none of these studies was directed at the route level and all suffer from the shortcoming that indirect costs include an element determined not solely by technological considerations but instead by quality competition engendered by the nature of regulation imposed by the United States Civil Aeronautics Board.

Thus, the empirical evidence to justify treating the Crown airline as a price-discriminating monopolist subject to economies of scale is weak. But more important, the Canadian airline fails to behave in other ways which this approach would predict. The price-discriminating firm should be expected to discriminate not only amongst markets but also amongst passengers on the same route. That this has occurred on the cartel-controlled North Atlantic routes is well known.[4] Peak season, off-peak season fares, affinity group fares, and

[c]The elasticity of the industry demand curve $Q(P)$ and that of a dominant firm whose share is always $(1-k)Q(P)$ where k is a constant are the same.

[d]The most annoying anomaly unexplained by this alternative model is the failure of the general price level to move upwards on the northern Ontario and Quebec sector in 1971. With entry elsewhere, the existence of economies of scale should have led to a price increase. Since there was no entry thereon, it is more difficult to argue that the elasticity of demand faced by the airline should have suddenly increased. The lack of movement in the general price level thereon is however consistent with the support-maximizing model.

inclusive tour fares have been characteristic of the North Atlantic, but rarely seen in the Canadian market. The contrast between American and Canadian behavior is equally striking. Air Canada has consistently used less interpersonal fare discrimination than the American airline industry has employed. For instance, in the early sixties, the United States offered youth, military, "Golden Age," standby, night coach, and "Discover America" fares, none of which existed in Canada. This difference is consistent with the predicitions of the support-maximizing model—that is, a public airline finds it more costly to price discriminate than private carriers.[e] Thus, the alternative treatment of the public airline as a profit-maximizing monopolist is unsatisfactory.

There is another possible explanation for interdependence of market prices. Since for each city-pair some of the passengers carried thereon have originated on a different segment of the route system, the demand for air services on one route is rarely independent of that for services elsewhere. A passenger's decision to travel is a function of the total price of the trip—the sum of all the individual segment prices. Should the airline find itself unable to set special fares for interconnecting passengers, the prices established by a profit-maximizing airline on its different routes will be interdependent.

Consider such an airline to be operating in only two markets. Demand in each market consists of some who restrict their travels to that particular market and others who utilize both services. Then the demand curves (Q_i, $i = 1, 2$) can be written as follows:

$$Q_1 = Q_1(P_1, P_2) = f(P_1 + P_2) + g(P_1), \qquad (12\text{–}1a)$$

$$Q_2 = Q_2(P_1, P_2) = f(P_1 + P_2) + k(P_2)\,. \qquad (12\text{–}2b)$$

Assuming the necessary conditions for use of the inverse function theorem, the price in each market can be written as a function of both Q_1 and Q_2. The profit-maximizing firm will maximize:

$$Q_1 \cdot P_1(Q_1, Q_2) + Q_2 \cdot P_2(Q_1, Q_2) - C(Q_1) - D(Q_2)\,,$$

where C and D are the cost functions of the first and second markets respectively. The first-order conditions are:

$$\left\{ P_1 + Q_1 \frac{\delta P_1}{\delta Q_1} + Q_2 \frac{\delta P_2}{\delta Q_1} \right\} - \frac{\delta C}{\delta Q_1} = 0, \qquad (12\text{–}2a)$$

$$\left\{ P_2 + Q_2 \frac{\delta P_2}{\delta Q_2} + Q_1 \frac{\delta P_1}{\delta Q_2} \right\} - \frac{\delta D}{\delta Q_2} = 0. \qquad (12\text{–}2b)$$

[e]This does not imply there will be no interpersonal fare discrimination nor that conditions will not change so as to make it more feasible and more desirable. For instance, it

The first order condition may be totally differentiated to analyze the effects of lowering the marginal cost in the second market. Let the change in marginal cost be represented by dC_2. Then

$$\begin{bmatrix} A \end{bmatrix} \begin{bmatrix} dQ_1 \\ dQ_2 \end{bmatrix} = \begin{bmatrix} 0 \\ dC_2 \end{bmatrix}, \qquad (12\text{–}3)$$

where

$$A = \begin{bmatrix} 2\frac{\delta P_1}{\delta Q_1} + Q_1 \frac{\delta^2 P_1}{\delta Q^2} + Q_2 \frac{\delta^2 P_2}{\delta Q_1{}^2} - \frac{\delta^2 C}{\delta Q_1{}^2}; \frac{\delta P_1}{\delta Q_2} + \frac{\delta P_2}{\delta Q_1} + Q_1 \frac{\delta^2 P_1}{\delta Q_1 \delta Q_2} + Q_2 \frac{\delta^2 P_1}{\delta Q_1 \delta Q_2} \\ \frac{\delta P_2}{\delta Q_1} + \frac{\delta P_1}{\delta Q_2} + Q_2 \frac{\delta^2 P_2}{\delta Q_2 \delta Q_1} + Q_1 \frac{\delta^2 P_1}{\delta Q_2 \delta Q_1}; 2\frac{\delta P_2}{\delta Q_2} + Q_2 \frac{\delta^2 P_2}{\delta Q_2{}^2} + Q_1 \frac{\delta^2 P_1}{\delta Q_2{}^2} - \frac{\delta^2 D}{\delta Q_2{}^2} \end{bmatrix}$$

Now $$\frac{dP_1}{dC_2} = \frac{\delta P_1}{\delta Q_1} \frac{dQ_1}{dC_2} + \frac{\delta P_1}{\delta Q_2} \frac{dQ_2}{dC_2}$$

$$= \frac{\delta P_1}{\delta Q_1} \left(\frac{-a_{12}}{D} \right) + \frac{\delta P_1}{\delta Q_2} \left(\frac{a_{11}}{D} \right) \text{from (12–3)} \qquad (12\text{–}4)$$

where a_{ij} is the element in the i'th row and j'th column of A, and D is the determinant of A.

Now consider the effect of introducing a competitor to the route on which the profit-maximizing airline had a monopoly—route 2. This may be represented by introducing a shift parameter α in P_2 and $\delta P_2/\delta Q_2$. Entry will shift P_2 to the left ($\delta P_2/\delta\alpha < 0$), but may cause $\delta^2 P_2/\delta Q_2 \delta\alpha > 0$. Then totally differentiating (12-2a) and (12-2b) including this effect gives:

$$\begin{bmatrix} A \end{bmatrix} \begin{bmatrix} dQ_1 \\ dQ_2 \end{bmatrix} = \begin{bmatrix} 0 \\ -\frac{\delta P_2}{\delta \alpha} d\alpha - Q_2 \frac{\delta^2 P_2}{\delta Q_2 \delta \alpha} d\alpha \end{bmatrix}$$

---

has become more widespread in the late sixties—a period when the Crown airline suddenly was faced with entry on both its transcontinental and regional routes. It was argued in Chapter Eleven that the existence of competitors made it easier to introduce changes in the fare structure. To the extent that entrants reduced profits available for cross-subsidization, they also increased the pressure to engage in price discrimination.

Therefore $$\frac{dP_1}{d\alpha} = \frac{\delta P_1}{\delta Q_1}\frac{dQ_1}{d\alpha} + \frac{\delta P_1}{\delta Q_2}\frac{dQ_2}{d\alpha}$$

$$= \left[-\frac{\delta P_2}{\delta\alpha} - Q_2 \frac{\delta^2 P_2}{\delta Q_2 \delta\alpha} \right] \left[\frac{\delta P_1}{\delta Q_1}\left(\frac{-a_{12}}{D}\right) + \frac{\delta P_1}{\delta Q_2}\left(\frac{a_{11}}{D}\right) \right]$$

$$\frac{dP_1}{d\alpha} = K\frac{dP_1}{dC_2} \text{ from (12–4).} \qquad (12\text{–}6)$$

Similarly, it can be shown that

$$\frac{dP_2}{d\alpha} = K\frac{dP_2}{dC_2}\,, \qquad (12\text{–}7)$$

but $dP_1/d\alpha > 0$ and $dP_1/dC_2 > 0$ were the results predicted by the support-maximizing model.[f] In order to yield the same results here, K must be greater than zero.

Therefore, $sgn\ dP_2/dC_2 = sgn\ dP_2/d\alpha$. If prices are reduced on the mainline routes in response to decreases in costs thereon, entry to the same sector should increase its prices. Thus the model would also explain the movement of absolute prices described in earlier chapters. But it does not explain the movement in price differentials.

For $$\frac{dP_1}{d\alpha} - \frac{dP_2}{d\alpha} = K\left[\frac{dP_1}{dC_2} - \frac{dP_2}{dC_2}\right] \text{from (12–6) and (12–7).}$$

If K is positive, should a decrease in marginal cost on route 2 cause the price spread to increase, then entry to route 2 will cause the price spread to decrease. While the former situation is in accordance with the Crown airline's behavior, the latter is opposite to what would have been predicted by the support-maximizing model and what was actually observed.

There is a more compelling reason to reject the interdependence of the demand curves as an alternate explanation. This approach assumes the airline cannot set a special fare for the connecting passengers. Yet, examination of Air Canada's 1970 timetable shows ample evidence of fares for city-pairs that have no direct flights yet differ from the sum of the fares for each segment.

There may be those who would not regard profit-maximizing models of the public firm as the relevant alternatives. The public firm, they might argue, exists

[f]See Table 5–1. The subscript ordering used here is the opposite of that found in this table.

to correct the defects of the market system and as such it will act so as to maximize consumer welfare. Treating the public firm as maximizing a welfare function subject to a budget constraint yields well-defined pricing rules. For instance, if substitution effects are ignored, for each product *i*, the public firm should set its price so that

$$t_i \frac{dq_i}{dp_i} = - \beta q_i \text{ [5]}$$

where t_i is the difference between price and marginal cost. Using these conditions and the profit constraint, it is not difficult to show that the behavior of the support-maximizing and welfare-maximizing firm in response to shifts in marginal cost and demand curves will be qualitatively the same. Admittedly, the prediction of cross-subsidization does not result from a simple welfare-maximizing model. This can be remedied by postulating an additional interest by the Crown airline in distributional issues.[6]

But to postulate this as the relevant motivational model is as sensible as developing the theory of the privately owned firm by first assuming that private managers will operate so as to satisfy the first-order conditions for Pareto optimality. In order to do so, one would have to argue that should they fail to satisfy these conditions, the government would step in and rectify the situation. Otherwise, there is no connection between motivations and actions. While it is not impossible to argue this position, it is implausible. The model developed herein stems from the body of thought that governments attempt to maximize the present value of benefits they are able to bestow upon their supporters. Whether this satisfies the economist's first-order conditions seems doubtful.

The strength of neoclassical economic theory is the demonstration that individual firms, acting in their own interest, maximize society's welfare. Parallel development in the evolution of the theory of the public firm requires an examination of whether the public firm acting in response to pressures from the political arena will produce results deemed to be optimal in the Pareto sense.

This has not been the purpose of the present exercise. Instead, it has concentrated on the first step—that of providing positive models of institutional behavior. In particular, it focused on the behavior of two institutions often chosen to influence an industry's performance—a regulatory agency and a public firm. While the issue as to whether either or both produces the optimum result from a welfare standpoint will not be dealt with here, the relative desirability of these two institutions will be examined. For in a world of second bests—where government intervention is bound to occur even when not required—to be able to say something about which form of intervention will do the least harm is not unimportant.

A CROSS-COUNTRY COMPARISON OF THE EFFECTS OF REGULATION VERSUS PUBLIC OWNERSHIP

In order to be manageable, this section shall concentrate upon the difference between the price-cost mark-ups produced by regulation of the airline industry in the United States and public ownership in Canada. The models developed herein suggest that public ownership may produce less of a discrepancy between prices and average costs than a regulatory agency. It was argued that both institutions would adopt similar objective functions. The difference in the performance of the industry in each case arises because the regulatory agency is constantly engaged in a bargaining process with private firms. Some of the funds the public firm would utilize to support lower prices or higher quality of service on "regional" routes would under a regulatory scheme be diverted to shareholders of the regulated airlines in an attempt to reward them with more than a competitive rate of return. This suggests that regulation will lead to larger price-cost differences than will the existence of a state-owned monopoly.

As a test for this hypothesis, the performance of the airline industry under regulation in the United States will be compared to the performance that resulted in Canada from the existence of a publicly owned firm. But before examining the quantitative evidence as to the effects of the different institutions, certain qualitative evidence that would support treating the behavior of the Civil Aeronautics Board as falling within the confines of the model of the regulatory process is presented.

Regulation has been treated as a compromise process—the outcome of which was determined by an evolving set of bargains struck between the regulated and the regulator. That this was the case in the United States is evidenced by the fact that the legislation that established the Civil Aeronautics Board instructed this agency to consider the interests of both consumers and producers.[7]

The very nature of the compromise process, it was argued, implies the necessity of a regulatory agency being able to offer something to the participants. In the case of the industry, this is likely to involve both explicit payments such as subsidies and indirect benefits such as those stemming from reduced competition. The use of the latter instrument implies that transportation regulatory agencies should be found to exercise tight control over entry.

Since its inception in 1936, the Civil Aeronautics Board (CAB) has effectively blocked entry to the industry. Admittedly pressure by Congress served to prevent CAB-initiated annihilation of the "supplementary" carriers [8]—whose existence eventually aided in the weakening of the North Atlantic cartel—and the 1960s saw the expansion of a number of "local" service carriers to small "trunk" status.[9] However, it is generally agreed that the rate of new entry has been well below what it would have been otherwise.

The regulatory agency should also have been expected to benefit certain consumer groups. Throughout this book, emphasis in this area has been focused on the resulting manipulation of the fare structure. As long as the American industry relied almost completely on subsidies, the regulatory agency was able to maintain substantial equality between routes in terms of the fares that were charged. As late as 1952, when operating subsidies were being phased out, the fare structure provided no variation in the fare per mile with respect to distance.[10] Throughout the fifties, the CAB devoted considerable time and effort to perpetuating the internal subsidy that existed between dense long-haul routes and shorter less dense markets.[11] Its efforts involved not only protection of existing carriers from new ones but also an attempt to resist pressures leading to fare reductions—especially on the profitable routes.[12] Even when selective reductions were permitted—such as the introduction of coach service—the CAB attempted to restrict their impact by severely limiting the availability of this service.[13]

As soon as the regulatory process is regarded as one of compromise, the opportunities for strategic bargaining become evident. In the Canadian case, the regulatory agency found itself unable to control all aspects of the regional airlines' equipment or route policies. The history of American experience exhibits a similar pattern. As a result of a lack of downward price flexibility forced upon the industry by the Civil Aeronautics Board and improved technology, which reduced costs on the longer stage-lengths, the price-cost margins increased thereon. Trunk carriers concentrated their efforts in this area and gradually abandoned many of their shorter or lightly travelled routes. As a result, the Civil Aeronautics Board attempted to arrest this trend, first by attempting to strengthen the weaker trunk carriers, then by nurturing a second level of air carrier—the local service airlines.[14] As in Canada, the success of the American regulatory agency was limited. Eads concludes that service to those cities depending exclusively on local service carriers declined in quality between 1959 and 1969.[15]

In light of this evolution, it would not be surprising to find that prices on some American routes were well above that level that would have characterized a competitive industry. Caves, after analyzing the American fare structure in 1958, concludes that average costs tended to be below average revenues on the longer and denser routes.[16] Jordan compares fares during the middle 1960s on the unregulated intra-state Los Angeles-San Francisco route with those on comparable but regulated East Coast interstate markets. He concludes that regulation raised fares on these short-haul routes by between 32 and 47 percent.[17] While Jordan's analysis rests on a comparison of a relatively small number of dense short-haul routes, Keeler extends the comparison to 30 high density city-pairs of varying stage-length.[18] By assuming that in the absence of regulation seating densities and load factors would have approximated those achieved in the unregulated California market, Keeler concludes that in 1968 prices were about 20 percent above average costs on short-haul routes, but 80 to 90 percent above costs on the longest routes.[19] Keeler's study shall provide the benchmark for a comparison of the performance of the American and the Canadian markets.

The year 1966 is chosen for estimates of the Canadian price-cost margins since this is the last year in which the Canadian public airline clearly dominated the domestic industry. In the following four years, Air Canada increasingly shared its trunk market with CP Air and its regional traffic with carriers like Quebecair and Eastern Provincial Airways. The routes chosen for the analysis are those on which direct flights were offered. Appendix B describes the generation of cost estimates for each route. While direct operating costs for each route are relatively easy to estimate, indirect costs—consisting of such items as passenger service, promotion and sales, aircraft and traffic servicing, and general administration expenses—are not. Thus two approaches are followed. The first allocates this expense partially on a passenger basis, partially on a per-mile basis. The second, more comparable to Keeler's analysis, allocates all indirect expenses on a per-mile basis. Both the cost and mark-up estimates so generated are presented in Table 12–1. The cost for all routes of less than 1,000 miles distance assumes the use of a DC-9; that for all longer stage-lengths a DC-8 or a stretched DC-8 (the DC-8L). The figures for the DC-8L are included in parentheses.

Examination of the table indicates that no matter which costing method is chosen, the Canadian market performed better under a public carrier than the American market did under regulation. Using the first method of allocating indirect costs, Canadian long-haul mark-ups for the DC-8 were between 20 and 40 percent; for the DC-8L, they ranged between 45 and 60 percent. Keeler reports long-haul mark-ups in the United States of at least 80 percent. Using the first method of cost allocation yields short-haul mark-ups that were negative in Canada, whereas they were about 20 percent in the United States. Using the second method of indirect cost allocation yields Canadian short-haul mark-ups of 20 to 40 percent—a result that is indistinguishable from American results. But this method produces a marked difference in long-haul mark-ups—only 30 to 40 percent for Canada as compared to the 80 percent Keeler found for the United States. The correct method of allocating indirect costs probably lies somewhere between the two methods chosen here. If this is the case, both long- and short-haul mark-ups in Canada were less than those in the United States.

While the quality of the cost data prevents much confidence being placed in the figures for individual route mark-ups, it does not invalidate the cross-country comparison. Moreover, the method used to generate Canadian costs consistently imparts a downward bias to their estimates and thus an upward bias in the price-cost mark-ups reported above. In the first place, load factors on most Canadian domestic routes were below seventy percent—the figure chosen to generate the Canadian price-cost margins reported in Table 12–1. Secondly, neither the long-bodied DC-9 nor the DC-8—the two aircraft used in this study—had been introduced in Canada by 1966. Their shorter predecessors showed mark-ups only about half of those reported for the DC-9-30 and the

DC-8-60. Thus, the results in Table 12–1 substantiate the contention that regulation of the air transport industry in the United States did indeed produce price-cost margins that were greater than those established by the Crown airline in Canada.[g]

THE USE OF POSITIVE MODELS IN THE POLICY PROCESS

The purpose of this work has been to develop positive models that explain the behavior of transportation regulatory agencies and state-owned transportation companies. Much of the exposition has attempted to show that the behavior of both the Canadian regulatory agency and the Crown airline accords with that predicted for each by the positive model. The previous section provides one use to which the models can be put—predicting the comparative performance of these institutions. Judiciously applied, they can also yield insights into other policy issues.

Both models serve to explain, but not to justify, the existence of certain aspects of behavior often criticized by observers of these institutions. For instance, implicit in the very creation of a regulatory agency is the requirement that the agency satisfy all parties involved. Regulatory agencies should, therefore, be expected to seek support whenever the benefits of such a policy outweigh the costs. This suggests we should not be surprised to discover producers receiving "side payments." Similarly, for both the regulatory agency and the Crown airline, the practice of cross-subsidization is seen to be the natural outcome of these institutions following survival-motivated policies. It immediately follows that, should this be true, remonstrations on the part of political economists as to the undesirability of this practice are likely to have little impact. It is a futile gesture to request that the agency change its ways irrespective of the environment in which it operates.

Nor is it true that these models imply that should we wish different results, the complete abolition of an institution is required. Although capable of predicting the regulatory body's behavior, this in no way should be interpreted as meaning the model is deterministic. For instance, the discussion of regional aviation policy illustrates the effect that the introduction of subsidies had on the outcome of the regulatory process. By changing the nature of the bargaining process, it enabled regional carriers to break down entry barriers which had previously faced them. At the same time, this event illustrates the major shortcoming of the regulatory process. The implicit nature of the bargains reached between agency and industry produces an uncertain outcome. What does appear evident from Canadian experience is that the introduction of

[g]The relative size of the welfare loss from regulation as compared to public ownership will be less than a simple comparison of price-cost margins would suggest, because load factors and thus the time cost of a trip were lower in the United States than in Canada.

Table 12–1. Canadian Route Costs and Fare Mark-Ups, 1966

City Pair	*Distance*	*Fare*	*Cost Method 1*	*Cost Method 2*	*Mark-up Method 1*	*Mark-up Method 2*
Victoria-Vancouver	42	8	15.65	5.85	.51	1.37
Vancouver-Calgary	454	31	27.18	22.42	1.14	1.38
-Edmonton	539	33	29.42	25.83	1.12	1.28
-Winnipeg	1,182	63	51.19	55.78	1.23	1.13
			(43.42)	(48.01)	(1.45)	(1.31)
-Toronto	2,123	109	79.90	96.34	1.36	1.13
			(66.98)	(83.42)	(1.63)	(1.31)
Calgary-Edmonton	164	13	18.97	10.76	0.69	1.20
-Regina	430	28	26.42	21.46	1.06	1.30
-Saskatoon	342	26	24.11	17.92	1.08	1.45
-Winnipeg	746	43	35.13	34.17	1.22	1.26
-Toronto	1,686	89	66.64	77.51	1.34	1.15
			(56.11)	(66.98)	(1.59)	(1.33)
Edmonton-Regina	485	30	27.90	23.68	1.08	1.27
-Saskatoon	325	24	23.58	17.23	1.02	1.39
-Winnipeg	765	43	35.61	34.93	1.21	1.23
-Toronto	1,705	89	67.17	78.33	1.33	1.14
			(56.54)	(67.69)	(1.57)	(1.31)
Regina-Winnipeg	340	23	23.90	17.84	0.96	1.29
-Toronto	1,280	75	54.56	60.01	1.37	1.25
			(46.25)	(51.70)	(1.62)	(1.45)
Saskatoon-Winnipeg	443	30	26.85	21.98	1.12	1.36
Winnipeg-Thunder Bay	383	27	25.19	19.57	1.07	1.38
-Windsor	913	50	39.68	40.89	1.26	1.22
-Toronto	946	52	40.21	41.80	1.29	1.24
-Ottawa	1,056	58	47.41	50.36	1.22	1.15
			(40.32)	(43.27)	(1.44)	(1.34)
-Montreal	1,152	63	50.36	54.50	1.25	1.16
			(42.74)	(46.88)	(1.47)	(1.34)
Thunder Bay-Sault Ste. Marie	262	23	21.94	14.70	1.05	1.56
-Toronto	582	37	30.71	27.57	1.20	1.34
Sault Ste. Marie-Toronto	311	25	23.28	16.67	1.07	1.50
Windsor-Toronto	196	17	19.98	11.98	0.85	1.42

London-Toronto	88	9	16.85	7.70	0.53	1.17
Toronto-Ottawa	244	19	21.29	13.98	0.89	1.36
-Montreal	340	23	23.90	17.84	0.96	1.29
Ottawa-Montreal	104	9	17.25	8.34	0.52	1.08
Montreal-Saguenay	248	21	21.49	14.14	0.98	1.49
-Quebec	158	13	18.82	10.52	0.69	1.24
-Sept Isles	499	32	28.36	24.23	1.13	1.32
Saguenay-Three Rivers	69	11	16.48	6.94	0.67	1.58
-Quebec	131	11	18.03	9.43	0.61	1.17
Quebec-Sept Isles	353	27	24.44	18.36	1.10	1.47
Toronto-Sudbury	235	19	21.06	13.61	0.90	1.40
-Timmins	377	27	25.10	19.33	1.06	1.40
-North Bay	192	17	19.88	11.88	0.86	1.43
Ottawa-Val d'Or	221	19	20.71	13.06	0.92	1.46
Sudbury-Timmins	141	13	18.39	9.83	0.71	1.32
-North Bay	68	9	15.87	6.90	0.57	1.31
Toronto-Fredericton	674	40	33.17	31.27	1.21	1.28
-Halifax	829	48	37.48	37.51	1.28	1.28
Montreal-Moncton	459	29	27.20	22.66	1.07	1.28
-Fredericton	369	25	24.74	19.00	1.01	1.32
-St. John	398	27	25.57	20.17	1.06	1.34
-Halifax	523	33	29.01	25.20	1.14	1.31
-St. John's	1,033	60	46.88	49.37	1.28	1.22
			(39.91)	(42.41)	(1.51)	(1.41)
Quebec-Fredericton	277	22	22.27	15.30	0.99	1.44
Moncton-Halifax	116	10	17.62	8.81	0.57	1.13
Fredericton-Halifax	183	17	19.65	11.52	0.86	1.48
St. John-Halifax	137	12	18.24	9.67	0.66	1.24
Halifax-Yarmouth	159	13	18.84	10.56	0.69	1.23
-Sydney	191	17	19.85	11.84	0.86	1.44
-St. John's	552	37	29.96	26.37	1.24	1.40
Sydney-Stephenville	180	17	19.58	11.40	0.87	1.49
Stephenville-Gander	189	17	19.80	11.76	0.86	1.45
Gander-St. John's	139	11	18.23	9.75	0.60	1.13

Note: Method 1 uses the equation C($) = 10.01 + .00783 Miles + .0528 Fare for indirect costs; method 2 uses the equation C(¢) = .023 Miles for indirect costs. The figures in parentheses refer to the DC-8L.

Source: Appendix B.

subsidies (resulting from a reduction in their cost to the regulatory agency) emasculated the attempt of the regulatory agency to provide service via a scheme of cross-subsidization to short-haul, low-density points.

While the model of a regulatory agency provides a framework within which the effectiveness of the subsidy program can be analyzed, that of the Crown airline permits evaluation of the changes in market structure that were billed as "competition" policy. Introduction of private carriers to the transcontinental and regional routes has generally increased the prices in both sectors. Although the consumer is now presented with a choice of carriers, this has been accomplished at a cost.

Failure to recognize the relevance of the model has led to a complete neglect of the cost of competition. Most discussions treated the policy as unquestionably beneficial. But this must be the result of implicitly considering the public airline to be similar to a privately owned price-discriminating monopolist. If joint cost effects and economies of scale had existed, the standard model of the firm would have suggested that price increases could result from the introduction of a competitor to the Crown airline. The difficulty inherent in cost function estimation meant this possibility was ignored. Adoption of what, it is claimed, is the more realistic model would have had the desirable effect of focusing the debate on whether provision of choice was worth the increase in prices or whether there were alternative methods of achieving the same objective, for to blame the Crown airline for initiating price increases is pointless. As long as the airline continued to act rationally in order to maximize its survival, this is the result we should have expected of this policy. Any blame must be assigned to the formulators of policy. Had they wished to avoid this result, they could have countered with either increased opportunities for cross-subsidization elsewhere—via international route awards to the Crown airline—or by direct payments for the losses suffered by the Crown airline on its social routes.

Although the use to which these models might have been put is most evident after the event, certain suggestions as to the future course of Canadian air transport policy can be evaluated with their aid. The primary use of these models lies in their ability to predict whether the instruments available for government manipulation permit attainment of a desired objective. For instance, the prescription that the regulatory board be given absolute control over the government airline is meaningless in the absence of an understanding of the results of such an act. The positive models permit just such prognostications.

With similar objectives and the same set of instruments at its control, at first glance the regulatory agency might be expected to take an equal interest in provision of service to outlying areas and thus to perpetuate the Crown airline's policies. However, the agency can only continue to function by producing policies equally satisfactory to its other constituents—the industry. The primary participant apart from the Crown airline is CP Air. Its persistent demands for a satisfactory share of the transcontinental market would have to be met by the regulatory agency. The most likely outcome would be an even or fifty-fifty split of traffic between Air Canada and CP Air.[h]

In the past, policies that have tended in this direction have increased the spread between price and average cost on the transcontinental route. Unless price were already at the joint profit-maximizing point, there seems to be little likelihood that this would not be repeated. In the first place, the immutability of the fifty-fifty focal point means that CP Air would have little to gain from price competition. On the other hand, Air Canada might fail to increase prices further only if the losses sustained on its social routes were to be eliminated. It would be unlikely to do so itself—its very nature as a support-maximizing entity necessitates this view.[i] Nor would the regulatory agency be likely to alleviate the cost of these social routes by paying direct subsidies to the Crown airline. It has already been shown that this method of financing is unsatisfactory to both parties.[j] The regulatory agency's other option would be to replace Air Canada with the regional carriers on many of these routes. However, the evidence cited suggests that in the absence of subsidies to these carriers this would either lead to increased fares or decreased services on these routes—a prospect the regulatory agency would be likely to avoid in order not to lose support. Besides, given the present tendency of these carriers to abandon low density points, the pressure on the regulatory board to aid these carriers has been considerably reduced. Therefore, we should generally expect the fares of the transcontinental route to increase relative to costs should the regulatory agency have its power extended.

However, this tendency may be inevitable within the present institutional context. CP Air has been allowed to expand its share of the transcontinental market on two occasions since 1958. Despite this, prices have moved upwards on this route resulting in a higher degree of cross-subsidization. The policy of "competition" has resulted in perverse price movements. It is, therefore, interesting to speculate on future performance in this market. The fifty-fifty split is too strong a focal point to ignore. Even without the regulatory body, government policy probably will tend to this result. Therefore, if we extrapolate past performance and assume monopoly profits can still be wrung from this route, we might well expect this sector to have its burden of cross-subsidization increased without any change in the institutional setting.

Thus, the issue appears to resolve itself into the question of which system is more likely to lead the Crown airline to drop its social routes. Since neither

[h]This result, it has already been pointed out, was achieved in Australia under these circumstances.

[i]Similarly, the Crown airline's reluctance to give up these routes to regional carriers during the past eight years supports this contention.

[j]The fact that the regional subsidy program was billed as only "temporary" confirms this contention.

would appear likely to accomplish this, we are faced with determining not what the outcome will be, but how quickly it will be brought about.

However, both forecasts assume the Crown airline is a passive participant—a doubtful hypothesis in the light of recent events. The loss in profits Air Canada will incur from any future change in CP Air's share of the market will result in a reduction of support it receives from its social routes. A second best course of action for the Crown airline may be to reduce profits on the transcontinental route in the hope of forestalling future pressures for further expansion. There are indications that this policy is presently being pursued, for in the late summer of 1972, the Crown airline initiated a series of price reductions on the transcontinental sector.[k] Should this be the case, the present structure may lead to a more desirable outcome than if the regulatory agency were given complete control over the industry. If, as has been argued, the regulatory agency ends up by splitting the market evenly between CP Air and Air Canada, prices would probably move back up to the joint profit-maximizing level since the Crown airline would no longer have any incentive to practise this form of limit pricing.

No claim is made that this analysis of the future course of the Canadian airline industry is either comprehensive or conclusive. Rather, it is meant to show that a judicious application of positive theories to predict the behavior of a regulatory agency or a Crown airline promises to yield valuable insights as to the likely impact of a change in public policy.

[k]It is too early to conclude the exact nature of the outcome because, although price increases were announced for shorter (loss) routes initially, CP Air's failure to follow suit caused fares on both profit and loss sectors to fall.

Appendixes

Appendix A

Regional Carrier Subsidies

Table A–1. Estimates of Subsidies Paid to Regional Carriers, 1967–1970 ($000)

Year	*Quebecair* (1)	*Eastern Provincial Airways* (2)	*Total*[a] (3)
1967	....	629[b]	629
1968	770[c]	780[d]	1,548
1969	685[e]	1,355[f]	2,040
1970	455[h]	1,400[g]	1,855

[a]Canada, Canadian Transport Commission. *Annual Report,* various years.

[b]Canada, Canadian Transport Commission, *Annual Report 1968,* p. 12, reports that only one carrier received subsidies in 1967. Since the *Financial Post,* November 1, 1969, p. A3 indicates EPA received subsidies in this year the total is attributed to this carrier.

[c]*Financial Post,* November 1, 1969, p. A6

[d]Canada, Canadian Transport Commission, *Annual Report, 1969,* p. 14, reports that only two carriers received subsidies in 1968. Therefore EPA's subsidy is estimated as the residual of column (3) less column (1).

[e]International Civil Aviation Organization, *Digest of Statistics, Financial Data,* No. 121 (1969).

[f]The residual calculated from columns (3) and (1).

[g]Canada, Statistics Canada, Aviation Statistics Centre, *Air Carrier Operations in Canada, January-March, 1971,* Cat. No. 51–002, p. 70, reports that as of 1970 federal subsidies are shifted from operating revenues to non-operating revenues. Since this latter category is so insignificant prior to this year, the figure listed under this category for 1970 is used as the estimate of subsidies paid EPA. (See Table A–2).

[h]The residual from columns (3) and (2). This is almost identical to the entry under miscellaneous non-operating revenue for Quebecair in 1970–$447,000. Quebecair, *Financial Statement,* June 1971 reports federal subsidies for the first half of 1970 at $160,000.

Table A–2. Revenue Accounts Likely to Contain Subsidies Paid to Eastern Provincial Airways and Quebecair, 1965–1971 ($)

Year	*Eastern Provincial*			*Quebecair*		
	Operating Revenue	*Non-Operating Revenue*		*Operating Revenue*	*Non-Operating Revenue*	
	Non-Flying Services	*Interests & Discounts*	*Miscellaneous*	*Non-Flying Services*	*Interests & Discounts*	*Miscellaneous*
1965	150,227	......	40,685	161,383	....	–13,491
1966	203,976	836	40,529	347,358	....	....
1967	257,921	1,877	4,678	45,921	....	–19,068
1968	1,446,498	15,032	47,822	782	....	775,540
1969	1,972,609	3,619	21,777	308,864	695,668	....
1970[a]	261,053	1,138	1,400,204	27,436	275,165	447,467
1971	198,465	1,620	1,420,309	186,026	....	222,050

[a]Canada, Statistics Canada, Aviation Statistics Centre, *Air Carrier Operations In Canada,* January-March 1971, Cat. No. 51–002, p. 70, reports that as of 1970, federal subsidies for EPA were shifted from operating to non-operating revenues. It appears therefore that subsidies paid to this airline were included in non-flying services previous to 1970 and under miscellaneous non-operating income for the subsequent two years.

Source: Canada, Dominion Bureau of Statistics, Aviation Statistics Centre, *Civil Aviation–Annual,* Cat. No. 51–202, 1965–69. Canada, Statistics Canada, Aviation Statistics Centre, *Air Carrier Operations in Canada, October-December 1970,* and ibid., 1971.

Appendix B

Estimation of Airline Route Costs in Canada

The purpose of this section is to develop an estimate of Canadian route costs so as to compare fare-cost differentials between the United States and Canada. Keeler's article provides estimates of the amount by which American fares exceed costs.[1] The method adopted here to develop estimates of Canadian route costs will follow his approach whenever possible. However, Keeler's cost estimates cannot simply be transferred to Canada. Neither factor prices nor system characteristics in Canada and the United States were identical during the 1960s. For instance, between 1965 and 1969 the cost of jet fuel to Air Canada grew from 10.8¢ to 12.5¢ per U.S. gallon.[2] In the United States, the trunk carriers paid between 9 and 10.5¢ per gallon for jet fuel during the same period.[3] In addition, Canadian carriers faced an excise tax on aircraft used on domestic flights that their American counterparts did not pay. On the other hand, average pilot salaries in Canada were below those in the United States—though this may be partially the result of a different mix of long- and short-haul equipment. In 1966, Air Canada's pilots received an average salary of $15,600 while American pilots were paid an average of between $18,000 and $23,000.[4]

Differences in system characteristics of airlines in Canada and the United States may also have led to differences in costs. Table B–1 compares certain features of the two Canadian trunk carriers and a sample of the American trunk airlines. Air Canada ranked about equal to the smaller American carriers in terms of passengers carried, but conveyed a smaller number of passengers per flight. As measured by the number of route miles flown per network mile, the traffic density of its route system was below almost all of the American carriers. Thus, if there are economies of scale either at the system or route level, American carriers should have exhibited lower costs.

These differences preclude an outright transfer of American cost estimates to the Canadian route system. A comparison of average costs sheds some light on

Table B–1. Comparison of the System Characteristics for Canadian and American Scheduled Carriers, 1968

	Air Canada	*CPAir*	*American*	*Braniff*	*Delta*	*Eastern*	*National*	*Pan Am*	*TWA*	*United*
Passengers (000)	6,380	1,032	18,298	5,749	11,225	20,705	5,265	8,579	13,557	26,939
Passengers per Flight	32	34	44	33	34	41	35	46	43	41
Average Stage-Length[a]	482	768	632	408	372	406	456	1,228	872	576
Average Passenger Hop[a]	870	1,592	845	626	680	581	791	1,623	1,123	795
Miles Flown per Route Mile	749	272	13,908	3,938	8,592	8,948	11,849	663	1,242	21,031

[a]Measured in miles.

Source: International Air Transport Association, *World Air Transport Statistics*, 1968.

the magnitude of the differences. Table B–2 presents a comparison of average costs per available tonne-kilometre for Canadian and American carriers. Even though it had one of the shortest average stage-lengths, Air Canada's direct operating costs were generally less than those of American carriers. On the other hand, the indirect costs of both Canadian trunk carriers were 20 to 30 percent above those of the American carriers. The comparative disadvantage of the Canadian carriers in this area was greatest in two categories—aircraft and traffic servicing (station costs) and ticketing, promotion, and sales. As a result, Air Canada's total operating costs per available tonne-kilometre were above those of most of the American carriers. However, because Air Canada operated at a higher load factor, when cost is measured on a revenue tonne-kilometre basis, the public airline's costs fell in the middle of those reported for this sample of American carriers.

DIRECT COSTS

The period chosen for the estimation of Canadian route costs is the mid-sixties. Prior to 1967, Air Canada was virtually the sole carrier in the domestic market. Its chief competitor, CP Air, was restricted to one daily flight on the transcontinental route. After 1967, CP Air's share was substantially increased. Therefore, an examination of the effects of establishing a state-owned monopoly on fare-cost margins must rely upon the former period for evidence.

In 1966, the Air Canada fleet consisted of Viscounts, Vanguards, DC-9's, and the unstretched version of the DC-8. Because the first two aircraft were about to be phased out, estimates will be developed for the direct costs of the latter two. Since Keeler uses the stretched DC-8 (DC-8L) for his estimates of costs on the longer stage-lengths, its costs will also be considered—even though it was not extensively used until 1968. Including a cost estimate for the DC-8L provides a basis for comparison of the two systems. Of course, the mark-up of fare over cost obtained using this version of the DC-8 in 1966 is a theoretical construct with no real counterpart in that year.

Direct costs include those expenses that are required to move the aircraft from point to point. It includes such items as flight crew costs, fuel expenses, insurance, and depreciation. In order to estimate the direct flying costs for each route, the cost per flying hour for each aircraft was allocated to each route on the basis of the number of hours required to cover the relevant distance. This relationship was obtained from the 1973 route schedule of Air Canada. The year 1973 was chosen so as to omit the influence of Viscounts and Vanguards which had by then mostly been phased out.[a]

The resulting equation linking schedule flight time and block distance was estimated:

[a]The few routes where Viscounts were still used were either discarded or the Viscount flights removed from the data. In addition all B-747 or L-1011 flights were omitted. Only domestic flights were considered.

Table B–2. Comparison of Canadian and American Airline Costs, 1969 (U.S. ¢ per available tonne-kilometre)

	Air Canada	*CPAir*	*American*	*Braniff*	*Delta*	*Eastern*	*National*	*Pan Am*	*TWA*	*United*
Flight Operations	2.8	3.1	3.7	4.4	3.8	4.7	3.4	3.4	3.7	4.0
Maintenance	2.5	1.5	2.0	1.9	2.4	2.5	1.8	1.8	1.8	2.1
Depreciation	1.6	1.3	1.4	1.2	1.9	1.4	1.3	1.3	1.1	1.4
Total Direct	6.9	5.9	7.1	7.5	8.1	8.6	6.5	6.5	6.6	7.5
Station	3.1	2.1	2.5	2.4	2.9	2.6	2.1	2.4	1.9	2.3
landing	(0.5)	(0.4)	(0.2)	(0.2)	(0.2)	(0.3)	(0.2)	(0.4)	(0.2)	(0.2)
Passenger Service	1.6	1.7	1.4	1.4	1.4	1.5	1.4	1.5	1.4	1.3
Ticketing, Sales	2.4	2.9	1.5	1.5	1.8	2.2	1.9	2.0	1.9	1.5
Administration	0.7	0.8	0.6	0.7	0.5	0.7	0.5	0.6	0.6	0.6
Total Indirect	7.8	7.5	6.0	6.0	6.6	7.0	5.9	6.5	5.8	5.7
Total Operating	14.7	13.4	13.1	13.5	14.7	15.6	12.4	13.0	12.4	13.2
(per revenue t-K)	30.4	27.8	31.5	26.2	31.9	35.9	33.7	23.7	30.8	28.8

Source: International Civil Aviation Organization, *Digest of Statistics, Financial Data*, No. 121 (1969).

Minutes (0's) = 187.8 + 1.19126 Miles R^2 = .99 S.E.E. = 41.16

t = (23.5) (107.0) .

In keeping with Keeler, 10 minutes was added to the scheduled time to obtain block time on each route.[5]

The cost per block hour for each aircraft was obtained in the following manner. Direct operating costs in 1968 for the DC-9 were reported by Air Canada to be 1.48¢ per available seat-mile at a stage-length of 600 miles.[6] Using the above relationship to determine the time required for this length of trip and Air Canada's DC-9 seating capacity of 94 results in an estimate of $500 per block hour for this aircraft. In 1966, Air Canada and CP Air operated the DC-8 at an average cost of $855 per block hour on the transcontinental route.[7] There is no comparable estimate on record for the cost per hour of the stretched version of the DC-8. However an estimate of the ratio of the cost per available seat-mile for the DC-8 and the DC-8L is available.[8] Since Air Canada used an average seating capacity for the DC-8L of 194, and 133 for the DC-8, this ratio may be used to produce an estimate that the cost per block hour for the DC-8L was 7.37 percent higher than the DC-8 or $918.[b]

To be comparable to Keeler's study, an estimate of the rate of return on capital must be added to these figures. In order to do so, the capital cost of each aircraft is required. Keeler uses $9 million (U.S.) and $4 million (U.S.) for the stretched versions of the DC-8 and DC-9, respectively.[9] But Air Canada paid $3,800,000 for the original version of the DC-9[c] that Straszheim reports cost American carriers only $3,100,000 (U.S.).[10] Similarly, the standard DC-8 (the DC-8-50) cost Air Canada $7,800,000,[d] whereas the American cost was reported to be only $6,500,000 (U.S.).[11] During 1967, 1968, and 1969, Air Canada paid $308 million for flight equipment. If the costs applicable to the American market are used, the aircraft that were acquired would have cost only $255,500,000 (U.S.). After correcting for the exchange rate difference, Canadian capital costs during this period were 11.5 percent higher than American capital costs.[e] Therefore, in order to derive the Canadian capital cost, the American capital cost of each aircraft was increased by 11 percent. Finally, 20 percent was added to the price of each aircraft to account for spares and

[b]*Aviation Week,* April 12, 1965, p. 57, reported that Douglas initially predicted that the cost per block hour would be 6 percent per unit higher.

[c]Canada, Dominion Bureau of Statistics, *Civil Aviation–Annual,* Cat. No. 51–202, 1968, p. 22. The only aircraft retired in 1968 were DC-9-10's.

[d]See footnote c above. Air Canada retired a DC-8-50 from its books after a crash in 1967, and this provides us with an estimate of the Canadian capital cost of this aircraft.

[e]After correcting for exchange rate differences, the additional cost for the DC-9-10 and DC-8-50 mentioned above was 11 and 14 percent, respectively.

ground equipment.[f] Together with the exchange rate differential, these corrections yield a capital cost of \$12,947,000 for the DC-8L, \$9,351,000 for the DC-8, and \$5,754,000 for the DC-9.

Keeler's annual capital costs were derived from gross investment multiplied by a capital rental rate. This rate (ρ) is estimated from

$$\rho = \frac{r}{1 - e^{-rL}} ,$$

where r is the interest rate and L the life of the capital good. Air Canada utilized a 14-year life on its jet equipment.[12] Its cost of capital was the government long-term bond rate (see Chapter Six). This averaged 6 percent in the 1960s (see Table 6–4). The difference between the rental rate calculated using these figures and the rate already included in the direct costs (1/14) times the above capital costs yields an additional annual cost of \$445,000 for the DC-8L, \$321,000 for the DC-8 and \$198,000 for the DC-9. Between 1968 and 1972, the average annual utilization rate for Air Canada's DC-8L's and its DC-9's was 3168 and 2774 hours, respectively. Between 1965 and 1969, the airline's average annual utilization rate for DC-8's was 3616 hours.[13] Dividing the additional annual capital cost by the average annual utilization and adding the result to the cost per block hour previously reported yields the following estimates of direct costs for the three types of aircraft (see Table B–3).

The direct cost per block hour can be translated into a cost per revenue passenger carried once the relevant seating densities and load factors have been specified. In his study of the U.S. airline industry, Keeler chose densities equal to or comparable to those used by Pacific Southwest Airlines—the large, unregulated California intra-state carrier.[14] The load factor he chose as "optimal" was 60 percent.[g] This yielded him estimates of 66 passengers per flight for the DC-9 and 150 for the stretched DC-8.

The average load factor on Air Canada's and CP Air's domestic scheduled services was 65.1, 67.1, and 68.0 percent in 1965, 1966, and 1967.[15] But as Table B–4 shows, most of the Canadian domestic routes have historically experienced lower load factors than the transcontinental routes. Vondracek

[f]At the beginning of 1969, spares and ground equipment amounted to 20 percent of Air Canada's investment in flight equipment. Straszheim, *The International Airline Industry,* pp. 76, 103, reports ground equipment traditionally runs at 10 percent of aircraft costs, spares from 18 to 20 percent.

[g]George W. Douglas and James C. Miller, III, "Quality Competition, Industry Equilibrium, and Efficiency in the Price-Constrained Airline Market" (unpublished paper, Department of Economics, Texas A & M University, 1973). The authors argue the efficient load factor varies according to the density and length of a route. However, since we are concerned with a cross-country comparison, what matters is a consistency of approach.

Table B–3. Aircraft Operating Costs per Block Hour, 1966 ($)

DC-8L	*DC-8*	*DC-9*
1058	944	571

Table B–4. Comparison of Load Factors in the United States and Canada, 1960–1965

	United States		*Air Canada*			
Year	*U.S. Trunk*	*California Intra-State*	*Montreal-Toronto*	*Trans-continental*	*Other Domestic*	*System*
1960	59.5	71.1	68.3	65.9	64.5	66.0
1961	56.2	72.1	68.9	67.4	62.4	64.1
1962	53.3	75.3	67.4	62.1	57.1	60.2
1963	53.8	72.8	66.1	59.8	57.3	59.6
1964	55.4	74.9	68.2	62.7	58.2	63.4
1965	55.2	63.8	66.8	68.2	59.1	65.2

Source: William A. Jordan, *Airline Regulation in America: Effects and Imperfections* (Baltimore: Johns Hopkins, 1970), p. 202 and Table 11–1.

reports the transcontinental load factor was 73.3 percent in 1966.[16] Table B–4 shows Air Canada maintained load factors on its densest route–Toronto to Montreal–near this figure. Since the comparison of fares to costs will use only those Canadian routes on which there were direct flights, and since these were generally the densest routes, a load factor of 70 percent was chosen for this study. With Air Canada's seating density, this yields 66 passengers per flight for the DC-9, and 93 for the DC-8. The former is identical to that used by Keeler. However, this procedure produces a figure of only 127 revenue passengers per flight for the DC-8L–a number that is lower than the 150 passengers per flight used by Keeler. Since the 73.3 percent load factor actually achieved on the transcontinental route in 1966 would have yielded 144 passengers per flight, just six short of the number used by Keeler, this figure will be used for the DC-8L.

INDIRECT COSTS

Indirect costs as reported by Canadian carriers are divided into four components: those related to passenger service, to aircraft and traffic servicing, to promotion and sales, and to general administration. In contrast to direct costs, indirect costs are more difficult to assign on a route by route basis. There are two reasons for this. First, the level of indirect costs is a function of market structure. Where prices are held well above average costs, whether it be by the cartel that controls the North Atlantic or the regulatory body that oversees the United States domestic market, competition spills over into service areas. More expensive food service increases passenger service expenses; more luxurious lounges and ground facilities increase aircraft and traffic servicing expenses; greater advertising increases promotion and sales expenses. Secondly, Canada lacks sufficient airlines for a complex cross-sectional analysis of those variables that determine the level of indirect costs. In what follows, studies of the American industry have been utilized to suggest the important determinants of indirect costs while time series regressions on Canadian data were performed where more than one determinant appeared to have been important.

Passenger Service

Passenger service expenses include those costs that are meant to satisfy the comfort of passengers. In 1967, crew salaries and materials (mainly food) accounted for almost equal proportions of the expenses reported in this category by the major Canadian scheduled airlines.[17] Crew salaries are incurred on an hourly basis and thus are higher per plane-mile for shorter routes. On the other hand, meal expenses are higher for longer routes. The two effects seem to offset one another to yield a relatively equal cost per passenger mile for airlines with different average stage-lengths.[18] Caves, in his cost studies, also allocated this expense on a passenger-mile basis.[19]

Table B–5 presents Air Canada's passenger service expenses per passenger mile from 1965 through 1969. In addition, the constant 1966 dollar cost calculated using an index constructed from the annual wages of flight crew attendants is presented. It can be seen that following the introduction of the DC-9 in 1966, the cost per passenger-mile remained relatively constant. Thus, passenger service expense will be allocated on the basis of .5540¢ per passenger-mile.

Table B–5. Air Canada Passenger Service Expenses per Passenger-Mile, 1965–1969

Year	*Absolute Cost (¢)*	*Constant 1966 Cost (¢)*
1965	.5152	. . . . .
1966	.5540	.5540
1967	.5978	.5457
1968	.6304	.5183
1969	.6880	.5367

Source: Canada, Dominion Bureau of Statistics, *Civil Aviation–Annual,* Cat. No. 51–202, various years.

Ticketing, Promotion, and Sales

This category includes all expenses related to the selling of tickets such as advertising, the preparation of schedules, and the making of reservations. It has been found to vary across airlines both with respect to number of passengers carried and average length of flight.[20] One reason average stage-length is important is that the longer the flight the greater the choice of interconnections and the resulting complexity of ticketing a customer. More important is the fact that longer flights are generally performed in markets where prices have been artificially maintained above average cost and where heavy advertising expenditures have resulted.

Table B-6 presents the percentage of passenger revenues accounted for by selling expenses for the Canadian trunk carriers and two regional airlines. As the two regional airlines expanded into mainline service, this ratio increased rapidly. CP Air's selling expense ratio, although higher than Air Canada's, does not differ markedly from other carriers whose primary market is international. For example, in 1968, the relevant percentage for Swissair was 25.3, for Iberia 23.0, for Alitalia 25.4, for El Al 26.4, and for Qantas 26.0.[21]

In order to obtain a cost per passenger in this category for the Canadian system, promotion and sales expenses (C) for both Air Canada and CP Air were regressed on number of passengers (P), passenger revenue (R), and a time trend. A dummy variable for CP Air was entered as an intercept but was not found to be significant. The resulting estimates are reported in equation (B–1) below:

$$\text{Costs (\$)} = 5.881 + 4.025 \text{ Passengers} + .0528 \text{ Revenues} + 1934T$$

$$t = (6.0) \quad (2.3) \qquad (1.3) \qquad (3.8) \qquad \text{(B–1)}$$

$$R^2 = .9986; \text{D.W.} = 2.13; F(3,4) = 985.$$

The coefficient on the revenues variable (5.28 percent) is close to the commissions rate the airlines allowed travel agents (5 percent). The size of the constant term indicates there may be significant economies of scale in this

Table B-6. Promotion and Selling Expense as a Percent of Passenger Revenues, Canadian Carriers, 1965–1969

Year	*Air Canada*	*CP Air*	*Eastern Provincial*	*Pacific Western*
1965	17.6	23.6	....	....
1966	18.4	24.2	4.6	6.5
1967	18.1	24.8	6.7	7.6
1968	17.2	24.9	8.7	12.9
1969	19.0	24.5	10.3	12.6

Source: Canada, Dominion Bureau of Statistics, *Civil Aviation–Annual,* Cat. No. 51–202, various years.

category and would explain why American carriers have lower ticketing costs per revenue tonne-kilometre performed (Table B–2 above). Using this equation and the 1966 Air Canada passenger volume yields a cost per passenger of $5.51 plus 5.28 percent of the fare charged.

Aircraft and Traffic Servicing

Aircraft and traffic servicing expenses include passenger handling expenses at the airport, preparing and servicing aircraft, scheduling and preparing the crew, and controlling the in-flight movement of the aircraft. Table B–2 indicated that on an available tonne-kilometre basis, Air Canada experienced higher aircraft and traffic servicing costs than American carriers. Since aircraft and traffic servicing expenses is a function of number of departures and varies by aircraft type,[22] this may be the result of longer average stage-lengths or the use of larger aircraft in the United States. If the cost of aircraft and traffic servicing per departure is compared, the apparent disadvantage suffered by Canadian carriers reported in Table B–2 is reduced. For instance, in 1968 the largest four American trunk carriers averaged $318 (U.S.) per departure; the other trunks $210 (U.S.), while Air Canada's cost was $268 (U.S.). Table B–7 presents Air Canada's traffic and servicing costs per departure for the late sixties. The 1965 constant dollar estimate presented in the same table was generated using an index derived from the average wage of traffic and servicing personnel.

Since a large percentage of costs in this category relate to traffic handled, Air Canada and CP Air's aircraft and servicing costs were regressed on number of passengers carried (PASS), number of tons of freight handled (FRT), and a time trend for the period 1965 to 1968. A second equation using constant 1965 costs but without the time trend was also used. Both are reported below. The first yields a cost of $4.45 per passenger for Air Canada in 1966, the second $4.68.[h] For route allocation purposes, the figure of $4.50 was adopted for the cost per passenger in 1966.

$$\text{Cost} = -318 + 1603T + \$3.90\ \text{PASS} + \$236\ \text{FRT} \quad R^2 = .99;\ \text{D.W.} = 1.45;$$

$$t = (.22) \quad (3.3) \quad (2.2) \quad (2.1) \quad F(3,4) = 473 \qquad \text{(B–2)}$$

$$\text{Constant Cost} = 2261 + \$4.27\ \text{PASS} + \$185\ \text{FRT} \quad R^2 = .98;\ \text{D.W.} = 2.31;$$

$$t = (.62) \quad (3.2) \quad (2.8) \quad F(2,2) = 85. \qquad \text{(B–3)}$$

General Administration

Table B–8 presents the general administration costs per revenue ton-mile for Air Canada during the late 1960s. A revenue ton-mile is arbitrarily chosen as the

[h]This assumes that all fixed costs are allocated to passenger traffic. This leads to an upward bias in the price-cost spread.

Table B–7. Air Canada Aircraft and Traffic Servicing Costs per Departure, 1965–1968

Year	*Absolute Cost ($)*	*Constant 1965 Cost ($)*
1965	242	242
1966	257	248
1967	265	238
1968	290	245

Source: Canada, Dominion Bureau of Statistics, *Civil Aviation–Annual*, Cat. No. 51–202, various years.

relevant output measure determining expenditures in this classification. Assuming no fixed costs and a division of general administration costs between freight and passenger traffic on the basis of ton-miles performed yields a cost of .212¢ per passenger-mile for 1966.

Finally, to be comparable to Keeler's estimates, an allowance for the cost of working capital must be made. Air Canada's working capital averaged $15.3 million between 1966 and 1969. Using the 6 percent interest rate and the figure for revenue ton-miles produced by Air Canada in 1966 yields an estimate of .1726¢ per revenue ton-mile or .0173¢ per revenue passenger-mile.

Together these five categories yield the following estimating equation for indirect costs per passenger in 1966:

$$\text{Costs (\$)} = 10.01 + (.00783)\ \text{Distance} + .0528\ \text{Fare}. \qquad \text{(B–4)}$$

Although this equation has been developed from data and techniques that lack a certain degree of precision, it yields results not greatly different from the much more complex routine required by the Canadian Transport Commission of the Canadian carriers when reporting their costs by route. For instance, the above equation produces an estimate of $13.90 for Toronto-Montreal. Yet, in 1968,

Table B–8. Air Canada General Administration Costs per Revenue Ton-Mile, 1965–1969 (¢)

Year	*Costs*
1965	2.162
1966	2.117
1967	2.186
1968	2.170
1969	2.300

Source: Canada, Dominion Bureau of Statistics, *Civil Aviation–Annual*, Cat. No. 51–202, various years.

Air Canada using the Canadian Transport Commission allocation method reported an indirect cost per passenger of between $12.20 and $14.80 for this route.[i] For the Toronto-Vancouver route, the estimating equation adopted here predicts indirect costs per passenger of $32.38. Using the Transport Commission formula, Air Canada and CP Air's indirect costs (excluding working capital costs) averaged 1.26¢ per seat-mile [23] on this route. With the 73.3 percent load factor achieved on the transcontinental route in 1966, this translates to $36.48 per passenger. Therefore, the bias likely to be introduced using the equation developed here—relative to that which would have been obtained using the regulatory board's method of cost allocation—will result in an understatement of the indirect costs on lengthier routes and an overstatement of the mark-ups on these routes.

On the other hand, neither of the formulae may be correct. Both in essence assume there is a substantial proportion of indirect costs that vary not with mileage but only with number of passengers boarded. Keeler's cross-sectional analysis finds little in the way of fixed costs per passenger. In his analysis, costs per passenger are a function only of mileage travelled—cost per passenger-mile is virtually constant.[j] In 1966, total indirect costs per revenue ton-mile for Air Canada equalled 22.836¢. Adding the cost of working capital derived above yields a cost of 2.3¢ per passenger-mile. This will be the second method chosen to allocate indirect costs by route.

The sum of direct and indirect costs provides an estimate of the cost per passenger for each route. These results are reported in Table 12–1 in the concluding chapter.

[i] Canada, Canadian Transport Commission, Research Branch, *Operating Costs for Conventional and STOL Aircraft,* Report No. 08 of *Inter-city Passenger Transport Study,* prepared by G.A. Clark and J.W. Sobeniak (Ottawa: Canadian Government Printing Bureau, 1971), p. 53 and Figure 1–4. By using the formula derived from U.S. sources, indirect costs on the Montreal-Toronto route are calculated to range from 2.8¢ per passenger-mile for a 70 percent load factor to 3.4¢ at a 50 percent load factor. The study also reports this formula understated Air Canada's costs for corridor routes on average by 78 percent when such costs were calculated from regulatory board regulations.

[j] T.E. Keeler, "Airline Regulation and Market Performance," *Bell Journal of Economics and Management Science* III, no. 2 (1972):415 adopts the formula: Cost per passenger (¢) = 29 + 1.17 (Distance).

Notes

INTRODUCTION

1. Any one of a number of standard textbooks on regulation provides examples of this point of view. For instance, see Charles Franklin Phillips, Jr., *The Economics of Regulation: Theory and Practice in the Transportation and Public Utility Industries,* The Irwin Series in Economics (Homewood, Ill.: Irwin, 1965), pp. 742–44.

2. Such a position had been advocated generally by Harold Demsetz in "Why Regulate Utilities?" *Journal of Law and Economics* XI (April 1968): 55–65, as well as for specific industries by Alfred Edward Kahn in *The Economics of Regulation: Principles and Institutions,* 2 vols. (New York: Wiley, 1970–71), Vol. II, pp. 178–93, where deregulation of the trucking industry is proposed.

3. Anthony Downs, *An Economic Theory of Democracy* (New York: Harper and Row, 1957), p. 283. Downs implicitly advocates this approach when he states, "The economist does not suggest that men stop being selfish. Instead he attempts to achieve some social ordering which benefits society through the very leverage of that selfishness."

CHAPTER ONE

TOWARDS A POSITIVE THEORY OF THE REGULATORY PROCESS IN TRANSPORTATION INDUSTRIES

1. Downs, *Theory of Democracy,* p. 11. Downs postulates that a government maximized the number of votes it would obtain. Albert Breton, "A Theory of the Demand for Public Goods," *Canadian Journal of Economics and Political Science* XXXII, no. 4 (1966):455. Breton argues that governments will maximize the probability of their re-election. George J. Stigler, "Economic Competition and Political Competition," *Public Choice* XIII (Fall

1972):91–106. Stigler more properly points out that if a government maximizes net benefits to supporters it will want enough supporters to ensure re-election, but not so many that per capita benefits are not maximized.

2. Downs, *Theory of Democracy*, p. 80.

3. Ibid., chapter vii.

4. Gordon Tullock, *Toward a Mathematics of Politics* (Ann Arbor: U. of Mich. Pr., 1967), chapter ix.

5. Downs, *Theory of Democracy*, pp. 55–60.

6. Aaron B. Wildavsky, *The Politics of the Budgetary Process* (Boston: Little, Brown, 1964): Otto A. Davis, M. A. H. Dempster, and A. Wildavsky, "A Theory of the Budgetary Process," *American Political Science Review* LX (September 1966):529–47.

7. Breton, "Demand for Public Goods," p. 464.

8. James M. Buchanan and Gordon Tullock, *The Calculus of Consent: Logical Foundations of Constitutional Democracy* (Ann Arbor: U. of Mich. Pr., 1967).

9. James Samuel Coleman, "The Possibility of a Social Welfare Function," *American Economic Review* LVI (December 1966):1105–22.

10. Gordon Tullock, "A Simple Algebraic Logrolling Model," *American Economic Review* LX (June 1970):419–26.

11. Kenneth Joseph Arrow, "Political and Economic Evaluation of Social Effects and Externalities," in *The Analysis of Public Output*, ed. by Julius Margolis, Universities–National Bureau Conference Series, No. 23 (New York: National Bureau of Economic Research, distributed by Columbia U. Pr., 1970), p. 19.

12. R. H. Coase, "The Problem of Social Cost," *Journal of Law and Economics* III, no. 1 (1960):1–44.

13. D. H. Regan, "The Problem of Social Cost Revisited," *Journal of Law and Economics* XV, no. 2 (1972):427–38.

14. E. J. Mishan, "The Postwar Literature on Externalities: An Interpretative Essay," *Journal of Economic Literature* IX, no. 1 (1971):18–21.

15. Tullock, "Logrolling Model," p. 425.

16. Emmette S. Redford, *The Regulatory Process: With Illustrations from Commercial Aviation* (Austin: U. of Texas Pr., 1969), p. 33. Redford stresses the acceptance of the institution of private enterprise and the need to guarantee its profits.

17. Marver H. Bernstein, *Regulating Business by Independent Commission* (Princeton, N.J.: Princeton U. Pr., 1955), p. 250.

18. George M. Miller, "Origins of the Iowa Granger Law," in *United States Economic History: Selected Readings*, ed. by H. N. Scheiber (New York: Knopf, 1964), p. 326.

19. Paul W. MacAvoy, *The Economic Effects of Regulation: The Trunk-Line Railroad Cartels and the Interstate Commerce Commission Before 1900* (Cambridge, Mass.: MIT Pr., 1965), p. 204.

20. G. J. Stigler, "The Theory of Economic Regulation," *Bell Journal of Economics and Management Science* II, no. 1 (1971):3–21.

21. Gabriel Kolko, *Railroads and Regulation, 1877–1916* (Princeton, N.J.:

Princeton U. Pr., 1965). Kolko describes the support evinced by the United States railroads for legislation apparently meant to regulate them.

22. Richard A. Posner, "Taxation by Regulation," *Bell Journal of Economics and Management Science* II, no. 1 (1971):22–50. Posner recognizes this function of the regulatory agency.

23. Buchanan and Tullock, *The Calculus of Consent,* p. 82.

24. Matthew Holden, Jr., *Pollution Control as a Bargaining Process: An Essay on Regulatory Decision-Making,* Cornell University Water Resources Center Publication, No. 9 (Ithaca, N.Y.: C.U.W.R.C., 1966), p. 11.

25. Bernstein, *Regulating Business,* p. 274.

26. Redford, *The Regulatory Process,* p. 37.

27. Ibid., p. 35.

28. Bernstein, *Regulating Business,* p. 262.

29. Redford, *The Regulatory Process,* p. 34.

30. Arthur R. Wright, "An Examination of the Role of the Board of Transport Commissioners for Canada as a Regulatory Tribunal," *Canadian Public Administration* VI, no. 4 (1963):351–2.

31. Harvey C. Mansfield in "Commissions, Government," *International Encyclopedia of the Social Sciences,* ed. by David L. Sills, III, p. 16, recounts the focus of early studies on public law and due procedure in the regulatory process—an interest that either focused on the rights of private property or the bias the legal profession brought to the judging of these issues.

32. Wright, "Board of Transport Commissioners," p. 350.

33. Ibid., p. 351.

34. Ibid., p. 353.

35. Ibid., p. 358.

36. Anthony Downs, *Inside Bureaucracy,* A Rand Corporation Research Study (Boston: Little, Brown, 1967), p. 7.

37. Holden in *Pollution Control,* p. 11, states that "successful regulation depends on the consent of the regulated."

38. Redford, *The Regulatory Process,* p. 20.

39. Gordon Tullock, *The Politics of Bureaucracy* (Washington, D.C.: Pub. Aff. Pr., 1965), p. 157.

40. Bernstein, *Regulating Business,* p. 272.

41. Ibid., p. 231.

42. Roland Neely McKean, "The Unseen Hand of Government," *American Economic Review* LV (June 1965):496–506.

43. Bernstein in *Regulating Business,* chapter iii, adopts this attitude.

44. Merle Fainsod, "Some Reflections on the Nature of the Regulatory Process," *Public Policy,* Yearbook of the Graduate School of Public Administration, Harvard University, Vol. I (Cambridge, Mass.: Harvard U. Pr., 1940), p. 298.

45. William A. Jordan in "Producer Protection, Prior Market Structure and the Effects of Government Regulation," *Journal of Law and Economics* XV, no. 1 (1972):151–76, summarizes the debate as to whether producers are actually aided by regulation.

46. Richard E. Caves, *Air Transport and Its Regulators: An Independent*

Study, Harvard Economic Studies, Vol. CXX (Cambridge, Mass.: Harvard U. Pr., 1962), p. 445.

47. Fainsod, "Nature of the Regulatory Process," p. 309.

48. Bernstein, *Regulating Business*, p. 219.

49. Peter B. Clark and James Q. Wilson in "Incentive System: A Theory of Organizations," *Administrative Science Quarterly* VI, no. 2 (1961):129–66, develop this point more fully.

CHAPTER TWO

THE TRANSPORTATION REGULATORY AGENCY: A MODEL

1. John Charles Harsanyi, "A General Theory of Rational Behavior in Game Situations," *Econometrica* XXXIV (July 1966):613–34.

2. Thomas Crombie Schelling, *The Strategy of Conflict*, A Galaxy Book (New York: Oxford U. Pr., 1963), pp. 70–71.

3. Stanley Brogden, *Australia's Two-Airline Policy* (Melbourne: Melbourne U. Pr., 1968).

CHAPTER THREE

INTERACTION BETWEEN THE REGULATORY AGENCY AND THE POLITICAL PROCESS

1. Canada, *Trans-Canada Air Lines Act, 1937*, 1 George 6, ch. 43, *Statutes of Canada*, 1937; *Revised Statutes of Canada*, 1952, ch. 268.

2. Canada, *Transport Act, 1938*, 2 George 6, ch. 53, *Statutes of Canada*, 1938 (parts 1–11).

3. Canada, Department of Reconstruction and Supply, Directorate of Air Development, "Development of Commercial Air Services in Canada, 1919–1944" (unpublished paper prepared by H. Cunningham, Ottawa, 1946, mimeographed), p. 21.

4. Ibid., p. 36.

5. J. W. Pickersgill, *The Mackenzie King Record*, Vol. I, 1939–44 (Toronto: U. of Toronto Pr., 1960), pp. 646–7.

6. Ibid., p. 648.

7. Ibid.

8. Wright, "Board of Transport Commissioners," pp. 351–2.

9. Canada, Parliament, House of Commons, *House of Commons Debates*, 5th Sess., 19th Parl., 8 George 6, Vol. II (1944), p. 1627.

10. Trans-Canada Air Lines, *Annual Report 1942*, p. 7; Canada, *House of Commons Debates*, 3rd Sess., 19th Parl., 6 George 6, Vol. III (1942), p. 2191.

11. David C. Corbett, *Politics and the Airlines* (London: Allen and Unwin, 1965), p. 164.

12. Canada, *House of Commons Debates*, Vol. IV (1944), p. 3962.

13. Pickersgill, *The Mackenzie King Record*, pp. 647, 649.

14. Canada, *House of Commons Debates,* Vol. I (1944), p. 956

15. Caves, *Air Transport and Its Regulators,* chapter iv; William A. Jordan, *Airline Regulation in America: Effects and Imperfections* (Baltimore: Johns Hopkins, 1970), p. 191.

16. Canada, *An Act to Amend the Aeronautics Act, 1944,* 8 George 6, ch. 28, *Statutes of Canada,* 1944.

17. Canada, *Transport Act, 1938.*

18. Canada, *House of Commons Debates,* 1st Sess., 24th Parl., 7 Elizabeth 2, Vol. II (1958), pp. 2206–7.

19. Canada, *House of Commons Debates,* 3rd Sess., 24th Parl., 8–9 Elizabeth 2, Vol. II (1960), p. 1800.

20. Ibid.

21. *Financial Post* (Toronto), March 2, 1963, p. 44.

22. Ibid.

23. *Globe and Mail* (Toronto), November 5, 1963, p. B2.

CHAPTER FOUR

REGIONAL AVIATION POLICY

1. Canada, Air Transport Board, *Circular,* No. 62/66 (October 31, 1966), pp. 1–2.

2. Canada, Air Transport Board, *Report on Review of Licenses Respecting Commercial Air Services Pursuant to Section 13 of the Aeronautics Act* (Ottawa, April 1947), p. 12.

3. Canadian Pacific Railway Company, *Annual Report, 1947,* p. 14.

4. K. W. Studnicki-Gizbert, "The Structure and Growth of the Canadian Air Transport Industry," *Papers of the Canadian Political Science Association Conference on Statistics* (Toronto: U. of Toronto Pr., 1960), p. 246.

5. Caves, *Air Transport and Its Regulators,* pp. 80–82.

6. Canada, Department of Transport, *Airline Competition in Canada: A Study of the Desirability and Economic Consequences of Competition in Canadian Transcontinental Air Services,* prepared by Stephen Wheatcroft (Ottawa, May 1958), p. 36.

7. Ibid.

8. Canada, Air Transport Board, *Report to the Minister of Transport on Transcontinental Air Services* (Ottawa, December 1958), pp. 18–19.

9. Ibid.

10. *Winnipeg Free Press,* December 5, 1960.

11. Ibid.

12. Ibid.

13. Canada, *House of Commons Debates,* 3rd Sess., 26th Parl., 13 Elizabeth 2, Vol. II (1965), p. 1814.

14. Canada, Parliament, House of Commons, Standing Committee on Railways, Canals and Telegraph Lines, *Minutes of Proceedings and Evidence,* No. 3 (June 22, 23, 1964), p. 352.

15. Canada, Department of Transport, *Press Release,* April 24, 1964.

16. Statement by the Minister of Transport to the House of Commons, June 1, 1965. Canada, *House of Commons Debates,* Vol. II (1965), p. 1814.

17. K. W. Studnicki-Gizbert, *The Regional Air Carriers' Problem,* a study prepared for the Air Transport Board (Ottawa: Queen's Printer, 1966), pp. 20–21.

18. Canada, Royal Commission on Transportation, 1959–1962, *Report,* M.A. MacPherson, Sr., Chairman, Vol. I (Ottawa: Queen's Printer, 1961), pp. 29, 72–73.

19. Canada, Parliament, House of Commons, *Bills,* Bill C–231, 1st Sess., 27th Parl., 14–15 Elizabeth 2, 1966: "An Act to define and implement a national transportation policy for Canada, to amend the Railway Act and other Acts in consequence thereof, and to enact other consequential provisions."

20. Studnicki-Gizbert, *The Regional Air Carriers' Problem,* p. 68.

21. Canada, Air Transport Board, *Circular,* No. 61/66 (October 31, 1966), p. 1.

22. Ibid., p. 7.

23. Canada, Air Transport Board, *Decision,* Serial No. 2550.

24. Ibid., p. 4.

25. Ibid., pp. 14–15.

26. Air Transport Board, *Decision,* Serial No. 2954, p. 7.

27. Fred Cleverley, "Transair Plans to Bring Jet Age to the Arctic," *Canadian Aviation* XLII, no. 3 (1969):27.

28. Canada, Canadian Transport Commission, Air Transport Committee, *Decision,* Serial No. 2913, p. 6.

29. Air Transport Committee, *Decision,* Serial No. 2954 (March 1970), p. 7.

30. Air Transport Committee, *Decision,* Serial No. 2623, p. 9.

31. Air Transport Committee, *Decision,* Serial No. 2687, "Dissenting Opinion," p. 5.

32. Ibid.

33. Mid-Canada Development Conference, 1st, Lakehead University, 1969, *Essays on Mid-Canada* (Toronto: Mid-Canada Development Foundation, 1970), Appendix B, using system average stage-length.

34. Air Transport Board, *Circular*, No. 62/66 (October 31, 1966), p. 1.

CHAPTER FIVE

A MODEL OF A GOVERNMENT AIRLINE

1. Important exceptions may be found in William A. Niskanen, Jr., *Bureaucracy and Representative Government* (Chicago: Aldine-Atherton, 1971) and Sam Peltzman, "Pricing in Public and Private Enterprises: Electric Utilities in the United States," *Journal of Law and Economics* XIV, no. 1 (1971):109–47.

2. Eirik Furubotn and Svetozar Pejovich, "Property Rights and Economic Theory: A Survey of Recent Literature," *Journal of Economic Literature* X, no. 4 (1972):1149–53.

3. Armen Alchian, "Some Economics of Property Rights," *Il Politico* XXX, no. 4 (1965):816–29; and Peltzman, "Pricing in Public and Private Enterprises," pp. 110–11.

4. Charles L. Schultze, *The Politics and Economics of Government Spending* (Washington, D.C.: Brookings, 1968), p. 50; and Wildavsky, *The Politics of the Budgetary Process*, pp. 13–18.

5. Peltzman, "Pricing in Public and Private Enterprises," p. 113.

6. Brogden, *Australia's Two-Airline Policy*, p. 72.

7. Ross Eckert and George Hilton, "The Jitneys," *Journal of Law and Economics* XV (October 1972):294.

8. R.H. Coase, "The British Post Office and the Messenger Companies," *Journal of Law and Economics* IV (October 1961):63.

CHAPTER SIX

THE CANADIAN CROWN AIRLINE: THE LEVEL OF SYSTEM PROFITABILITY AND THE PRACTICE OF CROSS-SUBSIDATION

1. Canada, *House of Commons Debates*, 2nd Sess., 18th Parl., 1 George 6, Vol. II (1937), p. 2042.

2. Canada, *Trans-Canada Air Lines Act, 1937.*

3. Corbett, *Politics and the Airlines*, p. 110.

4. Canada, *House of Commons Debates*, 2nd Sess., 26th Parl., 13 Elizabeth 2, Vol. II (1964), p. 2060.

5. Canada, *Trans-Canada Air Lines Act, 1937.* A summary of the legislation is also found in the first *Annual Report, 1937* of Trans-Canada Air Lines.

6. C.A. Ashley and R.G.H. Smails, *Canadian Crown Corporations: Some Aspects of their Administration and Control* (Toronto: Macmillan, 1965), p. 275.

7. Ibid.

8. A.W. Currie, *Canadian Transportation Economics* (Toronto: U. of Toronto Pr., 1967), p. 548.

9. Ashley and Smails, *Canadian Crown Corporations*, p. 291.

10. Ibid.

11. Great Britain, Parliament, *Parliamentary Papers* (House of Commons and Command), 1967–68, Vol. XXXIX (*Accounts and Papers*, vol. 6), Cmnd. 3437, "Nationalised Industries: A Review of Economic and Financial Objectives."

12. Trans-Canada Air Lines, "Initial Submission to the Air Transport Board in the Matter of Transcontinental Commercial Air Service" (unpublished paper, 1958, mimeographed), p. 110.

13. Canada, Dominion Bureau of Statistics, *Air Passenger Origin and Destination, Domestic Report, 1970*, Cat. No. 51–204 (Ottawa: Information Canada, June 1971). The Montreal-Charlo figure was calculated by adding up all traffic to Charlo and Chatham originating or terminating at Montreal and points west. The Charlo-Chatham figure was derived in a similar manner.

14. Mahlon R. Straszheim, *The International Airline Industry*, Transport Research Program (Washington, D.C.: Brookings, 1969), p. 85.

15. Ibid., p. 102.

16. Examples may be found in Canada, Sessional Committee on Railways, Airlines and Shipping, *Minutes of Proceedings and Evidence*, No. 4 (November 27, 28, 1962), p. 330; Trans-Canada Air Lines, *Annual Report, 1962*, p. 7; and . . . *Between Ourselves*, a newspaper for employees and their families, published by Air Canada, No. 361 (January 1972), p. 8.

17. Trans-Canada Air Lines, *Annual Report, 1955*, p. 17.

18. Ibid., 1958, p. 9.

19. Canada, *House of Commons Debates*, Vol. III (1958), p. 4362.

20. Air Transport Board, *Transcontinental Air Services*, p. 87.

21. Caves, *Air Transport and Its Regulators*, chapter iv.

22. Canada, Sessional Committee on Railways, Airlines and Shipping, *Minutes of Proceedings and Evidence*, No. 4 (November 27, 28, 1962), p. 334.

CHAPTER SEVEN

EQUIPMENT, EFFICIENCY, AND THE PUBLIC AIRLINE

1. For one example, see David G. Davies, "The Efficiency of Public versus Private Firms: The Case of Australia's Two Airlines," *Journal of Law and Economics* XIV, no. 1 (1971):149–66.

2. Robert T. Brown, "The 'Railroad Decision' in Chile," in *Transport Investment and Economic Development*, ed. by Gary Fromm (Washington, D.C.,: Brookings, 1965), p. 267.

3. Graham L. Reid and Kevin Allen, *Nationalized Industries*, Penguin Modern Economics Texts (Harmondsworth, Middlesex: Penguin, 1970), pp. 169, 177–8.

4. *Financial Post*, November 4, 1961, p. 70.

5. Reid and Allen, *Nationalized Industries*, p. 178.

6. Almarin Phillips, *Technology and Market Structure: A Study of the Aircraft Industry*, Heath Lexington Books (Lexington, Mass.: D.C. Heath, 1971), p. 95.

7. Ibid., pp. 97–98.

8. Canada, Parliament, House of Commons, Sessional Committee on Railways and Shipping, *Minutes of Proceedings and Evidence*, No. 4 (May 13, 1947), pp. 219–20, 225–6.

9. Comparisons may be found in A. Phillips, *Technology and Market Structure,* p. 38; Stephen P. Sobotka et al., *Prices of Used Commercial Aircraft, 1959–1965: A Research Report* (Evanston, I11.: Transportation Center at Northwestern University, 1959), Table 14, p. 45, as presented in Caves, *Air Transport and Its Regulators*, p. 68; George C. Eads, *The Local Service Airline Experiment*, Studies in the Regulation of Economic Activity (Washington, D.C.: Brookings, 1972), p. 58; and U.S. Congress, Committee on the Judiciary, *Monopoly Problems in Regulated Industries–Airlines, Hearings* before the Antitrust Subcommittee of the Committee on the Judiciary, House of Representatives, 84th Cong., 2nd Sess., 1957, Vol. III, p. 2067.

10. A. Phillips, *Technology and Market Structure*, pp. 144–5.

11. Aaron Jacob Gellman, "The Effect of Regulation on Aircraft Choice" (unpublished Ph.D. dissertation, Massachusetts Institute of Technology, 1968), p. 313.

12. Ibid., pp. 144–5.

13. Ibid.

14. Ibid., p. 88.

15. Canada, Sessional Committee on Railways and Shipping, *Minutes of Proceedings and Evidence*, No. 6 (April 4, 1950), p. 457.

16. Eads, *The Local Service Airline Experiment*, p. 22.

17. Ibid., p. 58.

18. A. Phillips, *Technology and Market Structure*, p. 103.

19. U.S., Antitrust Subcommittee, *Monopoly Problems*, Vol. I, p. 469; and Trans-Canada Air Lines, "Initial Submission," Exhibit 64C.

20. A. Phillips, *Technology and Market Structure*, p. 142.

21. Canada, Sessional Committee on Railways and Shipping, *Minutes of Proceedings and Evidence*, No. 6 (April 4, 1950), p. 457.

22. Trans-Canada Air Lines, "Initial Submission," Exhibit No. 416.

23. Gellman, "Regulation on Aircraft Choice," p. 295.

24. Ronald E. Miller and David Sawers, *The Technical Development of Modern Aviation* (London: Routledge and Kegan Paul, 1968), p. 143.

25. Caves, *Air Transport and Its Regulators*, p. 421.

26. Ibid.

27. *American Aviation* XVII, no. 24 (1954):81.

28. *American Aviation* XVIII, no. 25 (1955):92.

29. Canada, Department of Transport, *Airline Competition in Canada*, p. 19.

30. Trans-Canada Air Lines, "Initial Submission," Exhibits 64A through Q.

31. Gellman, "Regulation on Aircraft Choice," p. 325.

32. A. Phillips, *Technology and Market Structure*, pp. 38–41, 50–51. See also U.S., Antitrust Subcommittee, *Monopoly Problems*, Vol. III, p. 2067, for a comparison of the costs of these aircraft.

33. Trans-Canada Air Lines, "Initial Submission," Exhibit No. 416.

34. Gellman, "Regulation on Aircraft Choice," pp. 302–3.

35. Caves, *Air Transport and Its Regulators*, pp. 113, 313.

36. Ibid., p. 421.

37. Canada, Department of Transport, *Airline Competition in Canada*, p. 19.

38. Straszheim, *The International Airline Industry*, pp. 87–90; A. Phillips, *Technology and Market Structure*, pp. 38–41.

39. George Joseph Vondracek, "North Atlantic Versus Transcontinental Air Transport Passenger Services: Cost Analysis" (unpublished M.B.A. thesis, University of British Columbia, 1969).

40. Straszheim, *The International Airline Industry*, p. 86.

41. Canada, Canadian Transport Commission, Research Branch, *Operating Costs for Conventional and STOL Aircraft*, Report No. 08 of *Intercity Passenger Study*, prepared by G.A. Clark and J.W. Sobeniak (Ottawa Canadian Government Printing Bureau, 1971), p. 31.

42. For an account of this episode see Ashley and Smails, *Canadian Crown*

Corporations, pp. 323–5 and Canada, Sessional Committee on Railways, Airlines and Shipping, *Minutes of Proceedings and Evidence*, No. 1 (December 2, 3, 4, 1963).

43. Straszheim, *The International Airline Industry*, p. 158.

CHAPTER EIGHT

MANIFESTATIONS OF SUPPORT-MAXIMIZING BEHAVIOR--PRICE AND PRODUCT POLICY DURING THE 1950s

1. Canada, Dominion Bureau of Statistics, Aviation Statistics Centre, *Air Passenger Origin and Destination, Domestic Report, 1968*, Cat. No. 51–204 (Ottawa: Information Canada, June 1969).
2. U.S., Antitrust Subcommittee, *Monopoly Problems*, Vol. I, p. 224.
3. Caves, *Air Transport and Its Regulators*, p. 266. Caves suggests we at least consider this as one explanation of pricing behavior.
4. Ibid., pp. 373–6.
5. Ibid., p. 405.
6. U.S., Antitrust Subcommittee, *Monopoly Problems*, Vol. I, p. 222.
7. Canada, Sessional Committee on Railways and Shipping, *Minutes of Proceedings and Evidence*, No. 1 (March 16, 19, 1956), p. 88.
8. Ibid., No. 2 (March 21, 25, 26, 1957), p. 289.
9. Canada, Standing Committee on Railways, Canals and Telegraph Lines, *Minutes of Proceedings and Evidence*, No. 3 (June 22, 23, 1964), p. 331.
10. Canada, Department of Transport, *Airline Competition in Canada*, p. 19.
11. Trans-Canada Air Lines, "Initial Submission," Exhibit 64.
12. Trans-Canada Air Lines, *Annual Report, 1957*, p. 16.

CHAPTER NINE

COMPETITION AND GOVERNMENT POLICY: THE TRANSITION FROM MONOPOLY TO DUOPOLY ON THE TRANSCONTINENTAL ROUTE

1. Corbett, *Politics and the Airlines*, p. 163.
2. Ibid., pp. 163–5.
3. Canada, *House of Commons Debates*, 3rd Sess., 22nd Parl., 4–5 Elizabeth 2, Vol II (1956), p. 1869.
4. Ibid., 5th Sess., 22nd Parl., 5–6 Elizabeth 2, Vol. I (1957), p. 1037.
5. Trans-Canada Air Lines, "Initial Submission," p. 110.
6. *Globe and Mail* (Toronto), October 16, 1958, p. 10.
7. Statement of the Hon. G. Hees, Minister of Transport, made on February 4, 1958, Timmins, Ontario, quoted in Canada, *House of Commons Debates*, Vol. II (1958), p. 2055.
8. Canada, Department of Transport, *Airline Competition in Canada*; Air Transport Board, *Transcontinental Air Services*.
9. *Financial Post*, October 11, 1958, p. 19.

10. Robert Francis, "The McConachie Story: World Airline Looks Homeward," *Saturday Night* LXXIII (May 24, 1958):40.

11. Air Transport Board, *Transcontinental Air Services*, p. 16.

12. Canada, Department of Transport, "Further Airline Competition in Canada: A Study of the Consequences of any Further Development of Domestic Mainline Competition in Canada" (unpublished paper prepared by Stephen Wheatcroft, Ottawa, February 1966, mimeographed), Appendix 3.

13. Ibid., p. 4 and Appendix 3.

14. Since the average weight load factor for the transcontinental route in 1959 was unavailable, it was estimated by multiplying the ratio of the weight load factor to the passenger load factor in 1960 by the passenger load factor in 1959. Ibid., Appendix 3.

15. A. Phillips, *Technology and Market Structure*, Appendix D.

16. Canada, Standing Committee on Railways, Canals and Telegraph Lines, *Minutes of Proceedings and Evidence*, No. 3 (June 22, 23, 1964), p. 352.

17. Ibid., No. 4 (March 29, 1962), p. 330.

18. Ibid., No. 3 (June 22, 23, 1964), p. 352.

19. Caves, *Air Transport and Its Regulators*, p. 409, and Straszheim, *The International Air Transport Industry*, p. 96, report volume economies. N.K. Taneja and R.W. Simpson, *A Multi-Regression Analysis of Airline Indirect Operating Costs*, FTL Report R-67-2 (Cambridge, Mass.: MIT Flight Transportation Laboratory, June 1968); G.C. Eads, M. Nerlove, and W. Raduchel, "A Long-Run Cost Function for the Local Service Airline Industry," *Review of Economics and Statistics* LI (August 1969):258–70; and T.E. Keeler, "Airline Regulation and Market Performance," *Bell Journal of Economics and Management Science* III, no. 2 (1972):411, report no scale economies.

CHAPTER TEN

THE DEMAND FUNCTION FOR THE CROWN AIRLINE'S SERVICES

1. Caves, *Air Transport and Its Regulators*, p. 32.

2. Straszheim, *The International Airline Industry*, p. 275, in effect finds North Atlantic air traffic for 1948–64 is explained exclusively by a time trend. Samuel Brown and Wayne Watkins, "The Demand for Air Travel: A Regression Study of Time Series and Cross-Sectional Data in the United States Domestic Market," *Highway Research Record*, No. 213 (Washington, D.C.: Highway Research Board of the Division of Engineering and Industrial Research, National Academy of Sciences, National Research Council, 1968), pp. 28–29. Brown and Watkins find both fare and income elasticities highly sensitive to a time trend. Young Pyo Joun, "The Demand for Air Travel" (unpublished Ph. D. dissertation, University of Washington, 1966), shows the same sensitivity of fare, income, and price elasticities to the inclusion of a time trend.

3. Brown and Watkins, "The Demand for Air Travel: Regression Study"; Joun, "The Demand for Air Travel," and Hayle Carlyle Bartlett, "The Demand for Passenger Air Transportation, 1947–62" (unpublished Ph. D. dissertation,

University of Michigan, 1965). An important exception is Phillip K. Verleger, Jr., "A Point-to-Point Model of the Demand for Air Transportation" (unpublished Ph. D. dissertation, Massachusetts Institute of Technology, 1971).

4. R.G.D. Allen, *Mathematical Economics,* 2nd ed. (London: Macmillan, 1965), p. 709.

5. Verleger, "Demand for Air Transportation," pp. 22–24.

6. Caves, *Air Transport and Its Regulators*, p. 37.

7. Lester Dean Taylor, "The Principal-Components-Instrumental-Variable Approach to the Estimation of Systems of Simultaneous Equations" (unpublished Ph.D. dissertation, Harvard University, 1962).

8. Bartlett, "The Demand for Passenger Air Transportation," p. 264.

9. John R. Meyer and Mahlon R. Straszheim, *Pricing and Product Evaluation*, Vol. I of *Techniques of Transport Planning*, ed. by John R. Meyer, 2 Vols., Transport Research Program (Washington, D.C.: Brookings, 1971), p. 156. The authors list this as the major problem in route by route demand estimation.

10. Straszheim, *The International Airline Industry*; Joun, "The Demand for Air Travel"; and Brown and Watkins, "The Demand for Air Travel: Regression Study."

11. From J. Durbin, "Testing for Serial Correlation in Least-Squares Regression When Some of the Regressors are Lagged Dependent Variables," *Econometrica* XXXVIII, no. 3 (1970):410–21.

CHAPTER ELEVEN

PRICING POLICY ON THE TWO PROFITABLE SECTORS—THE NORTH ATLANTIC AND THE TRANSCONTINENTAL—DURING THE 1960s

1. Canada, Air Transport Committee, *Decision*, Serial No. 3026 (August 12, 1970), p. 2.

2. Vondracek, "North Atlantic Versus Transcontinental," p. 99.

3. Ibid.

4. Two descriptions of the operations and effect of the cartel may be found in K.G.J. Pillai, *The Air Net: The Case Against the World Aviation Cartel* (New York: Grossman, 1969), and Straszheim, *The International Airline Industry*.

5. William E. O'Connor, *Economic Regulation of the World's Airlines: A Political Analysis* (New York: Praeger, 1971), chapter ii.

6. Straszheim, *The International Airline Industry*, chapter ix.

7. Vondracek, "North Atlantic Versus Transcontinental," p. 98.

8. Pillai, *The Air Net*, p. 171.

9. Straszheim, *The International Airline Industry*, pp. 136–7.

10. Pillai, *The Air Net*, pp. 94–5.

11. Straszheim, *The International Airline Industry*, p. 137.

12. Stephen Wheatcroft, *Air Transport Policy* (London: M. Joseph, 1964), p. 82.

13. Vondracek, "North Atlantic Versus Transcontinental," p. 98.

14. Straszheim, *The International Airline Industry*, pp. 216–7.

15. David A.D. Saarty, "Future of the International Air Charter Market?" *Papers of the Tenth Annual Meeting of the Transportation Research Forum on Transportation Planning* (Washington, D.C., 1969), p. 293.

16. Straszheim, *The International Airline Industry*, p. 54.

17. Data from ibid., and Saarty, "International Air Charter Market," p. 292.

CHAPTER TWELVE

CONCLUSION

1. Straszheim, *The International Airline Industry*, p. 96.

2. Eads, *The Local Service Airline Experiment*, pp. 72–73.

3. Taneja and Simpson, *Airline Indirect Operating Costs*; Eads, Nerlove, and Raduchel, "A Long-Run Cost Function," pp. 258–70; and Keeler, "Airline Regulation and Market Performance," p. 411.

4. John Baldwin, "The Battle for the North Atlantic," in *Canadian Perspectives in Economics*, ed. by K. Acheson et al., No. J2 (Toronto: Collier-Macmillan, 1972).

5. Avinash K. Dixit, "On the Optimum Structure of Commodity Taxes," *American Economic Review* LX, no. 3 (1970):297.

6. L.S. Wilson, "Further Work with Feldstein's Pricing Rule" (unpublished paper, Public Economics Workshop Discussion Paper, No. 10, University of Essex, 1973).

7. Caves, in *Air Transport and Its Regulators*, chapter vi, examines the apparently conflicting nature of the goals embodied in the legislation.

8. Ibid., pp. 277–81.

9. Eads, *The Local Service Airline Experiment*.

10. U.S., Antitrust Subcommittee, *Monopoly Problems*, Vol. I, p. 224.

11. Caves, *Air Transport and Its Regulators*, pp. 402–11.

12. Ibid., pp. 159–60, 167.

13. Ibid., p. 145.

14. Ibid., pp. 201, 202, 204, 206, 213, 214, 220.

15. Eads, *The Local Service Airline Experiment*, p. 182.

16. Caves, *Air Transport and Its Regulators*, p. 409.

17. Jordan, *Airline Regulation in America*, pp. 110–3.

18. Keeler, "Airline Regulation and Market Performance," pp. 399–424.

19. Ibid., p. 416.

APPENDIX B

ESTIMATION OF AIRLINE ROUTE COSTS IN CANADA

1. Keeler, "Airline Regulation and Market Performance," pp. 399–424.

2. Dominion Bureau of Statistics, *Civil Aviation–Annual*, Cat. No. 51–202, 1965–69. This cost figure is derived using the U.S. gallon.

3. U.S., Federal Aviation Agency, *Direct Operating Costs and Other Performance Characteristics of Transport Aircraft in Airline Service*, 1965–69.

4. International Civil Aviation Organization, *Digest of Statistics, Fleet–Personnel*, No. 118 (1966).

5. Keeler, "Airline Regulation and Market Performance," p. 413.

6. Canadian Transport Commission, *Operating Costs for Conventional and STOL Aircraft*, p. 31.

7. Vondracek, "North Atlantic Versus Transcontinental," p. 75.

8. Canadian Transport Commission, *Operating Costs for Conventional and STOL Aircraft*, p. 8.

9. Keeler, "Airline Regulation and Market Performance," p. 405.

10. Straszheim, *The International Airline Industry*, p. 77.

11. *Aviation Week*, April 12, 1965, p. 56.

12. International Civil Aviation Organization, *Digest of Statistics, Financial Data*, 1965.

13. International Civil Aviation Organization, *Digest of Statistics, Fleet–Personnel*, various years; International Air Transport Association, *World Air Transport Statistics*, various years.

14. Keeler, "Airline Regulation and Market Performance," p. 415.

15. Dominion Bureau of Statistics, *Civil Aviation–Annual*, Cat. No. 51–202, 1965–67.

16. Vondracek, "North Atlantic Versus Transcontinental," p. 95.

17. Dominion Bureau of Statistics, *Civil Aviation–Annual*, Cat. No. 51–202, 1967, p. 17.

18. *Aviation Week*, June 8, 1970. p. 26.

19. Caves, *Air Transport and Its Regulators*, p. 74.

20. Ibid., p. 74, and Eads, *The Local Service Airline Experiment*, p. 67.

21. International Civil Aviation Organization, *Digest of Statistics, Financial Data*, No. 120 (1968).

22. Eads, *The Local Service Airline Experiment*, p. 64.

23. Vondracek, "North Atlantic Versus Transcontinental," p. 79.

Selected Bibliography

BOOKS

Allen, R.G.D. *Mathematical Economics.* 2d ed. London: Macmillan, 1965.

Ashley, C.A. and Smails, R.G.H. *Canadian Crown Corporations: Some Aspects of Their Administration and Control.* Toronto: Macmillan, 1965.

Bernstein, Marver H. *Regulating Business by Independent Commission.* Princeton, N.J.: Princeton U. Pr., 1955.

Brogden, Stanley. *Australia's Two-Airline Policy.* Melbourne: Melbourne U. Pr., 1968.

Buchanan, James M. and Tullock, Gordon. *The Calculus of Consent: Logical Foundations of Constitutional Democracy.* Ann Arbor: U. of Mich. Pr., 1967.

Caves, Richard E. *Air Transport and Its Regulators: An Independent Study.* Harvard Economic Studies, Vol. CXX. Cambridge, Mass.: Harvard U. Pr., 1962.

Cherington, Paul W. *Airline Price Policy: A Study of Domestic Airline Passenger Fares.* Boston: Division of Research, Graduate School of Business Administration, Harvard University, 1958.

Corbett, David C. *Politics and the Airlines.* London: Allen and Unwin, 1965.

Cross, John G. *The Economics of Bargaining.* New York: Basic, 1969.

Currie, A.W. *Canadian Transportation Economics.* Toronto: U. of Toronto Pr., 1967.

Downs, Anthony. *An Economic Theory of Democracy.* New York: Harper and Row, 1957.

——. *Inside Bureaucracy.* A Rand Corporation Research Study. Boston: Little, Brown, 1967.

Eads, George C. *The Local Service Airline Experiment.* Studies in the Regulation of Economic Activity. Washington, D.C.: Brookings, 1972.

Holden, Matthew, Jr. *Pollution Control as a Bargaining Process: An Essay on Regulatory Decision-Making.* Cornell University Water Resources Center Publication, No. 9. Ithaca, NY.: C.U.W.R.C., 1966.

Jane's All the World's Aircraft, 1948. London: Sampson, Low, and Marston, 1948.

Jordan, William A. *Airline Regulation in America: Effects and Imperfections.* Baltimore: Johns Hopkins, 1970.

Kahn, Alfred Edward. *The Economics of Regulation: Principles and Institutions.* 2 vols. New York: Wiley, 1970–1971.

Kolko, Gabriel. *Railroads and Regulation, 1877–1916.* Princeton, N.J.: Princeton U. Pr., 1965.

MacAvoy, Paul W. *The Economic Effects of Regulation: The Trunk-Line Railroad Cartels and the Interstate Commerce Commission Before 1900.* Cambridge, Mass.: MIT Pr., 1965.

Meyer, John R. and Straszheim, Mahlon R. *Pricing and Product Evaluation.* Vol. I of *Techniques of Transport Planning.* Edited by John R. Meyer. 2 vols. Transport Research Program. Washington, D.C.: Brookings, 1971.

Miller, Ronald E. and Sawers, David. *The Technical Development of Modern Aviation.* London: Routledge and Kegan Paul, 1968.

Niskanen, William A., Jr. *Bureaucracy and Representative Government.* Chicago: Aldine-Atherton, 1971.

O'Connor, William E. *Economic Regulation of the World's Airlines: A Political Analysis.* New York: Praeger, 1971.

Phillips, Almarin. *Technology and Market Structure: A Study of the Aircraft Industry.* Heath Lexington Books. Lexington, Mass.: D.C. Heath, 1971.

Phillips, Charles Franklin, Jr. *The Economics of Regulation: Theory and Practice in the Transportation and Public Utility Industries.* The Irwin Series in Economics. Homewood, Ill.: Irwin, 1965.

Pickersgill, J.W. *The Mackenzie King Record.* Vol. I, 1939–44. Toronto: U. of Toronto Pr., 1960.

Pillai, K.G.J. *The Air Net: The Case Against the World Aviation Cartel.* New York: Grossman, 1969.

Ramanadham, Venkata Vemuri. *Public Enterprise in Britain: Thoughts on Recent Experiences.* London: Frank Cass, 1959.

Redford, Emmette S. *The Regulatory Process: With Illustrations From Commercial Aviation.* Austin: U. of Tex. Pr., 1969.

Reid, Graham L. and Allen, Kevin. *Nationalized Industries.* Penguin Modern Economics Texts. Harmondsworth, Middlesex: Penguin, 1970.

Schelling, Thomas Crombie. *The Strategy of Conflict.* A Galaxy Book. New York: Oxford U. Pr., 1963.

Schultze, Charles L. *The Politics and Economics of Government Spending.* Washington, D.C.: Brookings, 1968.

Straszheim, Mahlon R. *The International Airline Industry.* Transport Research Program. Washington, D.C.: Brookings, 1969.

Tullock, Gordon. *The Politics of Bureaucracy.* Washington, D.C.: Pub. Aff. Pr., 1965.

———. *Toward a Mathematics of Politics.* Ann Arbor: U. of Mich. Pr., 1967.

Turvey, Ralph, ed. *Public Enterprise: Selected Readings.* Penguin Modern Economics. Harmondsworth, Middlesex: Penguin, 1968.

Wheatcroft, Stephen. *Air Transport Policy.* London: M. Joseph, 1964.

———. *The Economics of European Air Transport.* Manchester: Manchester U. Pr., 1956.

Wildavsky, Aaron B. *The Politics of the Budgetary Process.* Boston: Little, Brown, 1964.

ARTICLES IN PERIODICALS

Air Transport World VIII, no. 4 (1971):10.

Alchian, Armen. "Some Economics of Property Rights." *Il Politico* XXX, no. 4 (1965):816–29.

American Aviation XVII, no. 24 (1954):81.

——. XVIII, no. 25 (1955):92.

Averch, H. and Johnson, L.L. "Behavior of the Firm Under Regulatory Constraint." *American Economic Review* LII (December 1962): 1053–69.

Aviation Week. April 12, 1965; June 8, 1970.

Brannon, Peter et al. "TCA's First Quarter Century of Service." *Canadian Aviation* XXV, no. 9 (1962):41–77.

Breton, Albert. "A Theory of the Demand for Public Goods." *Canadian Journal of Economics and Political Science* XXXII, no. 4 (1966):455–67.

Brown, Samuel and Watkins, Wayne. "The Demand for Air Travel: A Regression Study of Time Series and Cross-Sectional Data in the United States Domestic Market." *Highway Research Record,* No. 213. Washington, D.C.: Highway Research Board of the Division of Engineering and Industrial Research, National Academy of Sciences, National Research Council, 1968, pp. 21–34.

Clark, Peter B. and Wilson, James Q. "Incentive System: A Theory of Organizations." *Administrative Science Quarterly* VI, no. 2 (1961):129–66.

Cleverley, Fred. "Transair Plans to Bring Jet Age to the Arctic." *Canadian Aviation* XLII, no. 3 (1969):27.

Coase, R.H. "The British Post Office and the Messenger Companies." *Journal of Law and Economics* IV (October 1961): 12–65.

——. "The Problem of Social Cost." *Journal of Law and Economics* III, no. 1 (1960): 1–44.

Coleman, James Samuel. "The Possibility of a Social Welfare Function." *American Economic Review* LVI (December 1966): 1105–22.

Davies, David G. "The Efficiency of Public Versus Private Firms: The Case of Australia's Two Airlines." *Journal of Law and Economics* XIV, no. 1 (1971):149–66.

Davis, Otto A., Dempster, M.A.H., and Wildavsky, A. "A Theory of the Budgetary Process." *American Political Science Review* LX (September 1966):529–47.

Demstez, Harold. "Why Regulate Utilities?" *Journal of Law and Economics* XI (April 1968):55–65.

Dixit, Avinash K. "On the Optimum Structure of Commodity Taxes." *American Economic Review* LX, no. 3 (1970):295–301.

Durbin, J. "Testing for Serial Correlation in Least-Squares Regression When Some of the Regressors are Lagged Dependent Variables." *Econometrica* XXXVIII, no. 3 (1970):410–21.

Eads, G.C., Nerlove, M., and Raduchel, W. "A Long-Run Cost Function for the Local Service Airline Industry." *Review of Economics and Statistics* LI (August 1969):258–70.

Eckert, Ross and Hilton, George. "The Jitneys." *Journal of Law and Economics* XV, no. 2 (1972):293–325.

Farrar, Donald E. and Glauber, Robert R. "Multicollinearity in Regression Analysis: The Problem Revisited." *Review of Economics and Statistics* XLIX (February 1967):92–107.

Francis, Robert. "The McConachie Story: World Airline Looks Homeward." *Saturday Night* LXXIII (May 24, 1958):40.

Furubotn, Eirik and Pejovich, Svetozar. "Property Rights and Economic Theory: A Survey of Recent Literature." *Journal of Economic Literature* X, no. 4 (1972):1149–53.

Harsanyi, John Charles. "A General Theory of Rational Behavior in Game Situations." *Econometrica* XXXIV (July 1966):613–34.

Jordan, William A. "Producer Protection, Prior Market Structure and the Effects of Government Regulation." *Journal of Law and Economics* XV, no. 1 (1972):151–76.

Keeler, T.E. "Airline Regulation and Market Performance." *Bell Journal of Economics and Management Science* III, no. 2 (1972):399–424.

McKean, Roland Neely. "The Unseen Hand in Government." *American Economic Review* LV (June 1965):496–506.

Mishan, E.J. "The Postwar Literature on Externalities: An Interpretative Essay." *Journal of Economic Literature* IX, no. 1 (1971):18–21.

Peltzman, Sam. "Pricing in Public And Private Enterprises: Electric Utilities in the United States." *Journal of Law and Economics* XIV, no. 1 (1971):109–47.

Posner, Richard A. "Taxation by Regulation." *Bell Journal of Economics and Management Science* II, no. 1 (1971):22–50.

Regan, D.H. "The Problem of Social Cost Revisited." *Journal of Law and Economics* XV, no. 2 (1972):427–38.

Stigler, George J. "Economic Competition and Political Competition." *Public Choice* XIII (Fall 1972):91–106.

——. "The Theory of Economic Regulation." *Bell Journal of Economics and Management Science* II, no. 1 (1971):3–21.

Tullock, Gordon. "A Simple Algebraic Logrolling Model." *American Economic Review* LX (June 1970):419–26.

Verleger, Phillip K., Jr. "Models of the Demand for Air Transportation." *Bell Journal of Economics and Management Science* III, no. 2 (1972):437–57.

Wenders, John T. "Collusion and Entry." *Journal of Political Economy* LXXIX, no. 6 (1971):1258–77.

Wright, Arthur R. "An Examination of the Role of the Board of Transport Commissioners for Canada as a Regulatory Tribunal." *Canadian Public Administration,* VI, no. 4 (1963):349–85.

ARTICLES IN BOOKS, YEARBOOKS, AND ENCYCLOPEDIAS

Baldwin, John. "The Battle for the North Atlantic." *Canadian Perspectives in Economics.* Edited by K. Acheson et al. No. J2. Toronto: Collier-Macmillan, 1972.

Brown, Robert T. "The 'Railroad Decision' in Chile." *Transport Investment and Economic Development*. Edited by Gary Fromm. Washington, D.C.: Brookings, 1965.

Fainsod, Merle. "Some Reflections on the Nature of the Regulatory Process." *Public Policy*. Yearbook of the Graduate School of Public Administration, Harvard University. Vol. I. Cambridge, Mass.: Harvard U. Pr., 1940.

Mansfield, Harvey C. "Commissions, Government." *International Encyclopedia of the Social Sciences*. Edited by David L. Sills. Vol. III. New York: Macmillan, 1968.

Miller, George M. "Origins of the Iowa Granger Law." *United States Economic History: Selected Readings*. Edited by H.N. Scheiber. New York: Knopf, 1964.

CONFERENCE PAPERS AND REPORTS

Alchian, Armen and Kessel, Reuben. "Competition, Monopoly, and the Pursuit of Money." *Aspects of Labor Economics*, a Conference of the Universities–National Bureau Committee for Economic Research. A Report of the National Bureau of Economic Research, New York. Special Conference Series, No. 14. Princeton, N.J.: Princeton U. Pr., 1962.

Arrow, Kenneth Joseph. "Political and Economic Evaluation of Social Effects and Externalities." *The Analysis of Public Output*. Edited by Julius Margolis. Universities–National Bureau Conference Series, No. 23. New York: National Bureau of Economic Research, distributed by Columbia U. Pr., 1970.

Mid-Canada Development Conference, 1st, Lakehead University, 1969. *Essays on Mid-Canada*, presented at the first session. Toronto: Mid-Canada Development Foundation, 1970.

Saarty, David A.D. "Future of the International Air Charter Market?" *Papers of the Tenth Annual Meeting of the Transportation Research Forum on Transportation Planning*. Washington, D.C.: 1969.

Sobotka, Stephen P. et al. *Prices of Used Commercial Aircraft, 1959–1965: A Research Report*. Evanston, Ill.: Transportation Center at Northwestern University, 1959.

Studnicki-Gizbert, K.W. "The Structure and Growth of the Canadian Air Transport Industry." *Papers of the Canadian Political Science Association Conference on Statistics*. Toronto: U. of Toronto Pr., 1960.

Taneja, N.K. and Simpson, R.W. *A Multi-Regression Analysis of Airline Indirect Operating Costs*. FTL Report R–67–2. Cambridge, Mass.: MIT Flight Transportation Laboratory, June 1968.

NEWSPAPERS

Financial Post (Toronto). October 11, 1958; March 2, 1963; November 4, 1961; November 1, 1969.

Globe and Mail (Toronto). October 10, 16, 21, 1958; November 5, 1963; June 26, 1971.

Winnipeg Free Press. December 5, 1960.

UNPUBLISHED MATERIAL

Bartlett, Hale Carlyle. "The Demand for Passenger Air Transportation, 1947–1962." Unpublished Ph.D. dissertation, University of Michigan, 1965.

Canada. Department of Reconstruction and Supply. Directorate of Air Development. "Development of Commercial Air Services in Canada, 1919-1944." Unpublished paper prepared by H. Cunningham. Ottawa, 1946. (Mimeographed.)

Canada. Department of Transport. "Further Airline Competition in Canada: A Study of the Consequences of any Further Development of Domestic Mainline Competition in Canada." Unpublished paper prepared by Stephen Wheatcroft. Ottawa, February 1966. (Mimeographed.)

Douglas, George W. and Miller, James C., III. "Quality Competition, Industry Equilibrium and Efficiency in the Price-Constrained Airline Market." Unpublished paper, Department of Economics, Texas A & M University, 1973.

Eckert, Ross. "Regulatory Commission Behavior: Taxi Franchising in Los Angeles and Other Cities." Unpublished Ph.D. dissertation, University of California, 1968.

Gellman, Aaron Jacob. "The Effect of Regulation on Aircraft Choice." Unpublished Ph.D. dissertation, Massachusetts Institute of Technology, 1968.

Joun, Young Pyo. "The Demand for Air Travel." Unpublished Ph.D. dissertation, University of Washington, 1966.

Taylor, Lester Dean. "The Principal-Components-Instrumental-Variable Approach to the Estimation of Systems of Simultaneous Equations." Unpublished Ph.D. dissertation, Harvard University, 1962.

Trans-Canada Air Lines. "Initial Submission to the Air Transport Board in the Matter of Transcontinental Commercial Air Service." 1958. (Mimeographed.)

Verleger, Phillip K., Jr. "A Point-to-Point Model of the Demand for Air Transportation." Unpublished Ph.D. dissertation, Massachusetts Institute of Technology, 1971.

——. "Theoretical Pitfalls in the Estimation of the Demand for Air Transportation." Unpublished paper.

Vondracek, George Joseph. "North Atlantic Versus Transcontinental Air Transport Passenger Services: Cost Analysis." Unpublished M.B.A. thesis, University of British Columbia, 1969.

Wheatcroft, Stephen. "Elasticity of Demand for North Atlantic Travel." Unpublished paper prepared for the International Air Transport Association. Montreal, 1964. (Mimeographed.)

Wilson, L.S. "Further Work with Feldstein's Pricing Rule." Unpublished paper. Public Economics Workshop Discussion Paper, No. 10, University of Essex, 1973.

PUBLIC DOCUMENTS

Canada

Air Canada. *Annual Report,* various years.

Bank of Canada. *Statistical Summary.* Ottawa: the Bank.

. . . *Between Ourselves.* A newspaper for employees and their families, published by Air Canada. No. 361. January 1972.

Canada. *An Act to Amend the Aeronautics Act, 1944.* 8 George 6, ch. 28. *Statutes of Canada,* 1944.

Canada. Air Transport Board. *Circular,* No. 61/66, effective October 31, 1966; No. 62/66, effective October 31, 1966.

——. *Decision,* Serial No. 2550 and 2954.

——. *Directory of Canadian Commercial Air Services.* Ottawa, January 1, 1965.

——. *Proceedings of Public Hearings* on Consideration of the need for additional Transcontinental Air Service in Canada. 23 vols. Ottawa, 1958.

——. *Report on Review of Licences Respecting Commercial Air Services Pursuant to Section 13 of the Aeronautics Act.* Ottawa, April 1947.

—— *Report to the Minister of Transport of Transcontinental Air Services.* Ottawa, December 1958.

—— *Transcontinental Route Hearings, Exhibit Book.* Ottawa, 1958. Canada. Canadian Transport Commission. *Annual Report,* various years.

——. Air Transport Committee. *Decision,* Serial No. 2623, 2687, 2801, 2803, 2913, 2954, 3026.

——. *Directory of Canadian Commercial Air Services.* Ottawa, August 15, 1972.

Canada. Canadian Transport Commission. Research Branch. *Operating Costs for Conventional and STOL Aircraft.* Report No. 08 of *Intercity Passenger Transport Study.* Prepared by G.A. Clark and J.W. Sobeniak. Ottawa: Canadian Government Printing Bureau, 1971.

Canada. Department of Transport. *Airline Competition in Canada: A Study of the Desirability and Economic Consequences of Competition in Canadian Transcontinental Air Services.* Prepared by Stephen Wheatcroft. Ottawa, May 1958.

——. *Press Release,* April 24, 1964, and October 20, 1966: "Statement of Principles for Regional Air Carriers."

Canada. Dominion Bureau of Statistics. Aviation Statistics Centre. *Air Passenger Origin and Destination, Domestic Report, 1970,* Cat. No. 51-204. Ottawa: Information Canada, June 1971.

——. *Air Passenger Origin and Destination, Domestic Report, 1968,* Cat. No. 51–204. Ottawa: Information Canada, June 1969.

——. *Civil Aviation–Annual,* Cat. No. 51–202.

——. *Civil Aviation–Preliminary Annual,* Cat. No. 51–201.

——. *International Air Charter Statistics,* Cat. No. 51–003. Vol. I, No. 3, July-September 1970.

Canada. Parliament. House of Commons. *Bills,* Bill C–231, 1st Sess., 27th Parl., 14–15 Elizabeth 2, 1966: "An Act to define and implement a national transportation policy for Canada, to amend the Railway Act and other Acts in consequence thereof, and to enact other consequential provisions."

——. *House of Commons Debates,* 2nd Sess., 18th Parl., 1 George 6, Vol. II (1937); 3rd Sess., 19th Parl., 6 George 6, Vol. III (1942); 5th Sess., 19th Parl., 8 George 6, Vol. I, II, IV and V (1944); 3rd Sess., 22nd Parl., 4–5 Elizabeth 2,

Vol. II (1956); 5th Sess., 22nd Parl., 5–6 Elizabeth 2, Vol. I (1957); 1st Sess., 24th Parl., 7 Elizabeth 2, Vol. II and III (1958); 3rd Sess., 24th Parl., 8–9 Elizabeth 2, Vol. I and II (1960); 2nd Sess., 26th Parl., 13 Elizabeth 2, Vol. II (1964); 3rd Sess., 26th Parl., 13 Elizabeth 2, Vol. II (1965); 2nd Sess., 27th Parl., 16 Elizabeth 2, Vol. I and IV (1967).

Canada. Parliament. House of Commons. Sessional Committee on Railways, Airlines and Shipping, owned and controlled by the Government. *Minutes of Proceedings and Evidence,* No. 3 (May 7, 1959); No. 4 (November 27, 28, 1962); No. 1 (December 2, 3, and 4, 1963).

Canada. Parliament. House of Commons. Sessional Committee on Railways and Shipping, owned, operated and controlled by the Government. *Minutes of Proceedings and Evidence,* No. 4 (May 13, 1947); No. 5 (April 3, 1950); No. 6 (April 4, 1950); No. 1 (March 16, 19, 1956); No. 2 (March 21, 25, and 26, 1957).

Canada. Parliament. House of Commons. Standing Committee on Railways and Shipping, owned, operated and controlled by the Government. *Minutes of Proceedings and Evidence,* No. 4 (October 30, 1945).

Canada. Parliament. House of Commons. Standing Committee on Railways, Canals and Telegraph Lines. *Minutes of Proceedings and Evidence,* No. 4 (March 29, 1962); No. 3 (June 22, 23, 1964).

Canada. Province of Manitoba. Royal Commission Inquiry Into Northern Transportation. *Report.* Winnepeg: Queen's Printer, 1969.

Canada. Royal Commission on Transportation, 1959–1962. *Report.* M.A. MacPherson, Sr., Chairman. Vol. I. Ottawa: Queen's Printer, 1961.

Canada. Statistics Canada. Aviation Statistics Centre. *Air Passenger Origin and Destination, Domestic Report, 1971,* Cat. No. 51–204. Ottawa: Information Canada, July, 1972.

——. *Air Carrier Operations in Canada, October-December, 1970,* Cat. No. 51–002.

——. *Air Carrier Operations in Canada, January-March, 1971,* Cat. No 51–002.

Canada. *Trans-Canada Air Lines Act, 1937.* 1 George 6, ch. 43. *Statutes of Canada,* 1937; *Revised Statutes of Canada,* 1952, ch. 268.

Canada. *Transport Act, 1938.* 2 George 6, ch. 53. *Statutes of Canada,* 1938.

Canadian Pacific Railway Company. *Annual Report,* 1947 and 1959.

Quebecair. *Financial Statement.* June, 1971.

Studnicki-Gizbert, K.W. *The Regional Air Carriers' Problem.* A Study prepared for the Air Transport Board. Ottawa: Queen's Printer, 1966.

Trans-Canada Air Lines. *Annual Report,* various years.

Great Britain

Great Britain. Parliament. *Parliamentary Papers* (House of Commons and Command), 1967–68, Vol. XXXIX (*Accounts and Papers,* vol. 6). Cmnd. 3437. "Nationalised Industries: A Review of Economic and Financial Objectives."

United States

U.S. Congress. Committee on the Judiciary. *Monopoly Problems in Regulated Industries–Airlines. Hearings* before the Antitrust Subcommittee of the Committee on the Judiciary, House of Representatives, 84th Cong., 2nd sess., 1957.

U.S. Civil Aeronautics Board. *Handbook of Airline Statistics.* Washington, D.C., 1965, 1967, and 1971.

U.S. Federal Aviation Agency. *Direct Operating Costs and Other Performance Characteristics of Transport Aircraft in Airline Service.* 1965–69.

International

International Air Transport Association. *World Air Transport Statistics,* various years.

International Civil Aviation Organization. *Digest of Statistics, Fleet–Personnel.* 1961–1971.

——. *Digest of Statistics, Financial Data.* 1965, 1968.

Index

About the Author

John R. Baldwin is an Associate Professor of Econcmics at Queen's University, Kingston, Ontario. His doctoral and post-doctoral studies were pursued at Harvard and Chicago respectively. Dr. Baldwin's research interests include micro-economic theory and political economy.

About the Author

John R. Baldwin is an Associate Professor of Economics at Queen's University, Kingston, Ontario. His doctoral and post-doctoral studies were pursued at Harvard and Chicago respectively. Dr. Baldwin's research interests include micro-economic theory and political economy.